Introducing English for Academic Purposes

Introducing English for Academic Purposes is an accessible and engaging textbook which presents a wide-ranging introduction to the field, covering the global and institutional position of EAP as well as its manifestations in classrooms and research contexts around the world. Each chapter provides:

- a critical overview introducing readers to theory- and research-informed perspectives;
- profiles of practice to guide readers in putting theory to use in real world contexts;
- tasks, reflection exercises and a glossary to help readers consolidate their understanding;
- an annotated further reading section with links to online resources to enable readers to extend their knowledge.

Covering both theoretical and practical issues, *Introducing English for Academic Purposes* is essential reading for students of applied linguistics, and pre-service and in-service teachers of EAP.

Maggie Charles is Tutor in English for Academic Studies at Oxford University Language Centre, UK. **Diane Pecorari** is Professor of English Linguistics at Linnaeus University, Sweden. Both writers have many years' experience of teaching and researching English for Academic Purposes in contexts around the world.

Routledge Introductions to English for Specific Purposes
Edited by Brian Paltridge and Sue Starfield

The Routledge Introductions to English for Specific Purposes series provides a comprehensive and contemporary overview of various topics within the area of English for specific purposes, written by leading academics in the field. Aimed at postgraduate students in applied linguistics, English language teaching and TESOL, as well as pre- and in-service teachers, these books outline the issues that are central to understanding and teaching English for specific purposes and provide examples of innovative classroom tasks and techniques for teachers to draw on in their professional practice.

Brian Paltridge is Professor of TESOL at the University of Sydney. He has taught English as a second language in Australia, New Zealand, and Italy and has published extensively in the areas of academic writing, discourse analysis and research methods. He is editor emeritus for the journal *English for Specific Purposes* and has co-edited the *Handbook of English for Specific Purposes* (John Wiley & Sons, 2013).

Sue Starfield is Associate Professor in the School of Education and Director of The Learning Centre at the University of New South Wales. Her research and publications include tertiary academic literacies, doctoral writing, writing for publication, identity in academic writing and ethnographic research methods. She is a former editor of the journal *English for Specific Purposes* and co-editor of the *Handbook of English for Specific Purposes* (John Wiley & Sons, 2013).

Introducing English for Academic Purposes

Maggie Charles and
Diane Pecorari

Routledge
Taylor & Francis Group

LONDON AND NEW YORK

First published 2016
by Routledge
2 Park Square, Milton Park, Abingdon, Oxon OX14 4RN

and by Routledge
711 Third Avenue, New York, NY 10017

Routledge is an imprint of the Taylor & Francis Group, an informa business

British Library Cataloguing-in-Publication Data
A catalogue record for this book is available from the British Library

Library of Congress Cataloging-in-Publication Data
Charles, Maggie, author.
  Introducing English for academic purposes / Maggie Charles and
Diane Pecorari.
    pages cm
  Includes bibliographical references and index.
  1. English language—Study and teaching—Foreign speakers.
2. Second language acquisition—Study and teaching. I. Pecorari,
Diane, author. II. Title.
    PE1128.A2C4455 2015
    428.0071—dc23
    2015021309

ISBN: 978-1-138-80510-1 (hbk)
ISBN: 978-1-138-80515-6 (pbk)
ISBN: 978-1-315-68212-9 (ebk)

Typeset in Sabon
by Apex CoVantage, LLC
Printed and bound in Great Britain by
Ashford Colour Press Ltd, Gosport, Hampshire

For Ruth, who started it all off, and for Alva,
who came along at the right time.

Contents

Figures

Tables

Acknowledgements

Many people have contributed to the writing of this book and we are very grateful to the numerous friends and colleagues who have always been ready with help and support. During our careers in EAP we have drawn on their research and benefited immensely from their insights. We cannot possibly name all those to whom we are indebted, but we would like to make special mention of Barrie Charles, David Charles, Suganthi John, Peter Saunders, Peg Shearer and George Taylor, whose help was much appreciated. Above all, we would like to acknowledge the contribution of our many students, without whose input and questions we could not have learned so much about English for academic purposes.

While every effort has been made to trace and contact copyright holders of material used in this volume, the publishers would be grateful to hear from any they were unable to contact.

How to use this book

This book introduces English for Academic Purposes (EAP), a growing and important area of English language teaching. The aim of EAP is to help English learners develop the skills they need to study through the medium of English. This introduction provides a brief orientation to the book, to help you find the best ways to use it for your own professional development.

Learning with this book

This book was written with an awareness of the extremely varied contexts in which EAP is taught around the world, and it is designed for readers from many different backgrounds. You may:

- have English as a first, second or foreign language;
- have prior EAP experience, general English teaching experience or little or no experience of teaching at all;
- have greater or lesser knowledge of basic concepts in applied linguistics and Teaching English as a Foreign Language (TEFL);
- use this book as part of a course, for example an MA TEFL, or read it on your own;
- teach students in an English-speaking country or in some other part of the world;
- have a current EAP course and group of students you can reflect on as you read, or not;
- have access to a good university library and the Internet, or have more limited resources.

The rest of this introduction describes the components of the book, and how people in different settings can make the best use of it.

The contents

This book consists of twelve chapters, each of which focuses on a different area of EAP. Section I deals with the contexts in which EAP instruction is offered. Given the variety of settings in which English is taught, learned and used around the world, teachers can benefit greatly from understanding how their own teaching situation fits into the big picture, and Section I provides that perspective. Section II deals with the process of planning and preparing to deliver EAP provision. Understanding this process is indispensable for teachers who are asked to develop courses, but it is also useful if you have 'inherited' courses from previous teachers, because it enables you to understand the choices which were made when the courses were designed. Section III treats aspects of delivering EAP provision, including the key types of academic texts which are taught, and the ways in which courses are assessed.

Although there is a progression throughout the chapters, it is not necessary to read them in order, and if you choose not to do so and encounter terms which are unfamiliar, you can consult the glossary at the end of the book. Terms in the glossary are highlighted in bold at the first mention in each chapter. Each chapter has several features which are intended to help you get the most out of the book.

Reflections

Each chapter begins with a task asking you to reflect on what you already know about the topic, and ends with another reflective task to help you consolidate what you have learned. These tasks are designed as reflective activities and do not require you to do more than think about the questions which are posed, or in some cases note down some brief answers.

Tasks

In each chapter there are tasks which will help you consolidate and apply what you have learned. The tasks take different forms and can be approached in different ways.

- Some tasks ask you to reflect on a course or a group of students with which you are familiar. If you are an in-service teacher, you can think about a course you are currently teaching. If you have interrupted your teaching career to pursue further study, you can think about a group you have had previous experience with. If you are preparing to be a teacher and have no previous classroom experience, you can think about a course in which you have been a student.
- Some tasks ask you to find materials on the Internet or to read something from an academic journal. Depending on your context, accessing these resources may be relatively easy or more difficult. If you find it impossible to do one of the tasks, please simply turn to the others. Before concluding that resources are not available, though, you should consult a librarian at your university or your public library, or someone else who is familiar with the information resources available to you.

- Some tasks ask you to gather information or perform an analysis and report back to your classmates. There are many ways this can happen, and if you are reading this book as part of a course, your teacher will tell you what form your report should take. If you are reading this book outside the framework of a course, you may find it useful to write brief written reports of your answers to these tasks to enhance your own learning.

Further reading and resources

The topics treated in this introductory book have been the subject of extensive study and have been written about in greater detail elsewhere, and each chapter ends with a selection of key texts, websites and further resources where you can find out more about the topics that interest you. Several of the chapters introduce tools and resources for studying and analyzing language and these too are listed in this section.

Teaching with this book

If you have assigned this book as reading in conjunction with a course you are teaching, the order in which the chapters are read is not critical, so you should feel able to vary reading assignments to suit the structure of your course.

The tasks are designed to allow varying levels of engagement; they can be carried out as in-class activities or as homework, and they range from short exercises to extensive writing or speaking assignments. A number of tasks ask students to report back after gathering and analyzing information, and these reports can be given in many different ways:

- as oral presentations in class;
- as written reports of varying length to be submitted for feedback;
- as group assignments;
- as postings in a discussion forum on the learning platform which other students can respond to.

Defining our terms

EAP is frequently taught at university, but it is also taught at private language schools, at secondary school level, and in other settings. The material in this book is relevant to all EAP teachers regardless of their institutional setting. However, for reasons of economy of expression, we frequently refer to universities, to lecturers, and to other aspects of academic life which are primarily found in tertiary institutions. Readers in other settings should overlook this and read with an understanding that broader EAP contexts are intended.

Academic institutions around the world use different terminology. We use the word 'course' to mean a specific class or module, and 'academic programme' to mean a course of study leading to a degree or other qualification. When we are speaking about EAP practitioners, we speak of 'teachers', and to distinguish them from people teaching other academic subjects, we refer to the latter as 'lecturers'.

A theme running throughout this book is that the features which characterize academic communication are not random or coincidental; scholars speak and write the kinds of texts they do, in the way they do, because it best serves the purposes of communicating about their subjects of research and study. In other words, there is a close and direct relationship between academic discourse and the ways knowledge is created in academic communities. This means that by learning about academic English, we gain direct insight into the ways scholars across the university work, the kinds of knowledge they value, and indeed the ultimate purpose of their disciplines. This makes EAP possibly the most fascinating, eye-opening area of English language teaching. We hope that by reading this book you come to share our enthusiasm for EAP.

Section I

The field of EAP

Chapter 1

The scope of EAP

All over the world there are students, teachers and researchers from many different subject areas who use English for some or all of their academic work, even though English is not their first language. Studying through the medium of a second or foreign language can be very challenging, and English for Academic Purposes (EAP) exists to support them.

By the end of this chapter you will have insights into four areas which, taken together, will give you a good starting point for digging deeper into EAP in the chapters which follow. They are: the relationship of EAP to other areas of English language teaching; the activities of the EAP practitioner; the nature of academic English; and the sorts of issues and concepts which EAP practitioners engage with.

REFLECTION

Here are some ideas about EAP. Think about them and decide to what extent you agree with them.

1   Academic English and general English have more similarities than they have differences.
2   Most EAP students need mostly the same content from their EAP courses.
3   The best EAP teacher for a specific subject (e.g. engineering) is a specialist in that subject.
4   Research in EAP should be driven by the needs of learners.
5   The roles of the EAP teacher differ substantially from those of the general English teacher.

The statements above relate to perceptions of EAP, and those perceptions are part of the background which teachers use to make decisions about course content and classroom practice. The rest of this chapter will provide a perspective from which these statements can be revisited.

EAP is part of a larger area of applied linguistics called English for Specific Purposes (ESP). The field of ESP developed in the period after the Second

World War when English began to grow into the important global language it is today. As English became essential for more and more professional and vocational purposes, the number of people learning English around the world also grew. In many contexts it became clear that traditional methods of teaching the language were not meeting all the demands of this new constituency of English learners, because the earlier methods presupposed that every learner was on the same trajectory. But when the ability to use English in specific work contexts became the driver for studying the language, then it was clear that different learners had different needs: airline pilots needed to be able to communicate with air traffic control about flight paths; nurses needed to be able to speak to doctors and patients about particular medical conditions; and industrial chemists needed to be able to read the latest research findings in chemistry.

The field of ESP was started by language teachers who realized that in order to deliver maximum value to their students, they needed to teach them to use the language for specialized purposes like these. Because teaching materials with such a specialized focus did not exist, the early ESP teachers had to write them themselves. In order to do this – since most language teachers are not experts in medicine or aviation or chemical engineering – they had to engage in a process of discovery to find out what sorts of language their students would need to understand and produce in their working lives. This is the source of the three major activities which take place today under the heading of ESP: materials development, teaching and research.

From the above it is clear that ESP is really a sort of umbrella term for many specific areas: English for nursing, English for aviation, English for chemical engineering and so on. In this sense EAP can be regarded as one specific strand within ESP: English for academic purposes is the English needed to be able to carry out activities in academic contexts.

In reality, though, the situation is slightly more complex than that. While it is true that there are certain general academic activities that all students need to be able to carry out, such as reading textbooks, listening to lectures and writing academic texts such as examination answers, all of these activities take place within specific subject areas or **disciplines,** such as chemical engineering and nursing. Thus there is a sense in which EAP cuts across many other areas of ESP.

However, the English needs of students in physics and history (for example) are very different; the physics student needs to perform experiments and write them up as research reports, while the history student has to use multiple sources to construct arguments in the form of essays. Thus in EAP it is frequently necessary to distinguish general academic needs from those that are specific to a given discipline or group of disciplines, and then we talk about **English for General Academic Purposes (EGAP)** and **English for Specific Academic Purposes (ESAP).**

What does EAP practice involve?

EAP activity, then, can be more general (EGAP) or specialized (ESAP), but what exactly does it involve? As noted above, the three main strands of EAP practice are materials development, teaching and research, and many EAP practitioners engage in more than one of these activities. In fact, we often use the term 'practitioner' to indicate that the roles of an EAP teacher can be wider than classroom teaching alone. Even if your present role is limited to teaching a specific class using an EAP textbook you have been given, an understanding of the contribution of these three activities to the practice of EAP is valuable in illustrating how EAP differs from general English language teaching (ELT).

A guiding principle underlying all three strands of EAP activity is that EAP is driven by the needs of the learners. In contrast to general ELT, where the assumption is that all students follow the same syllabus, the needs of different groups of EAP students can be extremely varied, and thus the content of EAP teaching is ideally based on an analysis of the needs of the particular group of learners. Chapter 5 provides more detail on this topic.

Teaching materials such as textbooks and worksheets are key elements in all language teaching, and there are many good commercially available materials for EAP. However, because of the specialized nature of much of EAP, it is frequently necessary for teachers to supplement or adapt the available materials, and sometimes even to produce materials from scratch. These processes are explored more fully in Chapter 6. Materials development thus plays a more central role in EAP, and ESP generally, than in general English teaching.

However, in order to be most helpful to learners, EAP course content and materials have to reflect the realities of the ways learners use the language, and here there is a potential difficulty: while a competent English teacher can be expected to know what constitutes good general use of the language, how can a teacher whose education has been in the English language know what is needed or appropriate in physics or archaeology? What sorts of written assignments do students in finance management have to do? What constitutes a good essay in comparative literature? Are listening skills or reading skills more important for students of biology? Is there a core vocabulary that all university students can benefit from knowing? Research in EAP has answered questions like these, and the research results, which are published in outlets like the *Journal of English for Academic Purposes*, are intended to inform both teaching practice and materials development.

The applied nature of EAP means that in performing all three of these roles, the EAP practitioner is positioned between students and subject specialists in the students' field and must negotiate rather complex relationships with them. In general ELT, the teacher knows the language and the student does not, but in EAP the situation is more complicated. While the teacher brings language expertise to the class, the learner often has disciplinary knowledge to contribute. Thus the expertise of language and discipline specialists can complement each other and learners can be a valuable resource for the EAP teacher to consult.

EAP practitioners also benefit greatly from collaboration with subject specialists, to become familiar with typical disciplinary texts (both spoken and written) and processes, and to collect information about specific requirements that affect the teaching of EAP. Collaboration, in which EAP and subject specialists work together to define student needs, research them, produce materials, teach and validate them, can result in extremely effective course delivery. However, this is a time- and resource-intensive option which requires the willing participation of the lecturers in the academic subjects, and that may well not be possible in your institution. Even so, you may be able to work with subject specialists on a smaller scale, for example by asking them to provide examples of texts or to recommend the most important **academic journals**. In many contexts it is possible to extend your knowledge of other disciplines and enhance your EAP teaching through informal contacts, departmental visits or even just by consulting departmental information online. All this may sound like a daunting prospect, but in fact discovering other disciplines, finding out how they use language and applying this knowledge to support students is one of the most interesting and rewarding aspects of work in EAP.

What is academic English like?

So far, then, we have defined the scope of EAP and seen the sorts of activities that EAP practitioners carry out, but what about the language itself? What is academic English like and how does it differ from general English?

TASK I What is academic language like?

Think back to when you were beginning your university education. You can answer the following questions about any language which you used for your studies.

1   Were any of the forms of academic communication (for example, lectures, textbooks, writing assignments) new to you, or different from what you had experienced before?
2   Was any of the language difficult to understand?
3   If you think about a specific form of academic communication, like a textbook, how is it different from something intended for a general readership, such as a newspaper or a novel?

In answering the questions above, you may have mentioned things like these: academic language contains long and unfamiliar words, many of which have specialized or technical meanings; it is often abstract and possibly even dry; written academic language often has footnotes and references. There may be other features, too, which are less easy to put a name to, but you very likely feel that even if you cannot fully describe the differences, you can reliably tell the difference between a textbook and a novel.

The textbook is an example of an academic **genre** or type of text, while the novel is a genre of general English. The fact that we can distinguish between examples of these two genres implies that there are particular characteristics of language use in academic contexts which are different from general English. That is, there must be features of the language or the way it is used which exist in a specialized **domain** and which can be distinguished from those found in a non-specialized domain. This has, indeed, been shown to be the case. For example, written academic discourse differs from fiction along a number of parameters, including the use of past and present tense (Biber, Johansson, Leech, Conrad & Finegan, 1999).

However, this distinction is not so clear when we look at it close up. We can illustrate this with the example of vocabulary. In answer to Task 1, you may have said that one of the differences between a textbook and a novel is the words they use, and it is true there are words which are typical of academic writing. However, what differentiates these 'academic' words is the *relative frequency* with which they occur in academic and non-academic texts. For example, the word *prioritization* occurs nearly three times more frequently in academic writing than in other sorts of texts, but it can be found in both. Furthermore, only about 14 per cent of the words in a typical academic text belong to this core **academic vocabulary** (Gardner & Davies, 2014). Thus in order to be able to read academic texts, it is necessary to know a great deal of **general vocabulary** as well. This demonstrates that the distinction between academic and general vocabulary is about tendencies; it is not absolute.

The same point can be made with another example, the academic essay. Essays are commonly used for assessment in many academic areas and are rarely written outside academic contexts. It is easy therefore to agree that essays are an example of a genre which can be labelled 'academic'. However, in order to write a good essay in English, a student must be able to do things like make accurate grammatical and word choices and use them appropriately. The writer also needs to be able to predict what things are likely to be new for a reader and need explanation and what can be taken for granted. These and many other skills are needed by all good writers, regardless of what they are writing. Thus, even though the essay is a typically academic kind of text, many general English skills go into producing it. Once again, we can see that 'academic English' is not fully distinct from 'general English'; rather, there is a continuum between them.

What do we research in academic English?

Now we have a clearer idea of what academic English is like, we can look at how we can research it, keeping in mind that teaching and developing materials drive research in EAP and that good EAP research aims to yield findings and applications which will be useful to learners. As a result, the issues which are of interest to EAP researchers are, broadly speaking, those which are of interest to teachers and materials developers. Before we look at some of these areas, however, we need to know how we can obtain language data on which to base our research.

A major source of the language data which underlie research comes from **corpora**. A **corpus** (plural: *corpora*) is a collection of texts (usually on computer) designed for a specific purpose and compiled according to predetermined criteria. Corpus-based work is dealt with in detail in Chapter 4; here we just want to emphasize that the use of large corpora and text analysis software enables generalizations to be made about the linguistic features of EAP which are founded on reliable empirical data.

There are three areas of inquiry and teaching which are particularly prominent in EAP work. The first is the linguistic forms which characterize academic communication. One example of this was seen above: vocabulary. Research has been conducted both on words that arise in many academic areas and on subject-specific **terminology**. Grammatical features have also been investigated, often using corpora; studies include, for example, the forms used to evaluate material (*This remarkable result*) or report material from sources (*As Bryson (2005) aptly notes*). Work by Thompson and Tribble (2001) using a corpus of doctoral **theses** illustrates the range of reporting structures available for referring to the literature and gives examples of how these data are used in teaching materials.

A second focus of EAP activity has been on genres. We have already referred briefly to the notion of genre when we used the research report in physics as an example above. Genres are kinds of texts which are written for a particular purpose. Academic genres such as the **research article (RA)**, the essay and the lecture are important for EAP learners to understand and/or produce. However, because they are found primarily or exclusively in academic contexts, even individuals who have acquired a good level of proficiency in general English may arrive at university needing support in these genres. An important approach within EAP has been to analyze the rhetorical structure of key academic genres. Much work in this area has identified the rhetorical **moves** and **steps** of a genre, that is, the objectives the writer or speaker wishes to accomplish and the strategies used to accomplish them. Work in this area is thus concerned with identifying broad discoursal features. For example, in his groundbreaking volume on genre analysis, Swales (1990) sets out the moves and steps that characterize research article introductions. The concept of genre is discussed in more detail in Chapters 4 and 7 of this book, while Chapters 9–11 review key academic genres.

We have also already mentioned disciplines, and a third important focus of EAP work has been to examine the influence of the discipline. Research in EAP has taken disciplinary difference into account in two ways. One approach is to conduct a comparative study and look at linguistic or discoursal characteristics in texts belonging to two or more academic disciplines. For example, Hyland (2000) compares the linguistic features that construct an expert identity in a corpus of textbooks selected from eight different disciplines. Other researchers make the tacit assumption that discipline influences how types of discourse are realized and focus on single disciplines in a case-study approach. Räisänen's (2002) work on the genres of a conference on automotive engineering exemplifies this approach.

These three trends are not kept separate in the research literature or in classroom practice, and many studies have attempted to identify systematicity in the relationships among them. For example, Ädel (2014) conducted a study which combined local linguistic features with generic structure, looking at anticipatory *it* constructions (constructions such as *it is interesting* or *it is important*) in a corpus of learner writing. She found that different completions of the *it is* construction were found in conjunction with different rhetorical moves. In addition, as noted above, disciplinarity is a factor taken into account in many studies, because it is such an important determinant of what other features are conventional in a text. In this book academic discipline is dealt with most directly in Chapter 7, but in line with its pervasive role in academic discourse, it is a thread which runs through many of the other chapters as well.

TASK 2 How can research help?

Imagine that at your institution there is a need for the following EAP classes. What type of research (on linguistic form, genre and/or discipline) would be necessary in order to develop appropriate materials for the students and how would you carry it out?

1   an advanced speaking class for a multidisciplinary group of graduate students
2   a pre-study listening class for intermediate-level social science undergraduates
3   an upper-intermediate/advanced-level writing class for final year undergraduates in business studies

---

On being a reflective practitioner

So far we have portrayed EAP as though there were no sites of contention and all practitioners were broadly in agreement as to the nature of EAP and the way in which it should be taught. However, as with any pedagogical activity, there are different perspectives. In this section we want to draw your attention to some of these contested areas, flagging them up so that as you read this book you can bear them in mind, reflect on where you stand and come to your own conclusions.

We have mentioned, for example, the huge increase in the number of those who use **English as a lingua franca** (i.e. English used as a means of communication between speakers who do not share a first language). However, this does not mean that everyone views this development as benign. On the one hand, it can be argued that the use of English as a lingua franca allows the dissemination of academic knowledge to take place smoothly and swiftly; on the other, it has led to the marginalization of scholars and research that do not use English and has caused a decline in the use of other languages for academic purposes. These matters are discussed in more detail in Chapter 2, but as a reflective practitioner you need to be aware of this issue and think about what it means in your own context.

Another socio-political issue of concern to EAP teachers is the extent to which EAP is politically and ideologically neutral. Researchers such as Benesch (2001) have criticized EAP for taking a stance of neutral pragmatism, pointing out that this position rests on unquestioning acceptance of current institutional arrangements. It implies that students should fit in with the status quo and that it is the job of EAP instructors to help them do this. By contrast, critical EAP researchers attempt to challenge prevailing academic structures in order to facilitate change and improvement for students.

We have also drawn attention to EGAP and ESAP teaching, another issue that has been much debated. While it is certain that there are substantial differences among disciplines, does this necessarily mean that all teaching has to be ESAP teaching? In many teaching circumstances it is a matter of convenience, and indeed cost-effectiveness, to have student groups that are multidisciplinary. Moreover, working alongside students from different disciplines can make learners more aware of the specific characteristics of their own discipline. Again, this issue demands your attention as you make decisions on the type of teaching that is desirable and achievable within your own context.

TASK 3 Being a reflective practitioner

Think about the extent to which each of the three issues raised above impacts upon your teaching context.

1   Within your teaching context, what are the advantages and disadvantages of the use of English? Give an example of how the use of English affects your EAP students either negatively or positively.

2   Should EAP practitioners help students to fit in with institutional require-
     ments or should they help students to change the institutions? Give an
     example of something that could be improved in your context. As an EAP
     practitioner, either say how you might help improve it or say why you
     would not be able to make any changes.
3   Do you expect to teach EGAP or ESAP in your context? Which do you
     think is more valuable for your students and which would you prefer to
     teach? Say why in both cases.

Profiles of practice

Some EAP practitioners were asked to describe their jobs. Read their
accounts and use the questions below to help you consider them from your
own perspective.

Fan

I teach EAP in a large university which has an emphasis on science and technology, so my students work in those areas. I trained in English literature,
so at first I wasn't very happy in my job. I couldn't understand why the students weren't motivated or interested in my classes. I expected them to love
English like I do. As I've continued, though, I've come to realize that they
can be motivated when they see the point of their classes, so now I try hard
to focus on what is most relevant to their needs and I'm very selective about
what I use from the textbook.

Felipe

I work in a language school, teaching an evening class to students who
want to study at English-speaking universities. The classes are very
focused on preparing the students for entry examinations and I have to
stick to the syllabus. I try to make the teaching interesting, for example,
by role-playing the oral examination and using games for testing
vocabulary. I can't include much supplementary material, though, because
if I do, the parents complain. I often help students with their university
applications as well, and seeing them get the grades they need is very
rewarding.

Ahmad

I've just started my career in EAP as a member of a large unit at one of the
top universities in my country. The unit has a good reputation and I have

plenty of practical help and support from my colleagues. At the moment I'm teaching a course for medical students and I'm lucky to have a resource bank of material I can draw on. Some of it is rather old, though, and we've set up a group of teachers and subject specialists to update the materials. I'm working on listening and I'm really enjoying going to lectures in medicine and finding out more about what the students have to do.

Beatrice

Two humanities departments, history and religious studies, asked our EAP unit to set up a course to prepare first year undergraduates for their reading in English. I am responsible for the course and I work very closely with the departments. We get a good level of support from them, because the course is assessed as part of the students' degree. But I have had to explain that reading is not just about learning lists of terminology – knowledge of discourse structure and skills training are important, too. I read books recommended by the specialists and ask students to suggest texts that they are finding particularly difficult. In that way, I get input from both sides and we work on material that is directly relevant to the students' course.

1   To what extent are these courses EGAP or ESAP?
2   To what extent do these EAP practitioners perform the roles of teacher, materials developer and researcher?
3   Compare these courses to those you expect to teach. What similarities and differences are there?
4   Do you think the courses described above would be appropriate within your own context? Why or why not?

TASK 4 Read and summarize

Ädel and Swales (2013) present an analysis of natural history guides, looking at how one species of butterfly is dealt with in a selection of guides in two languages. Although the guides were written in some cases by academics, the authors conclude that they 'all remain within the macro-genre of a "narrative of nature" since none bear much similarity to, for example, the scientific and highly scholarly genres of the systematic botanists described [elsewhere]' (p. 30).

1   Read the article.
2   Summarize the features described by Ädel and Swales which lead them to conclude that the texts they analyzed are not typical academic texts.

   The article is available at http://www.diva-portal.org/smash/record.jsf?pid=diva2%3A629596&dswid=-314

REFLECTION

At the beginning of this chapter you reflected on several questions. Revisit them now and consider what you know about:

- the extent to which academic and general English are similar or different;
- the circumstances under which an EGAP or ESAP approach is appropriate;
- how EAP teachers can increase their effectiveness if they lack subject-specific knowledge;
- the relationship between learner needs and EAP practice;
- how the roles of EAP and general English teachers differ.

Further reading and resources

BALEAP
This is an important membership organization for EAP practitioners (formerly known as the British Association of Lecturers in English for Academic Purposes). Their website contains information about conferences and other events, reviews of relevant titles and other resources: http://www.baleap.org/home/

English for Specific Purposes
This journal covers the area of ESP broadly, but many of the articles and other content have an EAP focus. Access to most content requires a subscription, although a limited amount is freely downloadable at http://www.journals.elsevier.com/english-for-specific-purposes/

English for Specific Purposes Special Interest Group of the International Association of Teachers of English as Foreign Language (IATEFL)
The web page of this special interest group contains a number of resources, including an online journal, which can be accessed freely at http://espsig.iatefl.org/

Hyland, K. (2006). *English for academic purposes: An advanced resource book.* London; New York: Routledge.
This provides an excellent set of readings and commentaries which give more detail on many of the topics of this chapter.

Journal of English for Academic Purposes
This journal publishes research articles, book reviews and other content related to EAP. Access to most content requires a subscription, although a limited amount is freely downloadable at http://www.journals.elsevier.com/journal-of-english-for-academic-purposes/

Swales, J.M. (2009a). *Incidents in an educational life: A memoir (of sorts).* Ann Arbor: University of Michigan Press.
In his autobiography, John Swales describes how his time spent teaching English to groups with very practical needs led him to develop approaches which became the cornerstones of EAP.

Chapter 2

The global context of EAP

English plays an important role around the world, and since higher education is one of the sectors in which the use of English is expanding, EAP is a global enterprise. However, the status of English differs from context to context: for example, some learners have English as a foreign language and others as a second language, and the amount of exposure to English which learners have in their environments also varies. These factors in turn greatly influence the specifics of how EAP can and should be taught.

The purpose of this chapter is to chart the rise of English in academic contexts and describe the many and varied settings in which EAP is taught, as well as the implications of these settings for instruction. By the end of this chapter you will understand how your teaching fits into a larger picture of global EAP practice. The reflection below provides a framework for thinking about the global settings of EAP.

REFLECTION

The sociolinguist Braj Kachru (1985) grouped the parts of the world into three categories according to the status of English. The countries in the **Inner Circle** are those in which English has first and/or official language status, for example, the UK, the US, Australia, and Canada. In the **Outer Circle**, including countries such as India and Malaysia, English has had an historical presence, typically through colonialism, and it has a strong status, sometimes as an official language alongside other local languages. What remains is the **Expanding Circle**, countries in which English is used as a foreign language for certain specified purposes or in certain contexts (for example, with tourists).

In which of these circles would you place the country where you grew up? What about the country in which you are currently studying, if it is not the same? Has the 'circle' you grew up in affected your development as an English speaker?

English as a lingua franca

Kachru's Circles model describes a use of English which stretches far beyond the places traditionally thought of as English-speaking countries, and as we saw in Chapter 1, this has been a rapidly growing trend throughout the period since the Second World War. English has become a global **lingua franca**; that is, a vehicle for communication among people who have other first languages. The phenomenon of **English as a lingua franca (ELF)** is widespread. For example, when a new paper manufacturing company was created by merging companies from two Expanding Circle countries, Sweden and Finland, a decision was made to use English as the corporate language, rather than Swedish or Finnish (Louhiala-Salminen, Charles & Kankaanranta, 2005). In Hong Kong, in the Outer Circle, people working in areas such as law, logistics and financial services were surveyed, and they said that written English was the most important form of communication in their professional lives; the more senior the respondents, the more likely they were to communicate in English (Evans, 2010). In short, English plays an important role in many vocational and professional **domains** around the world.

Academic activity is no exception: English is very much the lingua franca for academics, just as it is for people in many other professional and vocational sectors. The success of academic researchers is measured by the quantity and quality of their publications, and by the way their work is seen to have an impact on the work of their peers. In practical terms this means that researchers need to publish prolifically in prestigious outlets and to have their work cited as widely as possible, and this imposes a number of burdens on scholars outside the Inner Circle. To give their works the best chance of being widely read and cited, they are faced with a pressure to publish in English. However, writing is more labour intensive in a language which is not one's first language (**L1**), and that impacts productivity. Second language (**L2**) users are often subject to criticism for a lack of accuracy and fluency of their English, and responding to these criticisms entails either extending the peer review process (as a work goes through additional drafts) or submitting to a less demanding (and therefore less prestigious) outlet. (For a discussion of this topic, see Curry & Lillis, 2004; Hyland, 2015; Li & Flowerdew, 2007.)

English-medium instruction

Paralleling the rise of ELF has been a trend towards international mobility among university students. In the US, for example, the numbers of international students rose from under 50,000 in the mid-1950s (Spaulding, Mauch & Lin, 2001) to nearly half a million about forty years later. A similar development has occurred in other Inner Circle countries which receive large numbers of international students. This situation is one of the significant drivers for EAP: students who come from other countries to study at English-medium universities quite naturally need support in developing the advanced and specific skills in English which are a precondition for success.

A more recent trend is international student mobility towards the Outer and Expanding Circles. In 2012, of the ten countries with the highest proportion of foreign and international students (relative to total university enrolments in those countries), only four (Australia, the UK, New Zealand and Canada) were in the Inner Circle. The others were Luxembourg, Switzerland, Austria, Belgium, Denmark and the Netherlands (OECD, 2014, p. 349). Of course, not all of these newly mobile students are enrolled in academic programmes in English, but a significant proportion of them are, and a desire to attract them is one of the factors underlying an increase in the amount of teaching done in English, or **English-medium instruction** (EMI), in such countries. At master's level, for example, European universities had over 6,000 programmes taught in English in 2013. The Netherlands alone accounted for nearly a thousand of these and the Nordic region for just under 1,300. Across continental Europe these figures represented a 38 per cent increase since 2011 and a rise of over 1,000 per cent since 2002 (Brenn-White & Faethe, 2013). Here too, the rise in English-medium instruction creates a need for support in academic English.

A third trend which has led to increased prominence for English in higher education is the fact that it often has a presence in individual components of courses. For example, if a lecturer has been recruited internationally, that individual may lecture in English instead of the local language, at least for an initial period. Textbooks are also frequently in English, for various reasons. In Thailand, one objective of engineering education is to enable the transfer of technical know-how from the West, and giving engineering students English-language textbooks is one means of achieving that objective (Ward, 2001). In Sweden, with a population base of under 10 million, Swedish-language textbooks are not particularly remunerative for authors or publishers, so English-language books are frequently adopted for courses which are otherwise taught in Swedish (Pecorari, Shaw, Malmström & Irvine, 2011).

The wide use of English at universities around the world, both in specific, limited roles and as the main medium of instruction, means that many students must engage in academic activities in an L2. Study at university entails coming to grips with complex and cognitively demanding concepts, and the ability to understand and produce academic discourse is something which presents challenges to most students, even in their first language. Doing these things through an L2 only increases the demands on the learner. The implications of this situation are discussed below.

TASK 1 The role of EAP instruction in your context

1   Kachru's Circles model divides the world according to the status of English. Thinking about the circles in which you have experience as a teacher or student, can you name some practical differences which the context makes for teaching and learning EAP?

2   In the teaching context you are most familiar with, what is the role of EAP instruction? Is it to support students in full EMI, to help prepare them for an EMI context in the future, to support them in managing certain restricted aspects of English, such as the textbook or classroom English, or does it have some other purpose?

EAP settings and participants: Implications for EAP teaching

As we have seen, EMI arrived in the circles of English at different times and via different routes, and that has affected the way EAP has developed and is taught. This has resulted in several different EAP constituencies. In the Inner Circle, EAP students are generally either international students or students based locally who have not acquired English as their L1 and require EAP support. On their courses, both of these groups find themselves in classrooms in which the majority of students are typically L1 speakers of English. In the Expanding Circle the majority of students are *not* L1 users of English but may well have a common L1 (though this is not always the case).

The situation in the Outer Circle is frequently more complex. There often exists a proportion of the population who have had extensive lifetime exposure to English, possibly including some schooling through the medium of English, and who may well use English as a home language. On the other hand, others have had their formal education in another language and may have had much less exposure to English from other sources as well. Exposure to English and the ability to use it effectively for study purposes may be linked to social status, with an advantage going to an elite.

Kachru's model contains a necessary element of oversimplification, as the relationships among languages it attempts to capture are in fact highly contingent, and the model has been subjected to extensive critical examination (see e.g. Park & Wee, 2009). However, by highlighting the different contexts in which English is used, the model shows that there exist very different constituencies and settings for EAP instruction, and the specifics have a direct effect on the experiences of EAP students and teachers in important ways.

To the extent that English is influential in the setting in which a student has grown up, it is likely to be proportionally influential in the student's later working life. The implication of this is that some students may anticipate an extensive need for English later, and others may aspire simply to perform the necessary academic tasks in English.

This relates to the distinction which is sometimes made between a second language setting, characterized by extensive exposure to the target language, which is used as a primary means of communication in the setting, and a foreign language setting, in which exposure to the target language occurs primarily in the classroom. Although this distinction is somewhat contentious (see Pecorari, forthcoming for a discussion), it is helpful in highlighting some of the differences in EAP contexts. Students in the Inner Circle have the opportunity for more exposure to English than those in other settings, as English is necessary not only for academic purposes but for the tasks of everyday life. This offers the potential for more rapid development of English skills but also presents students with greater demands on their language skills. In many other contexts English is present for some instructional purposes only; for example, the textbook may be in English, while lectures are given in the local language. Some students, therefore, need the ability to perform only some tasks in English, while others need the full range of EAP skills.

Affect (that is, emotional response) is an important factor in language learning, and individuals who have made a choice to study abroad through the medium of English may be both more highly motivated and more confident about their abilities to use English in academic settings. In countries where English is associated with a colonial past, political sensitivities may cause responses ranging from negative affect towards a perceived imposition of English as the medium of instruction to ambivalence about the potential threat of English to the status of other languages.

The nature of the setting in which EAP is taught, and all it implies for learners' attitudes, abilities and aspirations, is a constraint rather than a matter of choice for most EAP teachers. However, with an understanding of how EAP operates in other contexts, it is possible to gain valuable perspectives and learn lessons which you can apply to your own teaching practice.

TASK 2 Changes in the role of EAP

In an overview of the situation in China, Cheng (2016) describes a view that university-level instruction in English

> should aim at developing in students a solid foundation of knowledge and skills in English. Those holding this view argued that students would have no difficulty communicating in academic and work settings once

they have mastered general English. Indeed, some even argued that a scientific variety of English did not exist, and there was only general English used for scientific purposes.

It is only recently that 'pedagogical realities . . . have led ELT scholars in China to call for a more prominent place for EAP courses in the tertiary-level ELT curriculum'.

1   Is the situation similar or different in other Expanding Circle countries with which you are familiar?
2   What advantages and disadvantages can you imagine to be associated with a move from teaching general English to teaching EAP?
3   How might your answer to question 2 be different if an Outer Circle country were undergoing the same change?

Problematizing global EAP

This chapter so far has provided an overview of some of the major trends and phenomena in the use of English worldwide which impact the forms in which EAP is needed, taught and learned. However, as noted in Chapter 1, few areas of pedagogical practice are uncontested. This section takes a critical perspective on phenomena presented in this chapter in order to reveal some of the assumptions which underlie them.

Is EMI good for learning?

As we saw above, one of the mechanisms behind the growth of EMI is a belief that it is good for students to be exposed to English, because knowledge of a language with global importance can only be beneficial to them in their later lives. This idea rests on a belief in the efficacy of incidental language acquisition, even if this is not always consciously articulated; that is, the idea that when individuals are exposed to a language and placed in circumstances where they have to use it, they learn the language. Even when EAP courses exist alongside or as a preparation for EMI, many students, teachers and educational administrators believe that exposure to more English in the subject classroom, in textbooks, etc. will promote language learning.

This assumption is problematic in two ways, though. First, the circumstances which would promote truly effective and efficient incidental learning are not always in place. For example, Ward (2001) found that at a Thai technological university where students were assigned reading material in English, their reading behaviour was selective and superficial. Simply because opportunities for exposure to English exist, students do not necessarily take them.

There is, in addition, mounting evidence that the use of EMI causes pedagogical problems, at least under some circumstances. For example, using an L2 causes lecturers to cover less material, and teachers report feeling awkward and constrained when they lecture in English, and have fewer resources to paraphrase or explain a tricky concept in a different way in response to student questions. For these and other reasons, students may learn less of the core subject content when working through English instead of their L1.

Thus while EMI can be beneficial and is often popular with students, there is a balance to be struck between costs and benefits. It is not clear at present which EMI contexts manage to achieve that balance and create a net positive effect. Perhaps more worryingly, the costs are also discussed relatively little, in contrast to the potential benefits, so it is not clear that when decisions are made about whether to offer EMI, where, when and how, both sides of the issue are taken into account.

Is EMI bad for other languages?

Setting aside the question of whether EMI produces sufficiently valuable gains to make it worth doing, concerns have been expressed about its potentially negative effects with regard to other languages. This concern has two dimensions: impact on the individual, and impact on the language itself. From the perspective of the individual learner, more exposure to English usually means less exposure to another language. This is manifestly the case when an entire academic programme is taught in English. In some settings, an attempt is made to create a parallel-language environment in which students are exposed to two languages, for example by listening to lectures in the L1 and reading the textbook in English. However, in practical terms, exposure is subtractive; that is, students do not double the time they spend on academic activities, so time spent on English is taken away from the L1.

There is a tendency to discount the loss of exposure to the L1 precisely because the learner has native proficiency in the L1. However, academic proficiency in the L1 has to be learned, so the risk is that individuals who have studied through the medium of English may not be able to manage discussions or reading or writing about their subject area in their L1, and this could have potentially serious repercussions for students who need good formal discourse skills in their L1 to complete their studies, or later in their working lives. This need not be a difficulty, and there are ways of surmounting it, but it is important to be aware of this issue.

There are also concerns about the potential threat to other languages themselves, a particular concern for languages spoken by relatively small numbers of users. In South Africa, the universities which traditionally used Afrikaans have now adopted English, to varying extents. If Afrikaans continues to contract as a language of instruction, we can wonder whether at some point the language will lose a contemporary academic **register** altogether. This phenomenon is known as domain loss, and while languages which are not used in some domains (e.g. university study) may still be used in others (e.g. social interaction), sociolinguists recognize domain loss as a warning signal. The risks associated with the expansion of English have been discussed in colourful metaphorical terms. Swales (1997) wrote of English as a *Tyrannosaurus rex*, rampaging across a linguistic landscape and gobbling up other languages. Phillipson (2008) has invoked an even more monstrous metaphor, English as a *lingua Frankensteinia*.

These concerns are minimized by some people who believe that a balance will be arrived at. Even those who perceive a problem do not all accept that it should be solved at the expense of an individual learner who will benefit personally from studying in English. However, this is both an important issue and one which provokes strong feelings, and as an EAP teacher you should maintain a critical awareness of it.

The deficit model and the native-speaker norm

A traditional view of language learning has been to see the ultimate objective as the attainment of native-like proficiency in the target language. Although it is widely acknowledged to be extremely difficult to learn to speak a second language as if it were one's first, this has nonetheless long been seen as the ideal. In this view, if the production of an L2 user of English (or any other language) differs from that of an L1 user, it indicates a deficit in the knowledge of the learner.

However, a relatively recent trend in the study of English as a lingua franca has been to problematize this starting point. Researchers in English as an academic lingua franca (ELFA) such as Mauranen, Hynninen and Ranta (2016), point out that most users of academic English are not native speakers of the language and that their divergence from the native-speaker norm does not ordinarily cause a breakdown in communication or, indeed, difficulty on the part of other participants in the interaction.

From this perspective, the native-speaker norm (that is, the idea that the standard for good English is what a native speaker would produce) is highly questionable. If good academic English is defined in terms of how effectively it works to communicate content, rather than in terms of how closely it conforms to the native-speaker norm, then many of the disadvantages which L2 users of English experience are mitigated.

The linguistic resources of ELFA users

Another tendency on the part of many teachers is to regard code switching (that is, switching between one language and another) as undesirable. Current language teaching pedagogies place a great deal of emphasis on the target language, and use of learners' L1 is often regarded with disapproval. However, this perspective has recently been challenged by a body of research which avoids the term 'code switching' in favour of the more neutral 'translanguaging'. Translanguaging, like code switching, involves shifting from one language to another, but in this perspective the analytical emphasis is placed on identifying how the two (or more) languages are used as a resource. For example, in a study of schools in Birmingham in the UK, Creese and Blackledge (2010) documented a head teacher addressing a group of pupils, teachers and parents at assembly and shifting back and forth between English and Gujarati, often in the same sentence. While the audience was bilingual, some members of it were more proficient in English and others in Gujarati, and the effect of using the two codes together created audience engagement in a way that one or the other alone would not have been able to achieve.

There is a certain irony in the fact that the expansion of EMI has led to more heterogeneous classrooms but has simultaneously led to a less diverse academic-linguistic landscape. Given that many students work in a language which is not the one in which they are most comfortable, it is worth asking how academic institutions, and by extension EAP classrooms, can involve other languages for positive, transformative purposes, rather than seeing their use as indicative of a shortfall from an ideal of native-like English-only interaction.

TASK 3 Code switching in class

Discuss the following questions in groups or on the learning platform.

1   What reactions from teachers have you encountered towards using languages other than English in the English classroom?
2   What reasons can you put forward for using English exclusively in the EAP classroom?
3   In your experience, do learners like to use their L1s in the classroom or do they prefer to use English only?
4   Is translanguaging more appropriate in some EAP contexts than in others?

Profiles of practice

Swedish universities have welcomed English-medium instruction enthusiastically, with many master's programmes taught in English and undergraduate degrees beginning to follow suit. However, the adoption of English at university has not been entirely unproblematic. This is reflected in the (often contradictory) responses which university teachers gave to a survey

(Pecorari, Shaw, Irvine & Malmström, 2011) about their perceptions of the role of English in Swedish universities.

Read their comments and answer the questions below.

- There are no non-introductory-level textbooks in my subject in Swedish, so English is essential.
- If you are going to do science or understand science, the (perhaps unfortunate) reality is that you need to understand English.
- English is key in economics. No one reads journals in Swedish. English is the most important language in economics and business.
- All of our courses on the master's level are given, and need to be given, entirely in English. This is partly because our students are from all over the world, but even more important is the fact that the world is their workplace.
- Students will not succeed as internationally recognized researchers without having strong verbal and written language and comprehension skills in English.
- All courses on the master's level are given in English. No exception. However, some students, especially international students, lack sufficient knowledge [of English] even if they have taken and passed the official tests.
- It's sad that so many students actually have difficulties in understanding a book in English. They ought to be able to manage it, I think. I don't have time or the desire to have to explain why they should be able to understand textbooks in English.
- Unfortunately there is great resistance from students; they often don't understand why it is important.
- It's a little overrated. A nurse has to learn the nuances in his/her own language to be able to understand patients' experiences and feelings – that is absolutely primary.
- If there's one thing we're missing in my subject area, it's the ability to express ourselves in writing and orally in Swedish.

1 Would a teacher in your context have given similar or different answers?
2 Can you explain why or why not?

TASK 4 Teachers' perceptions of English

In the study mentioned above, academics in a specific Expanding Circle context responded to a question about the role of English in their subjects in extremely varied terms.

1   Ask several teachers from your context to tell you their understandings of the role of English. Try to ask at least one person who is *not* a teacher of English.

2   Compare the answers you got to the themes reported above.
3   If you get contradictory answers, speculate as far as you can about the cause of the differences.
4   Prepare an informal report on your answers.

TASK 5 Read and respond

Kachru's Circles model has been the object of criticism on a number of grounds. Park and Wee (2009) supply both a discussion of some of these criticisms and an alternative approach to the model. Read the Park and Wee article and use it as a springboard for a discussion of English in your context.

1   To what extent do their criticisms of Kachru's model apply to English in your context?
2   Does their reframing of the model give useful insights for the teaching of EAP?
3   Write a reflective essay in which you relate the original distinction of the three circles and Park and Wee's later interpretation to EAP practice in your own context.

REFLECTION

As you have seen, the variety in EAP globally is considerable: established scholars as well as students are in need of academic discourse skills across settings in which English is more or less prominent for a broader or narrower range of purposes. The status of English as a lingua franca underlies much of this variety, but it also introduces an additional tension to the practice of EAP: if English is a lingua franca, is it reasonable to take the minority of L1 users of the language as a benchmark for good academic English?

Which of the ideas from this chapter shed the most light on your teaching practice? Can you apply them to your teaching in concrete terms, or are they simply things to keep in mind? Are there ideas from this chapter which you wish to explore in greater depth?

Further reading and resources

British Council
The British Council commissions books and reports about a range of issues relating to the role of English in the world, including volumes such as *English Next*, which describes the global status of the language, and *English as a medium of instruction: A growing global phenomenon*. These and other publications of

relevance to EAP teaching are free to download from the British Council website at http://englishagenda.britishcouncil.org/books-resource-packs
English as a Lingua Franca Academic corpus (ELFA)
The **corpus** contains the spoken output of L2 users of English in academic lingua franca contexts. It is freely available at http://www.helsinki.fi/englanti/elfa/elfa_distribution.html
Jenkins, J. (2014). *English as a lingua franca in the international university: The politics of academic English language policy*. London: Routledge.
This and the Mauranen volume below offer coverage of one of the important issues treated in this chapter, the consequences of the rapid expansion of lingua franca English in academic contexts.
Lillis, T., & Curry, M. J. (2010). *Academic writing in a global context: The politics and practices of publishing in English*. London: Routledge.
This volume highlights the situation of international scholars working in English as L2.
Mauranen, A. (2012). *Exploring ELF: Academic English shaped by non-native speakers*. Cambridge: Cambridge University Press.

Chapter 3

The institutional contexts of EAP

The heart of EAP, like all teaching, is in the structured learning experiences and interactions between students and teachers which take place inside and outside the classroom. However, this core activity takes place within the organizational framework of a university or other educational institution, and the organizational and administrative realities of the context shape teaching practice. As a classroom teacher, administrative decisions constrain your teaching, and your ability to influence them is limited. However, if you understand how and why they are made, you will be better able to identify the art of the possible and provide the very best instruction which your context supports.

Policy and administrative practice vary greatly from country to country and from institution to institution, and so the purpose of this chapter is to outline the factors which frequently are decided, or indirectly influenced, by administrators. By the end of this chapter you will understand how decisions made by people in roles close to the teacher (e.g. directors of studies), in institution-wide units (e.g. admissions officers) and in higher-level leadership roles (e.g. deans, vice-chancellors) affect your teaching.

REFLECTION

Think about an educational institution you know well. In that institution, who decides the following things? Is it the class teacher or somebody else?

- the size of student groups
- who teaches certain classes
- whether to hire additional teachers
- which textbook is used for a given course
- what sort of assessment is used
- whether EAP teaching is offered
- whether EAP teaching, if offered, is required or optional

It is likely that you answered 'somebody else' to many of the points above, and it is possible that, for some points, you answered 'I don't know'. The remainder of this chapter describes the choices which administrators have to make in five key areas: EAP course offerings; student intake; staffing; funding; and organizational structure.

EAP provision

Whether to offer EAP courses at all is an administrative decision, and if they are to be offered, then further decisions are needed about when, how often, how many classroom hours they will consist of, etc. In addition, although course content is properly a pedagogical matter to be determined in the planning process (see Chapter 5), whatever perceived need led to the decision to offer EAP instruction is also likely to lead the decision makers to specify some aspects of content, such as whether the course will be **EGAP** or **ESAP**, and whether it will cover a range of skills or focus on a particular area of need, such as academic writing. Perceived needs often are the basis for these decisions. For example, if an academic programme has a low success rate which is attributed to the students' English proficiency, the need to improve the success rate can be the impetus for an EAP course. Similarly, an institution may take the view that EAP provision is needed in order to enhance its attractiveness to student applicants. Another reason for deciding to offer EAP provision is a perceived opportunity, often to increase revenues, if the funding mechanism in place at that institution links revenues directly to student participation in courses. Thus, although the authority to decide about EAP provision usually rests with someone other than a classroom teacher of EAP, the most powerful arguments for influencing those decisions are those which address need and/or opportunity.

Two further areas of decision are: whether students will earn academic credit upon successful completion of the course, and if so, how much and at what level; and whether EAP will be mandatory for some or all students, or, if it is optional, whether all students who wish to enrol will be able to. Funding is generally closely implicated in these decisions as well, but in addition curricular pressures exist. Some curricular structures make it difficult to vary the number of academic credits students take, and so if a credit-bearing EAP course is introduced, it must replace something else. Other institutions permit greater flexibility, but ultimately there is a limit on the available hours for timetabling classroom teaching, and on the amount of time students will realistically spend on their studies in total.

This means that there is frequently some element of competition between EAP and core subject content. This competition can be played out at the curricular level, if staff in other subjects believe that students will opt out of other courses to make time for EAP, and that can lead to resistance to the idea of EAP generating academic credit or being required. The competition can also be felt in the classroom, if students have unrealistic demands on their time and have to choose whether to prioritize EAP or something else. The best arguments for a strong, stable, realistic positioning of EAP in the curriculum relate to outcomes. By enabling students to perform well in their academic programmes, leading to better pass rates, greater attractiveness to applicants, better outward mobility, etc., EAP can be shown to pull its weight in the curriculum.

TASK 1 Case study

The Department of Caring Sciences at a university in northern Europe initiated an exchange agreement with a university in Asia. Every year, 30 students were to travel to the European institution to study physiotherapy. The head of the hosting department suspected that many students would need English support and contacted the head of the language department to arrange an EAP course for the visitors.

It was agreed that the students would be offered a course which would meet once a week for the first term of their studies, for a total of about forty classroom instruction hours. These parameters were decided with regard to the available budget for the course and the students' available time, given that they had a heavy course load. The director of studies for English was told about these parameters.

When it was time to plan and staff the course, there was little interest in it, and it landed on the desk of an enthusiastic but relatively inexperienced teacher. She designed a course based on explicit grammar instruction aimed at the level the hosting department told her to expect, and short writing assignments, which were all she would be able to read and provide feedback for within the time constraints of the course.

When the course started, it was discovered that the students' proficiency levels in English were enormously varied, and the material the teacher had planned was too basic for some and too challenging for others. Nonetheless, the teacher established an excellent relationship with the students, and they indicated on their evaluations that they had learned from the course.

The students were able to complete their coursework, but at the end of the year, when it was time for them to write their **dissertations**, the hosting department got in touch with the language department again: a large proportion of the students were at risk of failing, because their academic writing skills were very weak. They wanted to arrange tutoring for the students, but further discussions revealed that the budget was not sufficient to cover the amount of tutoring which would be needed, and qualified staff were not available on the very short timeline required.

1   Who should take primary responsibility for these less than ideal outcomes?
2   Would it have been possible to plan for an ideal outcome?
3   What steps could have been taken to improve the situation?
4   Who could potentially have taken those steps?

Who are the students in EAP classes?

Another important influence on EAP teaching which is largely not subject to the teacher's influence is the composition of the class. Depending on the size of the institution, the number of EAP students and the purposes for which EAP is offered, groups can be made up of individuals from across the academic community or of students from a narrower group, and three factors are the primary sources of diversity or homogeneity. The first of these is level of study. At a small institution with a limited selection of EAP courses, members of the academic community who identify a need have little choice other than to take the course which is available; at the university level this could result in groups which include undergraduates, postgraduates and even established academics. By contrast, if EAP courses are offered so broadly that multiple groups run every term or every academic year, then they can normally be tailored to address the needs of people at different levels. Since the **genres** produced by undergraduates, graduates and established researchers are different, greater homogeneity in group composition in this respect is ordinarily a good thing.

The second factor taken into account in making admissions and grouping decisions is proficiency level. The same underlying logic applies here: the larger the number of students, the greater the opportunities for forming groups with similar ability levels in English. An additional consideration is that, in order to do so, it is necessary to have accurate information about students' proficiency levels. In many settings this is addressed by requiring students to submit a score on an established commercial proficiency test, or to sit a locally developed and administered test (see Chapter 12 for more on diagnostic assessment). Elsewhere there may be an assumption that students who have gone through the local education system and taken the required number of years in English have similar levels of proficiency. This is a questionable assumption, and the equation becomes more complex still if students come from a range of educational backgrounds (for example, if international students from China join a course in Japan). Having very diverse skill levels in a group makes it extremely challenging for a teacher to select activities and forms of assessment which are relevant and beneficial to all. The best administrative decisions about student intake and group composition are therefore supportive of a placement system which uses one or more methods to identify students' proficiency levels accurately and of a course structure which allows proficiency levels to be taken into account.

The third factor in the equation is students' disciplinary backgrounds. In ESAP courses it is naturally necessary to offer teaching in line with students' subject areas, although the lens can have a broad or narrow focus (e.g. English for the medical professions versus English for midwives). It is possible to offer EGAP courses to students from certain subject areas only, but a more common tendency is to open them to students from all areas of study (and indeed the decision process is often the opposite: the necessity of including students from many **disciplines** may be what dictates offering an EGAP rather than an ESAP course). As mentioned in Chapter 1, on this question it is less clear that specialization is always better. Students often believe that courses targeted at their subject areas are more beneficial, but many EAP teachers feel that the greater the degree of specialization, the more they are expected to demonstrate a degree of content knowledge they may not possess. Other teachers find that diversity of subject area in the classroom is enriching. Hearing classmates describe unfamiliar academic discourse practices can drive home important messages about EAP more effectively than just hearing the teacher assert them.

Who are the EAP teachers?

EAP teachers come to the field through diverse routes. Some started with a background in teaching general English and developed an interest in academic English as a specialization within their broader practice of teaching English as a Foreign Language (EFL) or English as a Second Language (ESL). Others have taken the opposite trajectory, beginning with a background in science or law or some other academic subject area, and then finding an outlet for that subject knowledge, in conjunction with good English skills, in the EAP classroom. This diversity of backgrounds comes about because EAP requires, by its nature, that teachers have a good knowledge both of the English language and of the way it is used in academic contexts.

This diversity is reflected in the formal qualifications held by EAP teachers. For example, when teachers are recruited for their subject-specific knowledge, they often have an undergraduate or even a postgraduate degree in a subject area but may lack formal post-secondary education in applied linguistics or English language teaching. Teachers who have arrived at EAP through teaching general English may have a qualification in Teaching English to Speakers of Other Languages (TESOL) or English applied linguistics but lack qualifications in other subjects. Some EAP teachers have made the transition from teaching English as a foreign language in the school sector, and their formal qualifications are likely to include a significant emphasis on teaching methodology and pedagogy, but possibly less about the structure of the language, or the content of other subject areas.

The fact that EAP requires twin competencies – in language and in the discourses of academic subject areas – means that administrators have three crucial functions to perform in ensuring good staffing. The first is recruiting a cadre of teachers with the right combined expertise to serve the institution's needs. The second is shaping opportunities for exploiting the pool of expertise, for example, by staffing EAP courses with a team of teachers, one from an English background and one from a disciplinary background. Solutions like this are often avoided, not because they are perceived as less valuable, but because they tend to be resource intensive. A third administrative function is ensuring that all teachers have good opportunities for professional development. This too is something which is often neglected in language teaching (Crookes, 1997) but is especially important in EAP, so that staff from disciplinary backgrounds have the opportunity to learn about language teaching, and vice versa. The teacher is hugely influential in the success of any course, and people in educational leadership roles can contribute to success by shaping these three factors.

How is EAP teaching funded?

Education is resource intensive and the funding levels and mechanisms have a great deal of influence on the way EAP instruction, among others, is provided. The question of how EAP teaching is funded actually resolves itself into two questions: how is education paid for and how does the larger funding model pass resources on to an EAP unit?

Funding for education comes from several sources: the societal bodies which operate the educational institutions (e.g. central government, religious organizations, foundations); tuition fees paid by students (or their parents); charitable donations (large or small); and income from assets or endowments. These models are closely related to beliefs about who should have access to education and ideologies about how it should be financed. The European Union, for example, has made a conscious decision to try to increase the proportion of citizens attending higher education. To enable access, most European countries charge modest tuition fees (in some cases none at all), at least to students from within the European Union, although students from outside it may pay high fees. In the US, by contrast, tuition fees are the norm, even in state-funded universities, and many institutions charge extremely significant amounts. However, it is common for fees to be linked to financial ability and to be waived in part or altogether for students who are talented enough to secure admission and can demonstrate financial need. In Australia, international students pay high fees both for university tuition and for EAP provision if they do not meet the entry requirements.

There is also great variety in the mechanisms which trigger funding at all levels. EAP units can receive a flat-amount budget from a university or be rewarded for the number of students enrolling in a course or performing well in it. The specifics play a great role in determining the availability of resources for teaching (and the willingness to make the resources available). If an EAP unit receives a flat amount as an operating budget, then the fewer the students admitted to courses, the more resources available for educating each one of them, and for other expenditures, such as professional development for teachers. If the funding model is linked to the number of students enrolled, then the opposite pressure exists, to admit more students but to control the costs associated with teaching them.

To some extent independent of the funding mechanism in place, there are two potential pitfalls which can negatively impact EAP units, and which higher-level administrators can guard against. The first is the risk of financial instability. A long-term budget is essential to enable good recruitment and staff development, but either of the funding models described above can threaten it. If funding comes directly from higher levels, the risk exists that it can be cut. Revenues triggered by student enrolments are protected in that sense, but are affected by fluctuations in student numbers, and those can be caused by factors outside the control of the EAP unit.

A second concern is the risk that EAP teaching can be seen primarily as a source of revenue. This is a relevant concern for teaching in all subjects, but because EAP is offered to fee-paying international students, in many contexts it is especially likely to be regarded as a cash cow. If administrators require EAP provision to generate profits, the actions necessary to make that happen may include setting high targets for numbers of admissions and meeting them by lowering standards; restricting the number of classroom teaching hours for students; increasing the number of classroom teaching hours for staff; increasing the number of students in a group; employing staff with fewer formal qualifications; cutting back on opportunities for staff professional development; and employing part-time staff without security of tenure. All of these measures can save money in the short term, but in the long term lead to decreased quality in education and worsened outcomes for students, and these in turn result in reputational damage for the institution, which will make it less attractive to applicants.

Funding decisions are made at a relatively high level. In the case of public universities, the first set of decisions, from which all others cascade, are usually made at the governmental level. The degrees of freedom for universities are few, and for the classroom teacher they are usually nonexistent. Here, too, a degree of understanding can be a useful tool for the teacher. For example, it was noted above that there is a pan-European political goal of encouraging 50 per cent of the population to try university. However, this goal has been set without a proportionate increase in the funding to higher education, and there has not been an outcry from the voters of Europe demanding an increase in their taxes. It is important for classroom teachers in this context to understand that the conditions under which they work are the ones which their societies have decided are acceptable. On those matters which universities can decide, the decisions that benefit EAP units are those that ensure long-term financial stability and see EAP as an instrument for quality in higher education rather than primarily as a revenue-generating enterprise.

Who 'owns' EAP?

EAP is cross-disciplinary, and for that reason it is placed in varying organizational spaces. Because EAP is a specialized form of EFL/ESL teaching, in one model it may find an institutional home in academic units such as departments of English or applied linguistics, or Teaching English as a Foreign Language (TEFL) programmes. However, most EAP students are not students of the subject English: they are students of accounting, or logistics, or civil engineering, or some other field, and for them English is a necessary skill for academic success, rather than an end in itself. For that reason, a second model is to house EAP provision in units with responsibility for providing ancillary support services, such as language centres, study skills workshops and university libraries. Sometimes the need for EAP is diagnosed by academic staff in other subject areas who become aware that their students are struggling with English. When that happens, a decision may be made by the department concerned to offer EAP provision in-house. A third model, then, involves an academic department hiring EAP teachers to provide instruction for their own students.

These scenarios have different implications, particularly for the teaching staff. In English or linguistics departments EAP teaching responsibilities go to staff with backgrounds in language teaching, while courses provided by subject departments are likely to be staffed by someone from that field with good English skills. In either case, EAP teachers in academic departments may feel somewhat isolated, as their teaching practice is very different from that of their departmental colleagues. Staff in a language or study support centre may benefit from having a pool of colleagues engaged in similar teaching, but are less likely to have the same academic qualifications and may be unable to pursue the same career and promotion path as EAP teachers in academic departments.

In deciding where EAP is to be housed within the organizational structure of an academic institution, it is important that administrators plan for a structure which will give EAP staff collegial support and opportunities for professional and career development. This is necessary to recruit and retain the best staff, and ultimately, therefore, to maintain quality in EAP provision.

The status of EAP

All of the considerations taken up so far in this chapter heavily influence a final one: the status of EAP within the institution. It is somewhat paradoxical that this is, in fact, a significant consideration. For all the reasons outlined in Chapter 2, English is a prominent part of academic life, and of life beyond university. The list of people who need EAP or can draw significant benefits from it is long: students who work through English; those who want to study abroad in the future; those preparing for professions which will require subject skills in English; academic staff who are required to teach or need to publish in English or wish to be visiting lecturers or guest researchers. Given the important role of English and the fact that, as a **lingua franca**, it is used by more **L2** speakers than **L1**, it might be thought that the academic community could agree that EAP provision is crucial and worth resourcing.

However, this is manifestly not the case, and in many institutions, EAP has a sort of Cinderella status, and staff do less well in terms of salary, opportunities to research and other benefits than staff in other subjects. There are a number of reasons for this situation. Universities (where much EAP teaching is done) tend to value staff with higher academic credentials and those who are active in research. Teaching is often taken for granted, and universities possess better developed mechanisms for measuring research productivity than effectiveness in the classroom. As a result, the skills which are most needed by an EAP teacher are not those which trigger the greatest rewards.

There is a widespread perception among academic staff outside EAP that using language correctly is a technical, mechanical matter, and that helping students to produce and understand academic discourse is as straightforward as showing them how to format their written assignments correctly. In fact, this is directly contradicted by the body of research on EAP (as Section 2 of this book shows), and there is a close relationship between the formal choices in academic discourse, which differ across academic disciplines, and the way knowledge is constructed in those disciplines. However, that understanding is not widely spread outside the circle of EAP specialists.

The status of EAP can be improved. Professional standards and accreditation schemes, like the one run by the professional body **BALEAP**, are a way of ensuring consistently high standards in EAP teaching, something which can only raise the status of the field. As this chapter has illustrated, many of the elements which can raise the professionalism and quality of EAP provision and improve outcomes for students are decided outside the classroom. Decisions made by people in administrative and leadership roles include:

- Will an EAP course be offered?
- How often will it be offered?
- When will it be offered?
- How many classroom hours of instruction will it include?
- Will the course be EGAP or ESAP?
- Will the course address a broad or narrow range of skills?
- Will it be open to all, required, optional?
- Will EAP courses be credit-bearing?
- Will EAP courses be offered concurrently with other content instruction?
- Will they be part of a normal course load or in addition to it?
- Can students count them towards their degrees?
- What range of proficiency levels will be offered?
- How many concurrent groups will be offered?
- How will proficiency be assessed?
- How will proficiency be taken into account in assigning students to groups?

- How will academic level be taken into account in assigning students to groups?
- How will area of study be taken into account in assigning students to groups?
- Which areas of expertise will be required from new teachers?
- How will teachers in the team be able to draw from each others' expertise?
- What opportunities for professional development will teachers be offered?
- How is EAP financed?
- Is EAP required to produce profits or break even, or can it be allowed to make a loss?
- Where is the EAP unit located in the organizational structure?
- What status do EAP staff have?
- Do EAP teachers have a career-and-promotion path?

If you are coming relatively new to EAP but have substantial experience of teaching, you may be familiar with administrative processes at your institution, or indeed may be a part of them. If you are new to teaching as well as EAP, an awareness of what decisions are made and by whom can allow you to understand both your limitations and your opportunities for shaping the setting in which you teach. In addition, opportunities to prepare for a decision-making role may present themselves, and as you consider them, it is worth keeping in mind the overarching lesson from this chapter: people in educational leadership roles have a tremendous ability to create good preconditions for teaching and learning.

Profiles of practice

A group of about thirty-five EAP teachers at an eastern European university were asked to say how much of their time they spent on various tasks. They said that in a typical working week during the academic year, their time was divided as follows on average:

- in the classroom, 32 per cent
- preparing lessons, 20 per cent
- marking and giving feedback, 16 per cent
- in meetings or on administrative tasks, 17 per cent
- professional development, 15 per cent

Imagine that you have an opportunity to speak to these teachers' managers.

1   Would you express a view that this situation is broadly desirable or that changes are needed?

2   If you advocated changes, what would they be?
3   What arguments would you put forward to support your evaluation of
    the situation?

TASK 2 Read and respond

A survey of English teachers in China (Cheng & Wang, 2004), 'Understanding professional challenges faced by Chinese teachers of English', *TESL-EJ*, 7(4), included the following findings:

- Over three-quarters reported spending ten or fewer hours in the classroom per week.
- The vast majority (over 80 per cent) said they had 50 or more students in their classes.
- Very few identified curriculum design as a main responsibility.

   Read the article, and then design a small study aiming to investigate the same questions in another context. The article is available here: http://www.tesl-ej.org/wordpress/issues/volume7/ej28/ej28a2/?wscr

---

TASK 3 The consequences of decisions

So far we have seen how administrative decisions impact realities in EAP teaching. This task asks you to take the opposite perspective; that is, to start with the details of EAP teaching and try to imagine what factors and decisions have led up to them.

1   Find descriptions online of two or more EAP courses or programmes with which you are *not* already familiar. Examples come from the University of Edinburgh   (http://www.ed.ac.uk/schools-departments/english-language-teaching/courses/academic-purposes/year-round-eap) and the University of Virginia (http://www.virginia.edu/provost/caelc/summer.html).
2   Compare them in terms of the decisions typically made at an administrative level (e.g. student numbers, timing, prerequisites).
3   Report back to your class in a short presentation about the similarities and differences you have found.

REFLECTION

Keeping in mind the administrative areas of decision identified in this chapter, reflect on your experiences as a teacher or student and identify a single administrative decision which could be made (or changed) to have the greatest positive impact on the student experience.

Further reading and resources

BALEAP

BALEAP is the UK's professional body for EAP and it runs an accreditation scheme. You can read more about it, and about what criteria BALEAP considers to be quality indicators for EAP provision here: http://www.baleap.org/accreditation/scheme

Crookes, G. (1997). What influences what and how second and foreign language teachers teach? *Modern Language Journal, 81,* 67–79.

This article, which looks at second and foreign language teaching generally, raises issues which are of great importance for the EAP classroom specifically.

Haque, E., & Cray, E. (2007). Constraining teachers: Adult ESL settlement language training policy and implementation. *TESOL Quarterly, 41,* 634–642.

This article examines teachers' understandings of policy and connects it to the ways in which administrative decisions and actions impact their work.

Pennington, M. C., & Hoekje, B. J. (2010). *Leading language programs in a changing world: An ecological approach.* Bingley, UK: Emerald.

This volume covers key issues in administering language programs.

Teachers of English to Speakers of Other Languages (TESOL) Program Administration Interest Section

TESOL is an international professional body. Its interest section on Program Administration is particularly for individuals who have to make the kinds of decisions dealt with in this chapter. The website is here: http://www.tesol.org/connect/interest-sections/program-administration

Section II

Planning for EAP

Chapter 4

Approaches informing EAP

So far we have dealt with issues that affect EAP teachers on an international and an institutional scale; now we turn to the subject matter of EAP itself and the approaches that inform research and teaching in the area. By the end of this chapter you will be familiar with corpus-based, genre-based and social context-based approaches and will be able to decide which approach or combination of approaches would be suitable for your own teaching circumstances. To get started, think about your answers to the following questions.

REFLECTION

Here are some questions asked by EAP students. How would you respond to the students' queries? What sources of information would you consult for help with each query? Would these sources be adequate for responding to the queries fully and accurately?

(a) Master's student in education: 'Can I say *broad variety*?'
(b) PhD student in psychology: 'Should I include information about my results in the introduction to my **research article**?'
(c) Undergraduate in environmental studies: 'Do I have to use references in my exam answers?'

Questions like those above have been asked many times by students, and the EAP teacher may not have ready answers. Question (a) can best be answered by consulting a **corpus**, as we will see in the next section. The answer to (b) can be provided by **genre** analysis, while a social context approach would offer a response to (c). We will look at each of these approaches in turn.

Corpus-based approaches to EAP

A corpus is a collection of texts, usually in electronic form, which has been built with a specific purpose in mind and designed according to specific criteria. A corpus can be searched to find out how people use language, so that as an EAP teacher, you can use corpora to learn more about academic English in your students' disciplines. For example, you could consult a corpus in order to find out whether *broad variety* is a commonly used expression or whether another combination of words would be preferable. Four corpora of EAP are freely accessible for teachers online: the **Michigan Corpus of Upper-level Student Papers (MICUSP)** and the **British Academic Written English Corpus (BAWE)**, both of which contain student written texts; the **Michigan Corpus of Academic Spoken English (MICASE)** and **the British Academic Spoken English Corpus (BASE)**, which consist of spoken language, including lectures and seminars. In addition, two large general corpora, the **Corpus of Contemporary American English (COCA)** (Davies, 2008) and the **British National Corpus (BNC)**, have academic components which can be accessed separately from the rest of the corpus. Access details are given at the end of this chapter.

Corpora have been very widely used in EAP and play both a direct and an indirect role in language learning. In the direct role, students work with the corpus data, using them to study aspects of the language; the indirect role of corpora is to provide the data upon which pedagogical materials such as dictionaries and reference grammars are based.

Indirect uses of corpora

The use of corpora to provide material for dictionaries and other reference works is now so widespread that you have probably already made indirect use of corpus data, although you may not be aware of the fact. Major dictionaries used in teaching and learning EAP, for example, the *Oxford Learner's Dictionary of Academic English* (2014), are corpus based, as are reference grammars such as the *Cambridge Grammar of English* (Carter & McCarthy, 2006), while corpora are increasingly used to inform student course books such as the *Cambridge Academic English* series by Hewings, Thaine and McCarthy (2012).

Corpora contribute to our knowledge about EAP by allowing us to observe repeated patterns of language in very large quantities of naturally occurring text. This enables us to provide descriptions of academic language which are based on evidence that is attested and extensive and can therefore serve as a reliable source for producing reference and teaching materials. For example, drawing on corpora of university discourse, Biber (2006) showed that spoken and written texts display substantial differences; class teaching is marked by features such as first and second person pronouns (*you, we*), while textbooks have high numbers of attributive adjectives (*academic texts, high achievement*). The differences between spoken and written academic discourse are dealt with in more detail in Chapter 7.

As we mentioned briefly in Chapter 1, corpus analysis has also been widely used to characterize and differentiate the discourse of individual disciplines and genres. For example, using a corpus of research articles, Hyland (2005) compared social sciences and humanities disciplines with natural sciences. He found that fields such as philosophy and sociology generally recorded higher frequencies of markers that show the writer taking an explicit position (*clearly, I agree*). Chapter 7 provides further detail on the differences between disciplines.

The investigation of learners' production is another area in which corpora have played a major role. In particular, the International Corpus of Learner English (Granger, Dagneaux, Meunier & Paquot 2009) provides large-scale data for examining **L1** and **L2** differences in writing and has been used to identify key difficulties experienced by learners when writing academic essays in English. For example, L2 writers often use items more characteristic of spoken than written language and have problems with **phraseology** or typical phrasal sequences; they might write *as a conclusion* instead of *in conclusion*. Thus the findings from learner corpora have an important contribution to make in the design of teaching materials for EAP.

Direct uses of corpora

The direct use of corpus data by students and teachers in class is less widespread than indirect use and has been applied primarily in the context of academic writing. Corpus software provides several tools which present language data in different ways, but the most frequently used for pedagogical purposes is the concordancer. This tool searches the corpus for every instance of a given word or phrase and presents each one with its context in a line on screen. The search term appears in the centre with a few words on either side of it. Figure 4.1 gives part of a **concordance** on the search term *variety*, retrieved from a corpus of **theses** in answer to the student who wanted to know whether she could say *broad variety*. Reading down the concordance lines shows that this **collocation** or combination of words is not normally used and that the most frequent adjective–noun collocation is *wide variety*, which occurs as part of the longer phrase *a wide variety of*.

From this example we can see that the concordance data provide a good basis for answering the student's query, allowing her to identify the phraseology of the noun *variety*. Corpus data, then, are particularly useful for providing guidance of this type, as they show **lexicogrammatical** information, that is, information on the way vocabulary (lexis) and grammar choices depend on each other. In this example, the lexical items *wide* and *variety* are associated with the grammatical items *a* and *of* to form the phrase *a wide variety of*. Although learner dictionaries often include a limited amount of

```
1.  imposed by Vico on the huge     variety    of human history - then we ar

2.  celebration of the "infinite    variety"   of subject-positions and an

3.  all contributing to the rich    variety    that makes up Humanity. Mazz

4.  tities of material, the wide     variety    of conditions within the conf

5.  lack in one batch of a given     variety    (e.g. Raven 430) has a large

6.  these qualifications a large     variety    of samples have been measured

7.  dies of treatments on a wide     variety    of materials. <p>The details

8.  that it depends upon a wide      variety    of factors. This has enabled

9.  experiments, we chose a wide     variety    of benchmarks, totalling ove

10. ering diets. Yet with a wide     variety    of foods available to north-w

11. mino acids occurs via a wide     variety    of metabolic routes, the car

12. bbey, and it contains a wide     variety    of types of material and writ
```

Figure 4.1 Concordance on the word *variety*

such information, corpora offer much more extensive coverage of lexico-grammatical patterns and thus provide a valuable supplement to traditional resources.

The approach in which students work directly with corpus data to make hypotheses and verify generalizations about language is called **data-driven learning (DDL)**. Johns (1991), who coined the term, regarded the learner as a 'researcher', whose task is to discover the language, and the corpus as an informant providing the learner with the necessary linguistic evidence. The role of the language teacher is to facilitate the learner's process of discovery. Thus DDL is an inductive approach: it offers students a large number of authentic examples from which they themselves derive linguistic descriptions and generalizations. This contrasts with more traditional approaches in which students are given linguistic rules and asked to apply them. It is suggested that discovery learning through DDL leads to deeper processing of the language and helps achieve long-term acquisition.

Since Johns's groundbreaking work, there have been many reports of corpus-based courses and materials in EAP at both advanced and intermediate levels. For example, a workbook on essay writing, *Exploring Academic English*, by Thurstun and Candlin (1997), uses concordances of lexical items in order to teach key rhetorical functions, such as stating the topic, referring to the literature and drawing conclusions.

TASK I Which resources use corpora?

1   Look at a dictionary, a reference grammar and an EAP textbook in current use.
2   Are corpus data used in these resources?
3   If so, what details are given about the corpus and how it is used?
4   Do you think the use or non-use of corpora affects the quality of these resources? If so, in what ways?

Genre-based approaches to EAP

Working with genre has become one of the most widespread and valuable ways of researching and teaching EAP, with three different approaches emerging from different educational contexts and traditions.

1   **Move** analysis was first developed in the context of work with international students in Britain and is now widely used throughout the world.
2   The Systemic Functional Linguistics approach to genre arose out of work with Australian primary school students and is now being applied in a number of higher education settings.
3   Rhetorical approaches to genre originated in the US university tradition of rhetoric and composition studies and are most frequently used in the context of North American higher education.

We deal with each of these genre approaches in turn.

Move analysis

In his seminal book *Genre Analysis*, Swales (1990) defines genre as follows: 'A genre comprises a class of communicative events, the members of which share some set of communicative purposes' (p. 58). For example, law essays can be considered a genre because they communicate information from the student to the lecturer and seek to achieve the purpose of demonstrating that the student has understood the legal point. These shared purposes provide the rationale for a genre, determining what contributions are allowed and shaping the structure of the discourse through a set of shared features; for example, law essays must identify the key legal principle and refer to relevant cases. Swales further explains that genres belong to **discourse communities**, groups of people who have common goals and practices which are carried out through the use of language. Discourse communities may own multiple genres, which may be related to each other in sets or networks.

In EAP, such communities arise within subject areas and form **disciplinary communities**. For example, one disciplinary community could consist of all those who work in the field of education, including experts conducting research, students taking a degree and the subject lecturers responsible for delivering and assessing the courses. This group shares the goals of researching, teaching and learning about education, and these goals give rise to a set of genres, including **research articles**, conference presentations, lectures, assignments, handouts and examination questions. Although genres may overlap to some extent, each has its own specific purposes which affect its content, structure and language. Thus an examination question does not include the same content as a lecture, and the language and structure of a research article differ from those of a handout.

Move analysis starts with a set of texts taken from a genre recognized and named by the **discourse community** and seeks to identify the structural and linguistic regularities that characterize the texts. Each text is analyzed as a series of stages according to the function being performed; these are called **moves** and may in turn be made up of a number of **steps**. The first and best known of these move analyses is Swales's structure of research article introductions, which is called the **Create a Research Space (CARS)** model, because the task of this genre is to show how the research article makes an important contribution within the field. Swales analyzes introductions into three moves, as shown in Figure 4.2.

Move 1 Establishing a territory

Move 1 provides the overall background to the study. It consists of steps that give generalizations about the topic which become gradually more specific.

Move 2 Establishing a niche

Move 2 shows that there is a need for the present work. It consists of steps that indicate a gap in the research, add to what is known or present a justification of the work.

Move 3 Presenting the present work

Move 3 shows how the work addresses the need outlined in Move 2. It describes the work or announces its purpose. Other steps may include presenting research questions/hypotheses, giving definitions, summarizing methods, announcing findings, stating the value of the work or outlining its structure.

(Adapted from Swales, 2004, pp. 230–232)

Figure 4.2 The CARS model

Since the publication of Swales's (1990) book, move analysis has formed the basis of many studies in EAP. The CARS model has been applied to draw attention to the differing features of introductions in different disciplines and languages and has been modified to analyze introductions to learner genres such as theses and **dissertations** (see Chapter 10). Other written and spoken genres, including results sections, syllabuses, funding proposals, lectures and seminars, have also been analyzed according to their move structures. Chapter 11 provides analyses of spoken genres.

The popularity of move analysis is due to the fact that for those genres with a sufficiently stable move structure, it offers an explicit account of this structure, along with its linguistic realizations, thereby providing a useful tool for teachers and students. Move analysis has been widely applied in EAP, with perhaps the best known examples being the series of books by Swales and Feak that deal with writing key graduate genres such as the abstract (Swales & Feak, 2009) and their volume *Academic Writing for Graduate Students*, now in its third edition (Swales & Feak, 2012).

Systemic functional linguistics approach

This approach is based on Halliday's (1994) theory of systemic functional linguistics (SFL) and defines genre as a 'staged, goal-oriented social process' (Martin & Rose, 2008, p. 6). This has similarities with Swales's definition in stating that genres are used by the members of a society to achieve specific goals, which are reached by means of a series of stages (moves). The SFL approach arose from the need to teach socially valued genres in schools and aims to provide a means of analysis that can be used throughout the educational system. The genres it proposes reflect general rhetorical functions (e.g. narrative, explanation, description), and texts are assigned to these genres according to linguistic criteria.

Because the SFL approach to genre emerged in response to educational needs, it has a detailed pedagogy, which seeks to develop genre knowledge through the 'teaching–learning cycle'. This cycle consists of three main stages.

1   Deconstruction: a genre is modelled and analyzed.
2   Joint construction: a new example of the genre is constructed with input from both students and teacher.
3   Independent construction: students write another example of the genre individually.

The cycle is entered at the stage most suited to the student's needs, and repeated cycles can be carried out. At each stage, students increase their knowledge of the content and context of the genre, and the goal is for students not only to achieve mastery of the genre, but also to develop a critical orientation towards it. The teaching–learning cycle offers learners a structure of support which 'scaffolds' the task, enabling them to complete it successfully.

A recent large-scale example of an SFL-based approach to genre description is the work of Nesi and Gardner (2012), which sets out to distinguish and analyze the genres of assessed writing in higher education. Nesi and Gardner use SFL genre methods to categorize the texts in the BAWE corpus, which consists of 6.5 million words of undergraduate and master's assignments which gained high grades. Thirty disciplines are represented, divided into four broad disciplinary areas: arts/humanities, life sciences, physical sciences and social sciences.

Nesi and Gardner classify the texts into thirteen genre families according to similarities found in their function, stages and purpose (2012, p. 34); these genre families are linked to the broad social purposes of a university education and require different levels of skill and knowledge. Table 4.1 shows the genre families that correspond to each of these purposes. Grouping the genres in this way allows us to see how university assignments reflect differing levels of learning and require different levels of skill and knowledge, ranging from the relatively straightforward exercise to the more complex and challenging research report.

Analysis of the genre families reveals that their members share characteristic linguistic features, and this provides the basis for selecting the key elements of a given genre for teaching purposes. Nesi and Gardner's work provides the most comprehensive analysis of assessed student writing to date and establishes a sound basis for further research investigations and pedagogical applications. You can find more detail on the essay and research report genre families in Chapter 10.

Table 4.1 Genre families and their social function

Genre family	Social function
explanation, exercise	demonstrate knowledge and understanding
critique, essay	develop powers of informed and independent reasoning
research report, literature survey, methodology recount	develop research skills
problem question, proposal, design specification, case study	prepare for professional practice
narrative recount, empathy writing	write for oneself and others

(Adapted from Nesi & Gardner, 2012, p. 34)

Rhetorical approaches to genre

In contrast to the prominence given to texts, which is apparent in both move analysis and SFL, rhetorical approaches focus on genres as forms of social action and place less emphasis on their content and form. This leads to a view of genres as dynamic entities which arise from a given social context, change, develop and decay. Thus the characteristics of a genre at any given time are just temporary phenomena, reflecting the circumstances of that time.

For those working within the rhetorical tradition, the challenge is to introduce genres into the classroom in a way that reflects their dynamism, complexity and the social context of their use. These practitioners are concerned with issues such as how students can learn to transfer genre knowledge, to critique genres and to produce alternative genres. To this end they often provide guidelines for analyzing genres in the classroom, such as those given below (Bawarshi & Reiff, 2010, pp. 193–194).

1   Collect samples of the genre.
2   Identify the scene and describe the situation in which the genre is used. This includes gaining information about the setting (where), subject (what), participants (who) and purposes (why).
3   Identify and describe patterns in the genre's features. This involves describing its recurrent regularities in terms of content, structure, language, etc.
4   Analyze what these patterns reveal about the situation and scene. Here the student focuses on issues such as the values, assumptions and goals of the genre, who is included and excluded by the genre, the roles of reader and writer, and the actions that the genre makes possible or unlikely.

Through the use of such guidelines, the student is encouraged to move between analyzing the context and analyzing the genre in a repeated process that establishes the dynamic interaction between the two.

Merging genre approaches

Recently, however, the three orientations towards genre have drawn closer together, with practitioners merging aspects of different approaches to achieve greater breadth and depth in research and pedagogy. For example, Johns (2011) suggests that novice academic writers should move from text to context and finally critique. Students would first examine how a text from a given genre is structured and then consider contextual issues such as the writer's role, the audience and the text's relation to other texts. Finally, they would evaluate the text as a member of its genre and/or the genre in relation to its communicative purposes.

TASK 2 Thinking about genre

1   Look back at Nesi and Gardner's list of undergraduate written genres. Which ones have you yourself produced?
2   Which ones, if any, do your EAP students have to produce?
3   What other genres might you need to add to this list in order to teach at the PhD level?
4   Select an example of one undergraduate genre and apply the guidelines of Bawarshi and Reiff given above.
5   To what extent do these questions shed light on the genre?
6   Do you think students would benefit from using these questions? Why or why not?

Social context-based approaches to EAP

Corpus-based and genre-based approaches to EAP both share an important focus on texts. However, as we saw in the section on rhetorical approaches to genre, this textual emphasis is challenged by some researchers, who stress the role of the social context and prefer to see EAP as a social practice. This section presents some of the research and pedagogy that takes this view.

Underlying this perspective is the theory of social construction, which holds that social phenomena are created through human interaction. For example, the texts and practices of the discipline of history are produced, developed and maintained by historians as they interact with each other in the process of constructing knowledge. To view history as a set of social practices, then, implies the importance of the social group within which the practices take place, the community of historians. In the section on move analysis, we introduced the notion of disciplinary community to refer to a group such as this, whose members share common disciplinary goals and make use of shared genres. Since our primary concern as EAP practitioners is with students, we must therefore ask how students become members of these disciplinary communities.

In answer to this question, it has been suggested that a process of socialization into the discipline takes place. As students begin to take part in disciplinary activities such as reading textbooks, attending lectures and writing reports, they are exposed to disciplinary practices and slowly begin to think, talk, write and act in ways that are appropriate within their field. This process entails the construction of a new identity as the student gradually becomes a physicist, an engineer or a lawyer. To see how this happens, we can observe the changes that occur over time in students' writing and thinking and see how they can be linked to the students' gradual adoption of ideas, values and practices specific to their disciplinary community (Berkenkotter & Huckin, 1995).

Not all social context approaches accept this notion of socialization, however. The academic literacies approach challenges the assumption that the student should adapt to the community's norms and emphasizes that there are many different literacy practices in academia. This approach views the student's own literacy practices as valuable and seeks to develop alternative institutional arrangements that would validate them (Lea & Street, 2006). For example, Wingate (2015) argues that an inclusive pedagogy in which academic literacy instruction is fully integrated into the curriculum can best respond to the needs of diverse student populations. Academic literacies researchers use ethnographic methods such as surveying, interviewing and collecting texts in order to gather data about the social context and use these data as the basis for engaging with the participants and developing EAP courses.

An example of the academic literacies approach is the Transkills project at the University of Cambridge, UK. Boz (forthcoming) describes how survey data from tutors and first-year students were used to identify issues that concerned both groups in terms of the transition from secondary to undergraduate study. Issues such as the students' perceived level of preparedness and the nature of effective feedback were addressed in academic writing workshops for tutors in the disciplines, and material from these was then incorporated into disciplinary writing resources for the students.

Critical EAP (see e.g. Benesch, 2001), which we mentioned briefly in Chapter 1, shares many of the socio-political concerns of the academic literacies approach. It seeks to question and problematize widely held assumptions and practices in EAP, urging practitioners to ask questions such as 'what sort of English is being taught?' and 'what are the purposes for which English is being taught?' Nonetheless, Benesch does not ignore the requirement to succeed in academia. She puts forward a dual aim for critical EAP: 'to help students perform well in their academic courses, while encouraging them to question and shape the education they are being offered' (2001, p. xvi). Thus both academic literacies and critical EAP approaches highlight the potential of EAP practices to be transformative and regard students as active agents of this change.

Chun (2009) offers an example of how critical EAP works in practice. Finding that his students were uninterested in the topic of emotional intelligence in their EAP textbook, he asked them to respond to the associated cartoon instead. The students then became fully engaged in the class and began to challenge the assumptions of the picture, commenting and questioning the gender stereotypes portrayed. In this way, the students critiqued the EAP textbook, revealed an aspect of its underlying ideology and simultaneously found a way of making the material meaningful within their own context. More recently, Chun (2015) provides a detailed discussion of the use of critical approaches in an EAP classroom over the course of a year.

TASK 3 Applying a critical EAP approach

Read the following scenario and consider the opportunities it offers to implement a critical EAP approach.

Michael has taught a course in EAP for first-year economics undergraduates for several years. The course has been fully funded by the department and is strongly recommended by subject lecturers, who have supported Michael by providing input. Although the course is non-credit-bearing, it is well attended and student feedback has been very positive. Because of financial cuts, the department has decided that it can no longer afford to fund the course and has suggested that students who want to attend should pay the full cost. As a critical EAP teacher, you want to respond to this situation in your class.

1   What materials and activities would you use and what outcomes would you aim to achieve?
2   What would students be likely to learn from the class?

Choosing approaches

With all these approaches to choose from, you may feel rather uncertain about which one to use. Although we have kept them separate, it is good policy to incorporate elements of all the approaches in your EAP practice. Each approach provides a different type of information, but they all have valuable insights to contribute. Thus you can use a corpus to answer lexicogrammatical queries and to teach students the phraseology of academic discourse. If you need to find out about the overall structure of a certain type of text, a genre analysis will provide the necessary information. Questions concerned with the practices carried out in the disciplines are best answered by taking a social context approach, while academic literacies or critical EAP procedures can be used to critique these practices. Thus taking a combination of approaches will allow you to build up a range of skills and methods to support your understanding and teaching of EAP.

Profiles of practice

Three EAP teachers, Nicole, David and Mariam, talk about the approaches they use as they respond to the needs of their students and the requirements of their institutions. Read their accounts and respond to the questions below.

Nicole

I teach a general EAP course for graduates from a range of disciplines. I think the most important issue for my students is linguistic accuracy. A lot of them need to publish articles in international journals and if their English is incorrect, they will be at a disadvantage. I use corpora like COCA and the BNC as a source of academic examples and I write tasks on difficult grammar points. We also refer to the corpora in class whenever they ask a question about language that I can't answer. I'm not a native speaker, so it's really useful to be able to do that. It can take time to get comfortable with the software, but I think it's worth it in the end.

David

One of the courses I teach is for final-year undergraduates in computer science who have to write a project report. I collected some samples of good reports from the department and did a move analysis on each part of the report. The CARS model was very useful for the introduction, but it was difficult to analyze some of the other sections. I'm not a computer scientist, and the lecturers in that department were too busy to help, so I just did the best I could. In class, I got the students to discuss what moves they expected in each section and then I presented the moves I'd found. We talked about the differences and then the students did another analysis on their own. They did say they found the analysis useful; it seemed to give them some guidelines for their own writing.

Mariam

I was asked to teach a class for first-year undergraduates in engineering because the content lecturers found that students were struggling with understanding the material at the beginning of the course. I interviewed the lecturers and students about what they needed, attended lectures, collected samples of work and generally familiarized myself with the department. The students had problems with listening and note-taking, so I recorded some lectures and used short sections to show them the way the lectures were organized and how each part was signalled. I also asked the lecturers to make structured notes of their lectures available online. This approach seemed to make lecturers more aware of students' difficulties and students more aware of lecturers' expectations, but it took up a lot of my time.

1   Have you used similar approaches in your own teaching? If so, what happened? Did you face the same problems and achieve the same results as these teachers?
2   If you have not used similar approaches, would you do so in future? Why or why not?

TASK 4 Researching and teaching a discipline-specific EAP course

A new one-year master's course in business administration has been set up at your university and you have been recruited to design and teach a discipline-specific EAP course to run during the first term.

1   How would you carry out preliminary research and what approach(es) would you use to teach the course? Why do you consider your chosen approach(es) suitable?
2   If you would implement more than one approach in your teaching, how much weight would you give to each? Why?

TASK 5 Researching an aspect of EAP

1   From your own experience and teaching context, choose one aspect of EAP that you could research as a classroom teacher.
2   Write down a specific research question or questions and a short justification for the research, saying why the issue is important.
3   How would you research this issue? Describe the approach(es) you would use and explain why they would be appropriate.
4   What do you expect to find out from this research and how could the findings be applied in your teaching?

REFLECTION

As you have seen, there are three major approaches to researching and teaching EAP: corpus-based, genre-based and social context-based. Have you applied any of these approaches in your own teaching circumstances? If so, which one(s) and to what extent? What other teaching approaches have you used in general or EAP classes? Were they successful? Why or why not? What approach(es) would work best in your own circumstances and why?

Further reading and resources

British Academic Spoken English Corpus (BASE)
   This corpus contains 1.2 million words of lectures and seminars. Details and access are at http://www.coventry.ac.uk/research-bank/research-archive/art-design/british-academic-spoken-english-corpus-base/

British Academic Written English Corpus (BAWE)

This corpus contains 6.5 million words of undergraduate and master's assignments which gained high grades. Details and access are at http://www. coventry.ac.uk/research-bank/research-archive/art-design/british-academic-written-english-corpus-bawe/

British National Corpus (BNC)

This corpus contains 100 million words, including an academic component, and contains texts from the late twentieth century. You have to register, but it is freely available at http://corpus.byu.edu/bnc/

Corpus of Contemporary American English (COCA)

This corpus contains 450 million words of texts from the period 1990–2012 and includes an academic component. You have to register, but it is freely available at http://corpus.byu.edu/coca/

Flowerdew, L. (2012). *Corpora and language education*. Basingstoke, UK: Palgrave Macmillan.

This book presents a good general overview of the many uses of corpus linguistics in language teaching. It will help you understand what corpora can do and how to interpret corpus data.

Michigan Corpus of Academic Spoken English (MICASE)

This corpus contains almost 1.8 million words of spoken academic genres, including seminars and lectures. You can access it here: http://quod.lib.umich. edu/m/micase/

Michigan Corpus of Upper-level Student Papers (MICUSP)

This corpus contains 2.6 million words of student writing, including reports and essays. You can access it here: http://micusp.elicorpora.info/

Nesi, H., & Gardner, S. (2012). *Genres across the disciplines: Student writing in higher education*. Cambridge: Cambridge University Press.

This is an important source text for all those who teach at the undergraduate or master's level.

Swales, J.M. (1990). *Genre analysis: English in academic and research settings*. Cambridge: Cambridge University Press.

This key text presents the ideas behind the genre-based approach which has become so influential in EAP.

Chapter 5

Planning EAP provision

Much of the success of a course depends on what happens before teaching starts, so this chapter is about the process of planning and developing EAP provision. Of course, not all courses are designed from scratch; many teachers 'inherit' courses which someone else has planned, or which must fall within some predetermined parameters. However, understanding the planning process as a whole will let you make effective choices where you can, so this chapter presents the planning process from beginning to end. By the end of this chapter you will know how to conduct a **needs analysis**, how to formulate learning objectives, how to select relevant and appropriate content, and how to apply the principle of **constructive alignment** to course design. Before you read, reflect on the questions below.

REFLECTION

Recall one or more courses with which you have been involved, either as teacher or as student, which have worked really well. What were the ingredients that made them successful? Think about areas such as the activities carried out during class time, how the teacher introduced new material, the textbook that was used, the tasks students were asked to do outside class, etc.

Needs analysis

The needs analysis (sometimes called the target situation analysis) is deeply rooted in the history of EAP and ESP, and this fact is explained by Hutchinson and Waters's observation that 'what distinguishes ESP from general English is not the *existence* of a need as such, but rather an *awareness* of the need' (1987, p. 53). The ESP movement was the product of the realization that there were some learners who needed to be able to use English in very specific **domains** and for very specific purposes, and that general English provision was letting them down in two ways: first, by providing instruction that was less than directly relevant; and second, by failing to provide what they did need, whether that was the ability, for an engineer, to write a technical specification or, for a pilot, to communicate with air traffic control. EAP, like other forms of ESP, aims to enable learners to acquire the skills in English they need for a particular purpose, and that is only possible if the purpose is clear.

The objective of a needs analysis is to identify the skills and knowledge which learners need to possess but currently lack. This means that a needs analysis is effectively a research project, in the sense that it is a process of gathering information and then drawing conclusions based upon it. The three key elements in the process are the areas of information needed; the sources of information; and the data-gathering methods (see Figure 5.1).

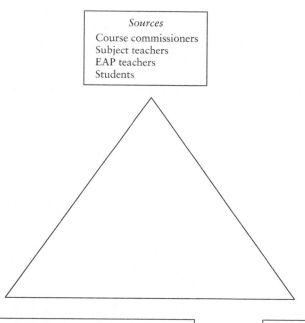

Figure 5.1 Areas of needs analysis

Areas of inquiry in needs analysis

When EAP staff are invited to plan a course, two stages in the planning process have effectively already happened: a need for English provision has been identified, and a decision has been made that a general English class is not suitable. The next question to resolve, then, is just how closely linked to a specific area the learning outcomes need to be; that is, whether an **EGAP** or **ESAP** course is to be planned. As Chapter 3 indicated, this is very often dictated by institutional constraints or by the preferences of the people who commission the course, so this, too, is a decision which has often already been taken by the time the planning stage begins.

A second question is what students need to be able to do. As a large-scale **corpus** study of academic language showed (Biber, 2006), the sorts of language use which can be called 'academic', in the sense that they are used in academic settings, are very broad indeed. To function at university, learners need to be able to understand both written and spoken instructional **genres**, such as the textbook and the lecture, and to take part in communicative events such as the tutorial and the discussion seminar, as well as being able to produce spoken and written assignments. In addition, they must be able to understand and/or participate in what could be called academic-administrative communication, including messages and information at the start of the lecture, and conversations with university staff about procedures such as how to register for classes.

Even if a decision is made to focus EAP instruction on academic discourse defined in a narrow sense to mean classroom and assessment genres, there is still a great deal of variety. As we saw in Chapter 4, Nesi and Gardner (2012) identified no fewer than thirteen genre families, including essays, case studies and literature surveys. Within these families are numerous variations on a basic theme; that is, a case study in one subject area may differ in many respects from a case study in another, and some subjects make heavy use of the case study genre, while others use it rarely if ever.

The genres students are called upon to produce for assessment purposes are often the subject of EAP teaching because the stakes are high; learning to produce them makes the difference between passing and failing. However, EAP learners also need to have the **receptive skills** to understand the instructional genres they read and listen to, as well as study skills (such as note-taking) to be able to get the most out of them. Because there is usually little if any overlap between the genres students are called upon to produce and those they must understand (that is, students are assigned to write essays and to read textbooks; they listen to lectures but are not asked to deliver them), the range of genres which could be included in EAP teaching is extensive. The needs analysis process involves considering how relevant each of these many kinds of language use is to students and, since few are entirely irrelevant, prioritizing among them.

A third area which must be understood as part of the needs analysis process is the level of attainment: how advanced are the skills of the learners in question, and how much more advanced do they need to be? The answer to these questions relates closely to the previous point, the sort of content which will be covered, as it indicates the priorities and dictates the art of the possible. For example, students on a master's course may ultimately need to learn to write a **dissertation**, but if they are struggling to understand their lectures, then teaching dissertation writing will not answer their immediate needs. Nor would teaching the dissertation be realistic if they were still developing the skills needed to write shorter, less complex academic texts.

Sources of information in needs analysis

EAP courses have four key stakeholders, and a thorough needs analysis process reveals the views of all four. The individuals or unit which commissioned or otherwise initiated the course have identified some sort of need, and the views of course commissioners are important, although they may not have been articulated very specifically. For example, if a department plans to send a group of students who have English as L2 on an exchange to an English-medium course at a partner university, the department may request a course because they simply feel (correctly) that additional support in English ahead of the visit is likely to improve the students' outcomes. On the other hand, the commissioners may have an awareness from past experience of likely problems, such as students not being able to keep up with the reading assignments or participate in seminar discussions, and have the more specific objective in mind that the course will deliver a solution for those particular problems.

A second group of stakeholders are the learners' subject-area lecturers. In many ways they are the people best placed to identify the target of EAP instruction, as they know what sorts of tasks their students are required to perform in English, and they are ultimately the people who set the standards for successful performance. They also have experience to be able to suggest what problem areas students typically encounter. As they are subject lecturers rather than language teachers, their views are most valuable about those things they can observe directly. That is, if a lecturer has noted that students routinely turn in written assignments which fall below the level for a pass, that can be taken as a good indication of a need for writing support. If the same lecturer diagnoses that students have weak oral proficiency on the basis that they are not active during in-class discussions, the observation is worth noting, but the cause could, alternatively, be that they are not confident about their understanding of the reading on which the discussion is based or that they are uncertain of the pragmatics of in-class discussions in that context.

A third set of perspectives informing needs analysis comes from EAP teachers. Unlike content teachers, their area of expertise lies in assessing language skills and planning to improve them. EAP teachers are well placed to understand the full range of proficiencies and areas of knowledge which need to be taken into account and what sorts of gains and attainments can reasonably be planned for within the scope of the course. The views of the teachers who will be involved in delivering the course are naturally of direct importance, but other teachers with relevant experience can also be consulted.

The fourth and arguably the most important stakeholders are the students themselves, in the sense that they have the most at stake: their academic success. In addition, it is they, ultimately, who must take responsibility for their own learning outcomes, so the success of the course rests largely on them. No matter how appropriate a course looks on paper, unless learners perceive it as relevant, they are unlikely to engage with it; and if they are not engaged in the process, then it is extremely unlikely to deliver the planned-for learning outcomes.

However, although the learners are of particular importance, it is essential for the success of a course that it has credibility with all four groups of stakeholders. In this respect it is unfortunate that perceptions of need so often vary. For example, Ferris (1998) demonstrated that the perceptions of teachers and students on oral/aural skill needs were quite divergent. In a study of Iranian EAP courses, teachers were more likely than students to say that students' low proficiency attainments were a problem, while students were more likely than teachers to say that the teachers' methods were a problem (Eslami, 2010). Reconciling the different perspectives is a challenge, but a foundation for it can be laid in the needs analysis process, by ensuring that all stakeholders perceive that their voices have been heard.

Methodologies for needs analysis

As an information-gathering process, a needs analysis can be thought of as a type of research, and that implies that a wide range of methodologies can be useful. One widely used approach is to ask the stakeholders directly, in surveys or interviews, about what they believe should be represented in the course. It is important to note that as valuable as these data directly from the interested parties can be, they only provide answers about peoples' *perceptions* and these are not always accurate.

Direct methods of understanding learner needs exist as well. To find out what students will be expected to do in their subject-area classes, it is possible to gather writing assignments and other course documentation and to observe teaching sessions. To find out the standard of performance in English which is required, assignments from previous years' students, both passes and fails, can be gathered. To find out about students' current abilities in academic English, scores from a test like the International English Language Testing System (IELTS) or the Test of English as a Foreign Language

(TOEFL) are useful. If those are not available, it is possible to administer a diagnostic test tailored for the particular context (see Chapter 12 for more on diagnostic assessment).

Of course, not all of these methods of gathering data are always available or practical. One frequent constraint on the methods used for needs analysis is the extent to which the course development is resourced. Activities like surveys, interviews and diagnostic testing take staff time, and staff time costs money. However, where resources are available, multiple methods of information gathering are ideal. In an account of an early needs analysis he conducted, Braine (2001) tells of sending questionnaires to students and staff. The return rate from the staff was low, and Braine reflects, with the perspective of time, that he did not even consider the option of following up on the questionnaire with interviews:

> Were the teachers offended that I took the more formal approach of a questionnaire, instead of meeting them informally? Were they, for reasons best known to themselves, reluctant to state their opinions and suggestions in writing? . . . . [A] few face-to-face meetings would have provided me with a rich source of data.
>
> (p. 199)

As this candid reflection reveals, in needs analysis, multiple sources of data can add up to more than the sum of their parts.

TASK 1 Read and respond

Tajino, James and Kijima (2005) adopt an approach from the field of management – soft systems methodology – and from it develop a new approach to needs analysis.

1   Read their article and consider what their proposal has to add to needs analysis.
2   Think about a course you have taught or taken. If you were given the task of redesigning it, what ideas for change might be thrown up by the approach Tajino et al. suggest?

Learning objectives

If the overarching objective of EAP provision is to close the gap between where learners are and where they need to be, then the things which need to be accomplished along the way can be expressed as one or more specific learning objectives (also called anticipated or expected learning outcomes). Learning objectives should be expressed as clear statements about specific things which the student will be able to *do* (as opposed to what the student will *know*) at the end of the course. Figure 5.2 shows a selection of learning objectives related to reporting the literature from a course on academic writing.

A framework for considering and describing learning objectives is provided by the SOLO taxonomy, developed by Biggs and Collis (1982). SOLO stands for Structure of the Observed Learning Outcome, and the taxonomy describes four levels of attainment. At the unistructural level, the learner has attained a single isolated understanding, skill, etc. The first learning objective in Figure 5.2, taken by itself, exemplifies an attainment at the unistructural level. The multistructural level consists of the attainment of multiple understandings. A learner who has achieved the first, second and third objectives in Figure 5.2 has reached this level. The fourth objective is an example of the relational level. At this level the multiple, isolated attainments can be integrated with or related to each other. Finally, at the extended abstract level (objective 5), the understandings can then be applied to a different domain.

Critics of the SOLO taxonomy point out that in practical terms it may be difficult to place an important skill, understanding, etc. neatly in one of these categories. However, the taxonomy provides a useful tool for thinking about learning in terms of a progression towards depth of understanding and ability. This is particularly useful in an area like language teaching, where the learning objectives are more often related to procedural and conditional knowledge (that is, knowing how and when to perform a skill), rather than declarative knowledge (knowing facts). Once decided, learning objectives then serve as a foundation for the rest of the planning phase.

A powerful concept for relating learning objectives to the elements of course design is **constructive alignment** (Biggs, 1996). Applying the principle of constructive alignment to a course entails harmonizing the course content, assessment and the learning objectives. In other words, the teaching and learning activities promote attainment of learning objectives, and all of the teaching and learning objectives are promoted by one or more of the activities. Similarly, the form(s) of assessment should measure attainment of the learning objectives.

Upon successful completion of the course, the student will be able to:

1   identify sources which are relevant to a research topic;
2   read and understand them;
3   provide an accurate explanation of their content;
4   write a meta-analysis showing how earlier studies on a topic relate to each other;
5   write an extended literature review which shows how the combined body of existing research on a topic can be applied to a new topic.

Figure 5.2 Selection of learning objectives from an academic writing course

---

TASK 2 Constructive alignment

The idea of constructive alignment was introduced in this chapter as a planning tool, to ensure that attainment of the learning objectives is supported by the course content and measured by the assessment. It has been pointed out, though, that constructive alignment is ultimately teacher-centred, in that it causes decisions about the course to be made with regard to objectives which are decided before the teacher meets the students, and therefore allows little flexibility to respond to students' wishes. This is somewhat at odds with the learner-/learning-centred focus to which many teachers aspire.

In groups in class or on the learning platform, discuss this question: how should students' expressed wishes for a class, their own diagnoses of their needs, and the teacher's understanding of the learning outcomes which will be desirable for them be balanced against each other?

Curriculum and syllabus design

With learning objectives established based on an analysis of learner needs, the next step is to translate the objectives for the course into a concrete plan. In some cases, EAP provision is planned as a series of courses or designed to be an integral part of an academic programme. 'Curriculum design' is the term used to refer to planning on this larger scale. An important principle in curriculum design is **progression**, the idea that learning objectives should be sequential and that there should be no gap between what learners can be expected to do at the end of one course and the abilities expected of them as a prerequisite for the next one. Even if a single course is being designed, rather than the entire curriculum, attention should be paid to the rest of the curriculum, to ensure that the new course fits into it well.

Syllabus design, the planning of the specific details of the course, takes four areas into account: timing and delivery; teaching and learning activities; assessment; and evaluation. The most significant aspects which come under these headings are treated in greater detail in other chapters, so the goal of this section is to provide an overview.

Timing and delivery

Timing is a key aspect, and important decisions to make include when in the academic calendar and within the framework of students' programmes the course should be delivered, along with duration. Should it run concurrently with other studies, or as a presessional course? Decisions there have knock-on effects on questions such as whether a course can be taught during the day or should meet in the evenings to avoid conflicts with students' other courses, and whether assessment deadlines need to be synchronized with those of other courses. Timing course delivery also includes deciding how many contact hours will be included (that is, how often the teacher meets the students in class) and how much work outside class students will be expected to do.

A decision is also needed about the balance which will be struck between teaching in a brick-and-mortar classroom versus activities online, ranging from discussions held in real time on a platform like Adobe Connect or asynchronous contact on a learning platform such as Moodle. In their simplest form, learning platforms can be simply an electronic repository of materials: a channel for distributing information, handouts, etc. which could otherwise be distributed in the classroom. However, they also have a potential to ease constraints. One constraint which is frequently relatively fixed is the number of classroom contact hours, since they are usually expensive to provide. If students are thought to need more contact with the subject than can be provided in the classroom, resources on a learning platform can provide a partial solution. Another common constraint is that either geography or conflicting schedules make it difficult for teachers and students to meet in a physical classroom, and here, too, learning platforms can provide a solution.

Teaching and learning activities

The learning objectives for a course drive the nature of the content which will be taught, but decisions need to be made about how to deliver the content. Teaching and learning activities (TLAs) include the things that teachers and students do in pursuit of the learning objectives. TLAs include assignments which students are asked to complete outside class as well as what happens during class time, and there are of course varied formats for the use of class time. The traditional lecture, involving an extended monologue from the teacher to which students listen passively, is not widely used in language teaching, although many teachers use mini-lectures to present chunks of declarative content, followed by discussions or activities to let students apply the content. In general, variation is good for learning, not least of all because it increases motivation. The nature of the activities in and out of class will be determined to a great extent by the EAP tradition within which the course is designed (see Chapter 4).

Practical constraints often steer the choice of TLAs. If a course involves many contact hours, then there is a need to provide variety and reduce fatigue by interspersing discussion activities or individual or small-group work on tasks in class. However, activities like those also lend themselves to being done outside class time and therefore tend to be deprioritized when contact hours are limited. Similarly, if the group is large and the only classroom available is a lecture theatre with seats which cannot be moved, small-group discussions become difficult.

The sorts of activities which are done in and out of class are also steered by the textbook and other materials which are used, and a decision in the planning process is whether there is a suitable textbook or whether materials need to be developed for the course. Chapter 6 discusses material selection and design in EAP.

Assessment

A number of decisions about assessment need to be made in the planning stage. One of these is whether any form of diagnostic assessment will be used. This can range from the very formal, such as requiring students to have standardized test scores, to the local and informal, such as conducting intake interviews. The extent to which diagnostic assessment is useful and should be planned for is determined by the freedom of the instructor and/ or the students to act upon the results. If a course is optional, then students who are shown by a diagnostic test to be very strong or very weak may be advised not to take it, in the first case because they have already mastered (many of) the learning objectives or in the second case because they do not have the necessary level to benefit. If there are multiple levels or groups, then a diagnostic test can help place students appropriately. However, if a given course at a given level is required, then there is less practical value in knowing how well or poorly students are likely to perform on it.

Decisions about final assessment for a course may be influenced, or indeed dictated, by institutional constraints, such as whether the course is credit-bearing and whether students are required to complete it for some purpose (to advance to the next level, to receive their degrees, to be eligible for study abroad, to gain admission to university study without having to take a test like IELTS or TOEFL, etc.). These questions are central in resolving the inherent tensions among various audiences for assessment: the student, university administrators, future employers. Consider, for example, a course on academic speaking. If students enrol in it out of personal choice and it does not generate academic credit, then a meaningful form of assessment could be to ask students to discuss a course-related topic in small groups and follow the discussion with a tutorial, commenting on the strengths and weaknesses of their performance and providing suggestions for addressing areas of weakness. However, if participants need to pass the course in order to be able to work as graduate teaching assistants, then the examiner needs evidence about whether they have passed a certain threshold level in their spoken performance, and the examination must be consistent not only across the group but from year to year. In that case, individual presentations would be more equitable than group discussions, to eliminate the risk that anyone is unfairly helped or hindered by their classmates' performance; the presentations might be video recorded so that the initial impressions can be revisited; and it might be necessary to use a formal marking rubric with headings for areas like the pronunciation of difficult phonemes, intonation and rate of speech, so that every student gets consistent feedback.

Chapter 12 offers a more in-depth discussion of forms of assessment, but it is important that these decisions be made early in the planning stage. Fairness requires that students have accurate expectations about how their attainment of the learning objectives will be measured and what criteria they will be measured against.

Evaluation

In many settings, teachers are required to give students the opportunity to evaluate a course. Even if evaluations are not required, they are valuable tools, as they provide indications of ways in which a course can be developed and improved. Course evaluations frequently come at the end, but if an additional round of evaluation takes place partway through a course, there is an option of addressing any problems which are discovered in time to make the remainder of the course as valuable as possible.

Student comments on a course, usually anonymous, are the most common form of course evaluation, but not the only one possible. A 360-degree evaluation (a concept better established in management studies than in higher education) involves feedback from a range of sources to provide a more complete perspective. Other sources of evaluation in EAP teaching include observations in the classroom from teaching peers and/or from directors of studies. It is also useful for teachers to set some time aside during and at the completion of a course to reflect on and document the successes and the opportunities for improvement.

Profiles of practice

Below, two teachers talk about the extent to which they plan their teaching or leave parts of it flexible.

Lena

I've been teaching a course on writing **research articles** for PhD students and staff for fifteen years. I was responsible for developing the course when it started – and the first few years it ran, I made lots of changes to the materials, borrowed ideas from colleagues, changed assignments back and forth and so on. As the course developed I started to understand what was needed better, and now I know what works and what doesn't. Students write a research article as they do the course, and I read it – in several drafts. In the evaluations they tell me that the feedback on their writing is very valuable, so I don't want to cut back the time I spend on that. As a result, it's my practice to spend minimal time on planning or redesigning the course. I pretty much do what I've been doing the past ten or twelve years.

Jim

When I started teaching at this university two years ago, I inherited a course which had been designed by a woman who retired; then it had been handed on to several other members of staff. My director of studies thinks the course works well, but the students are less positive. Last term, students asked questions about vocabulary in several classes, and so I asked them if they thought we should spend time on that. Most of them thought we should, so we added a book on **academic vocabulary** and did an exercise from it in class every time. The term before that, I noticed problems with basic grammar, and so we worked more with that in class. I think it's important to be responsive to the needs of my students and not just follow the plan to the letter.

1   Which approach is closer to the one you are most familiar with?
2   Are the explanations the teachers give for their approaches good ones?
3   If you were going to argue that one of these teachers should be more like the other, which one would it be, and what would you base your argument on?

TASK 3 Design an EAP course

Three different scenarios are presented below. Pick one of them and write a proposal for EAP instruction suited to the needs of the situation. Your proposal should contain the following:

- a description of the learners' needs;
- a set of expected learning outcomes;
- a description of the course content;
- an indication of the forms of teaching which will be used;
- a description of the forms of assessment which will be used;
- a list of materials which students will be expected to work with.

Your proposal should describe how the principle of constructive alignment has been applied to the planned provision and provide any commentary needed to make connections among the various elements clear (e.g. how the planned teaching will deliver the expected learning outcomes).

Scenario 1. A programme in midwifery at a university in Southeast Asia sends a group of 20 students to a teaching hospital in Australia every year. The students make this trip in the middle of their second year of study. They are in Australia for three months, and spend about half of their working time in classes and half shadowing an experienced midwife and taking part in all her working activities, including patient contact. The agreement between the university and the hospital in Australia indicates that students taking part in the exchange should have a level of English proficiency corresponding to 6.5 on the IELTS or 85 on the TOEFL. At the beginning of the course, students typically are at a level corresponding to 5.5 IELTS/55 TOEFL; some are even weaker.

Scenario 2. A large university in Denmark wishes to recruit more international students at master's level and, in order to attract applicants, has decided to design a series of EAP courses which can be taken concurrently with courses leading to a degree. Although the university's priority is to attract more students from outside Europe, the courses will be open to all students regardless of origin. The courses will also be open to students from across the university's very wide range of subjects. The admissions requirement for most of the university's programmes is an IELTS score of no lower than 6 overall, with at least a 5.5 on all components.

Scenario 3. An established, competitive UK university with a strong academic reputation sets a minimum IELTS score of 7 for most of its courses, and because it attracts applicants with very strong academic backgrounds, it is not felt that there is a need for large-scale EAP provision for international students. However, a course on academic writing for graduates is offered every year for those who are interested. Places in the course are strictly limited and tend to be filled by two rather different groups of students: those who feel they are weak in academic writing and those who are extremely motivated to develop their strong academic writing skills further still. A suggestion has been made that two different courses be developed to address these different groups.

TASK 4 Critical EAP needs analysis

Traditional approaches to needs analysis in EAP have started from several assumptions: that the learner's future needs can be identified; that the gap between the learner's current abilities and future needs can be described; and that EAP instruction can be planned to address the gap. In planning EAP provision, institutional constraints such as the number of teaching hours available and the forms of instruction (e.g. lectures, seminars) are frequently taken as fixed conditions to which the EAP instruction must adapt.

In response to this received view, Benesch (1996) proposed a critical approach to EAP needs analysis and curriculum design. Using the example of an EAP class which was intended to support students in a lecture-based psychology class, she pointed out that the lecture format was as much a barrier to the students' learning as their English proficiency was. This format was the direct result of funding cuts which had caused smaller discussion groups to be eliminated. She described actions which involved inviting the psychology lecturer to the EAP class to answer students' questions in a less impersonal setting and encouraging the students to write letters to the politicians responsible for the budget cuts. She concludes that 'EAP classes can be agencies for social change, both in and outside the academy' (p. 736).

Read Benesch's article and consider its implications for a teaching context you know well. Then write a position paper in which you argue for or against the sort of critical approach to planning EAP provision which Benesch advocated. Illustrate your response to Benesch with concrete examples of workable ways of implementing a critical approach in EAP planning (if your position is positive to Benesch's proposals) or with examples of obstacles to such an approach (if your stance is contra).

REFLECTION

The planning stage of an EAP course is the point at which many decisions are made which will constrain teachers' future choices, and there is a fundamental tension: teachers appreciate the freedom to use methods and approaches with which they are comfortable, but at the same time, planning course content is hugely time intensive, so the more latitude teachers are given to decide on aspects of their teaching, the less time they will have for other activities such as giving feedback. In your view, what is a good balance between comprehensive planning and leaving options open for the classroom teacher?

Further reading and resources

Huhta, M., Vogt, K., Johnson, E., & Tulkki, H. (Eds.). (2013). *Needs analysis for language course design: A holistic approach to ESP*. Cambridge: Cambridge University Press.

This volume offers a new approach to, and instructions for, needs analysis.

Liu, J.-Y., Chang, Y.-J., Yang, F.-Y., & Sun, Y.-C. (2011). Is what I need what I want? Reconceptualising college students' needs in English courses for general and specific/academic purposes. *Journal of English for Academic Purposes, 10*, 271–280.

This article provides a recent take on the question of needs analysis.

Nation, P. (2010). *Language curriculum design*. London: Routledge.

This volume presents a thorough treatment of important issues in designing a language curriculum.

Chapter 6

EAP materials

As we saw in Chapter 5, **needs analysis** is central to EAP teaching and is also of particular relevance to the production of materials, since it is key to both their selection and their development. We will use the term 'materials' to cover both texts and the tasks designed to exploit them for language learning purposes. The aim of this chapter is to explore the options in terms of commercially published materials or those written by yourself. By the end of the chapter you will understand the advantages and disadvantages of both types of materials and be able to take decisions on a sound basis. You will know the principles behind selecting and adapting materials as well as what is involved in writing your own. Before you read this chapter, think about your experience of language teaching materials and answer the questions below.

REFLECTION

Make a list of the different types of materials you have used as a language teacher and learner. Are the materials commercially produced or developed by yourself/others in the institution? Think about some language materials you have used for teaching. What help did the materials provide for you as a teacher? Think about some materials you have used to learn a language. What help did the materials provide for you as a learner?

The many diverse circumstances in which EAP is taught impact upon the type of materials that are used and the reasons for their use. For some teachers, a certain textbook is assigned and must be followed strictly, while others are free to select appropriate commercial materials or develop their own. When considering what help materials offer, you may have mentioned some of the following points. For teachers, materials supply examples of language for teaching along with explanations and tasks; they help organize and structure the teaching and can be a source of new ideas. For students, materials support learning, breaking it down into chunks to make it easier to manage and giving a sense of achievement. Materials can also be motivating and stimulating, providing variety so that students are not dependent solely on the teacher's input. Finally, both teachers and students can use materials as a reference resource.

Authenticity of materials

Before considering the two types of materials, commercial and self-developed, we must first examine the notion of authenticity, which underlies many decisions on materials' use and development. It has been suggested that authenticity is an essential attribute of EAP materials, but what counts as 'authentic' and how important is it to use authentic materials in the EAP classroom?

Authenticity of the text

Originally, the notion of authenticity became important in communicative language teaching and was used to refer to language 'produced by a real speaker or writer for a real audience and designed to convey a real message' (Morrow, 1977, p. 13); authentic texts were thus contrasted with texts produced solely for language learning purposes. This distinction is relevant to the demand for EAP materials to be authentic, so we begin by examining both sides of this issue.

There are two major arguments that proponents of using authentic texts put forward. First, and most importantly, there can be substantial differences in linguistic, pragmatic and discoursal features between the language of specially constructed texts and that used in examples of real academic discourse. Certain features may be over- or underrepresented, completely lacking or even misrepresented when compared with authentic texts. This is because academic texts arise from and are embedded within specific disciplinary contexts; in terms of both content and structure, they form part of what is sometimes called an ongoing 'conversation of the **discipline**'. As specially written materials do not emerge from this disciplinary context, they rarely reflect the features of academic discourse accurately. Many students, especially at pre-study or undergraduate level, have no other access to academic discourse except through their EAP materials, so it is vital that these reflect as closely as possible the discourse that they will encounter at university. It is argued that without a basis in authentic texts, there is a high risk that the materials will fail to meet the real-world communicative needs of the learners.

To counter these arguments, critics of the use of authentic texts point out that authenticity alone does not guarantee suitability for teaching purposes. Texts need to be contextualized within the classroom setting and must be appropriate for the learners and the learning aims of the class. A further, more practical point is that finding appropriate authentic materials can be extremely difficult and time-consuming. As Swales (2009b) points out, input texts must exemplify the target language in terms of **genre** and linguistic structure and be relevant, accessible and engaging in content, a highly demanding set of criteria to fulfil. In support of specially written materials, advocates also argue that constructed texts have the potential to provide a high density of examples of a target feature, thus giving the learner the key advantage of increased exposure to the feature studied.

The second major argument in favour of authentic texts for EAP learners is that they are considered to be intrinsically motivating. Where students have a specific academic goal in mind, they are likely to see the immediate relevance of texts that arise out of the academic and disciplinary context of their studies. Against this, it is argued that many authentic texts are neither interesting nor engaging in themselves and that they are often too difficult for lower-level learners, who may not be able to cope with the vocabulary requirements, or for pre-study learners, who may lack the necessary background in the discipline. In such circumstances, the use of authentic materials could certainly be a demotivating factor. However, it can be argued that by confronting learners with authentic but difficult texts, EAP teachers can help them not only to become more aware of the required level of English, but also to develop strategies for coping with these demands.

It is, of course, essential that authentic texts be carefully chosen so that they correspond to the learners' interests and goals and their English level and academic situation, but of equal importance is the way in which the texts are exploited and the degree of teacher mediation provided. Thus it is possible to assign a less demanding task on a difficult text or vice versa, and it is often suggested that the aim should be to vary the task rather than the text. For example, a reading text that is beyond the vocabulary level of the students can be read for gist, encouraging the students to guess the meaning of unfamiliar words and focus primarily on grasping the main points of the argument. With adequate teacher scaffolding, such a task can be highly motivating, since it has the potential to show students that they can successfully deal with texts that may initially seem too difficult.

TASK I Authenticity and suitability

The following texts can all be considered authentic in the sense that they were all produced under real communicative circumstances.

- Research article
- Video of a lecture given to master's students
- Undergraduate essay

- Recording of student chat before a class
- Email apologizing for arriving late for a seminar
- Instructions for an examination
- Twitter feed from an academic conference
- Article from a science journal for non-specialists
- Blog post on a specialist subject by a well known and respected academic professor

1   Would these texts be suitable for use as teaching material in an EAP context with which you are familiar?
2   Why or why not?

In the task above you may have noticed that all the texts arise within an academic context, but you may also have noted differences among them in producer, intended audience and communicative purpose; thus we would expect each of them to present very different language features. This would mean that some are more suitable for classroom use than others, and their appropriateness would depend upon the teaching context and purpose of the EAP class.

Authenticity of the learner, teacher and task

So far we have considered authenticity as a property of the text alone, but it can also be viewed as an attribute of the contextual circumstances in which the text is embedded. In other words, texts are truly authentic only in their original contexts of production and lose this authenticity when they are removed from that context and presented in class. For example, a research article abstract used for language purposes with an EAP class of graduates is divorced from the circumstances which led to its creation as a summary of the article, and no longer fulfils its communicative purpose of enabling members of the discipline to locate relevant material for their research. In this sense, it is no longer authentic. This argument would suggest that the goal of complete authenticity in the classroom is ultimately unattainable, but while this may be true, it does not mean that all attempts at authenticity should be abandoned. As Widdowson (1978) argues, it is possible for students to authenticate texts for themselves by relating them to their own circumstances and for teachers to make texts relevant and engaging so that they evoke authentic communicative responses from their learners. In this sense, then, we can refer to 'learner and teacher authenticity', the ability of learners and teachers to authenticate materials through their cognitive and **affective** engagement with them.

Considering authenticity in this way, as related to the activity of learning, leads us to the notion of 'task authenticity'. An authentic task is one which has a communicative purpose, involving the learner in a meaningful interaction with the text and/or others in the class. In EAP terms, such tasks often attempt to reflect the real-life purposes for which the language will ultimately be used. In such 'language-*use* tasks' (Widdowson, 1978), the focus is on the communicative purpose, and the outcome is judged on whether that purpose is successfully achieved. For example, an oral presentation could be deemed successful if the audience understood the speaker or asked relevant questions. However, students also need to perform 'language-*learning* tasks', in which the focus is on the language rather than on the communicative intent. Here task authenticity can be achieved through learners and teachers engaging in meaningful interaction which concerns the language itself. For example, analyzing an introduction to a research article and discussing its generic structure in groups does not necessarily reflect real-life procedures of language use, but could well be authenticated by teachers and learners within their own pedagogic situation. In this case, the outcome would be judged on the depth of engagement with the material and whether the students had learned how to structure an introduction. Both types of task can thus be considered authentic in the sense that both allow for the activity of authentication by learners and teachers to take place. Of course, working with authentic texts does not necessarily guarantee the authenticity of tasks, and devising authentic tasks is arguably as important as using authentic materials.

Working with published materials

The issue of authenticity in EAP materials surfaces again as we turn to look at the use of published materials. The role and value of commercially produced materials, primarily textbooks, has been much debated in English language teaching. Given their widespread use, it is important to understand the arguments as they relate to textbooks in EAP.

Arguments for and against EAP textbooks

Harwood (2005a) summarizes the anti-textbook and pro-textbook positions. The first argument adopted in the anti-textbook position is that the language taught in textbooks does not reflect the authentic language of academic work, as **corpus** studies of specialist EAP discourse show. For example, research by Hyland (2000), among others, has revealed extensive disciplinary differences which are often not represented in textbooks. As Harwood points out, this discrepancy is particularly important because where the textbook is inaccurate, both teachers and their students are likely to be misled. Compounding this issue is the fact that textbooks are 'officially sanctioned knowledge', which makes it difficult to challenge or find fault with them. The anti-textbook view also criticizes textbook writers for lacking the necessary theoretical and practical background in linguistics and pedagogy and argues that textbooks are commercial products, more concerned with marketing success than with pedagogical validity. Because textbooks need to reach a wide audience, they are unlikely to meet the specific needs of individual EAP groups adequately.

In opposition to these criticisms, the pro-textbook view holds that textbooks are the product of extensive research and consultation with teachers and publishers. Proponents point out that textbooks save time by easing the burden of preparation for teachers and provide a systematic syllabus and structure, which is difficult for individual teachers to achieve if they provide materials on a week-by-week basis. Textbooks are seen as resources which are used creatively by teachers, who adapt them to their own teaching circumstances rather than following them in every detail. Moreover, textbooks can stimulate teachers' professional development, providing suggestions for new approaches and activities.

Despite some of these undoubted advantages, like Harwood, we would conclude that a weak version of the anti-textbook view can be upheld, since textbooks can only aid teacher development and save preparation time if the contents are valid. The fact that many textbooks are not based on research evidence means that their potential benefits are often not realized. However, this is not an argument against textbooks themselves, but rather a call for them to be improved so that teachers and learners can gain access to the key features of authentic academic discourse.

Evaluating and selecting published materials

Despite their potential drawbacks, you may still prefer or be obliged to use published materials, but if you have the opportunity to choose your materials, how should you make the selection?

Many evaluation checklists have been proposed, but each tends to reflect the context in which it was produced. In consulting any such lists, then, the results of your needs analysis are of key importance in determining exactly the amount of weight to give to each aspect evaluated. The evaluation should take account of the needs and requirements of all those involved in the use of the material. This includes not only those within the classroom itself, the teachers and learners, but also those outside, at institutional (e.g. directors of studies, departmental heads) and societal levels (e.g. ministry of education). There may be external constraints on the selection of materials which need to be considered in addition to their suitability for classroom use.

A two-stage process is often suggested, in which an initial brief evaluation is used to eliminate the least likely materials, followed by an in-depth evaluation of the remaining options. The initial evaluation is based on a quick reading of the introduction, table of contents and publisher's description of the materials, while an in-depth evaluation should ideally involve a close analysis of at least two units of the materials.

Once you have the results of the needs analysis, you can make an initial assessment of the target materials, asking two types of questions: descriptive (What are the materials like?) and evaluative (Are they suitable?). These could include:

- Do the materials deal adequately with the needs identified?
- Is the level suitable?
- Is the content relevant?
- How are the materials organized?
- Can they be implemented in the given teaching circumstances?
- Is the pedagogical approach likely to be effective with students and acceptable to teachers?

Having reduced the number of possible choices, you can now carry out an in-depth evaluation. At this stage you would want to make a more detailed analysis on the basis of the questions above, including investigating the following factors:

- extent of the match between learning objectives and materials
- grading and sequencing of the materials
- treatment of skills and the balance between reading, listening, speaking and writing in multi-skill materials
- type of input used, including the authenticity of texts and whether the input is research-based
- type of activities and tasks, including their authenticity
- type of output expected from students
- roles of teachers both in class and in terms of preparation and feedback
- roles of learners both in class and independently
- affective and cognitive appeal of the materials
- outcomes expected

We should also bear in mind that this pre-use evaluation should be complemented by assessment of the materials during and after use and should form part of a constant and ongoing strand of course evaluation.

TASK 2 Evaluating materials

1 Choose a recent edition of an EAP textbook or other materials (e.g. a website) and carry out an initial evaluation.
2 Now focus on one unit and carry out an in-depth evaluation to determine whether it is suitable for an EAP teaching situation with which you are familiar.
3 Would you select it for your teaching situation? Explain why or why not in a short report.

Adapting materials

No matter how much effort you put into evaluation and selection, published materials are written to cater to a wide, often global, audience and it is therefore highly unlikely that they will meet all the needs of your specific group of students. Some adaptation will therefore be necessary and can be carried out in five ways: by adding, deleting, modifying, simplifying and reordering (McDonough, Shaw & Masuhara, 2013).

- *Adding* is either *quantitative* (providing more material of the same type, e.g. more comprehension questions for a listening task) or *qualitative* (adding new material, e.g. a completely new vocabulary task as a pre-listening activity).
- *Deleting* involves whole units and tasks or parts of them.
- *Modifying* can involve rewriting to change the content, or restructuring to change the way the task is carried out in class; for example an individual writing task could be restructured as a group activity.
- *Simplifying* usually involves adapting the language level of texts.
- *Reordering* can involve individual tasks or whole units.

The main impetus for adaptation is the necessity to align the materials more closely with the teaching circumstances and characteristics of your students. You can use your knowledge of local conditions, professional expertise and familiarity with your students to increase the impact and effectiveness of published materials.

Teachers' and learners' attitudes to and use of textbooks

Textbooks form a key element of teachers' practice and students' classroom experience, but how do users actually regard the books? One way of finding out is to look at the metaphors they employ to describe the book. According to a study by McGrath (2006), teachers saw their textbook in terms of four different functions: guidance (map), support (walking stick), resource (supermarket) and constraint (road block). The first three of these are similar to the roles we noted earlier and show that teachers primarily report positive images of the textbook, regarding it as helpful in various ways. However, there are also a minority of negative perceptions in which the textbook is seen as restrictive and inhibiting.

These metaphors can be mapped onto three categories which describe the roles of teachers in making use of textbooks: 'curriculum-transmitters, curriculum-developers and curriculum-makers' (Shawer, 2010, p. 173). Curriculum-transmitters tend to follow the textbook without deviation, using it as a script to be adhered to strictly, while curriculum-developers adapt the material, as described in the previous section, to make it more appropriate for their learners. Curriculum-makers use the textbook sparingly or not at all, devising their own materials based on an initial needs analysis, although the table of contents may sometimes be used as a stimulus to creativity.

These findings are corroborated in the EAP context by a study of seven teachers' use of the textbook in a medical English course in Saudi Arabia (Menkabu & Harwood, 2014). This research confirms the existence of both guidance and constraint metaphors but found that teachers had more negative perceptions of the textbook, due to their lack of specialist knowledge and insufficient time to cover the required material. Despite these constraints, however, teachers did adapt the textbook to make the materials more appropriate for their learners' needs, thus showing themselves to be curriculum-developers and curriculum-makers. Even in circumstances that are not ideal, then, it is possible to make textbooks work.

Turning to learners, McGrath (2006) showed that they, too, used the metaphors of support, guidance and constraint, but learners also proposed images associated with authority (great mind) and more negative metaphors, including boredom (sleeping pills), worthlessness (rubbish bin) and fear/anxiety (nightmares). Such images underline both the importance of the textbook to learners and the necessity of making an appropriate choice.

One study that addresses EAP students' attitudes to their textbook is by Yakhontova (2001), whose Ukrainian students evaluated Swales and Feak's (1994) *Academic Writing for Graduate Students*. In contrast to more theoretically oriented textbooks, students found the task-based approach refreshing and useful and were especially appreciative of the genre-based sections of the book. However, they also noted a mismatch between Ukrainian and Anglophone academic cultures and Yakhontova therefore argues for the production of modified versions of textbooks, which would take account of local contexts while still introducing students to the use of English in international academic communication.

TASK 3 Your attitudes to textbook use

1   What metaphors would you use to describe a recent language textbook you have used as a) a teacher and b) a student?
2   Are there differences between the two sets of metaphors?
3   What do these metaphors reveal about your attitudes towards textbooks as a teacher and student?

Developing your own materials

We have looked at how to evaluate published materials; however, after doing this, you may conclude that nothing suitable is available, and you may decide to create your own. In this section we look first at the process of developing your own materials and then discuss the advantages and disadvantages of doing so.

We can break down the process of developing materials into five stages, but we should stress that these overlap extensively and that the process is recursive, so that information from a later stage feeds back to modify decisions taken or materials written at an earlier stage. The process begins with general considerations and gradually narrows its scope to focus on the construction, piloting and assessment of specific materials. We start from the assumption that your needs analysis or evaluation of published materials has revealed a gap or insufficiency that you have to address.

Stage 1: Decide general approach

At this stage you need to decide your pedagogical approach and the aim and scope of the materials. Here are some examples of the questions that you need to think about. Will you use a traditional Presentation–Practice–Production procedure or a more inductive approach (see Chapter 4)? Is your aim to teach a specific genre, to practise a skill or something else? How will the materials address the learning objectives (see Chapter 5) and what outcomes are expected? Are you designing a whole course or just a single task? How many hours and weeks of instruction are planned?

Stage 2: Plan materials

At this stage you need to be more specific about exactly what is taught so that you can grade and sequence the materials. You need to take into account not only the linguistic level, but also the cognitive complexity of the tasks, including the demands placed upon learners in terms of the amount of language to be processed, the interaction and/or output required and the amount of support provided. Consider also how material from one unit can be recycled and built upon in later units.

Stage 3: Research the area

With a clear idea of what your materials are going to teach, you can research the area. Use all the approaches described in Chapter 4 to gain as much information as possible. Genre analysis of a set of texts is extremely valuable, especially when used in conjunction with corpus data to give you **lexicogrammatical** information and along with interviews and other data from subject specialists. Read the literature and take note of the findings of other EAP practitioners.

Stage 4: Construct the material

At this stage you are ready to begin writing the materials, incorporating the results of your research. Decide what input sources you will use and whether they will be authentic. Use corpora, subject specialists and your students to supply you with appropriate texts. Write the tasks, situating them within contexts and settings which are relevant to your students in order to achieve authenticity. Tasks should engage the learners both affectively and cognitively, providing them with content that is interesting and appealing and tasks that are challenging but achievable. Check that the tasks meet the learning objectives and ensure that the layout and instructions are clear.

Stage 5: Pilot and evaluate the material

Finally, your materials can be tried out in class. Afterwards, they should be evaluated by both teachers and learners, for example, using questionnaires and interviews. Take into account any test results and the quality of work produced by the students. Collect suggestions for improvement from as many sources as possible. If you are teaching the materials yourself, write a log of what worked and what did not as soon as possible after the class. Reflect on what happened and try to explain why, so that you can use these insights to make improvements. Ideally, there should be several iterations of the materials, so that feedback is not based on experience with a single group. This stage leads back into the design process once more.

Advantages and disadvantages of writing your own materials

With all these aspects to take into consideration, what are the advantages and disadvantages of writing your own materials? Taking the benefits first, producing your own materials ensures the availability of suitable tasks to address the specific needs of your students. Since they are tailormade for your group, tasks can also be interesting, motivating and effective. Moreover, the process of materials writing itself can be professionally rewarding, enabling you to develop new skills and insights into academic discourse, learning and pedagogy. Against these benefits, however, we should note the huge investment of time and effort involved in writing your own materials and the possibility that they may not be of high quality. The description of the process by Stoller and Robinson (2014) makes clear that extensive research and analysis underlie the production of successful materials and that several cycles of writing, piloting and rewriting are necessary before they can be considered ready for use. Not every EAP teacher has the means or opportunity to make such a commitment and where resources are lacking, the materials produced may be neither reliable nor effective.

> **TASK 4 Design a task**
>
> 1 Choose an EAP teaching situation with which you are familiar and specify its social and linguistic context.
> 2 Decide on an appropriate goal and task type.
> 3 Find suitable authentic content and construct your task.
> 4 Pilot and evaluate your task with an EAP group, or ask a colleague to evaluate it and suggest possible improvements.

Technology and materials

The technological developments that have revolutionized communication generally are having a similar impact upon materials design and development. There are two major ways in which this impact occurs: new technologies provide a means of discovering and accessing content and a means of producing and practising language. In other words they offer resources for language learning and frameworks within which language learning can take place. In the first of these roles, the Internet makes available a wealth of material that is suitable as the basis for EAP classes, including, for example, podcasts from university websites, massive open online courses (MOOCs) and other open access academic resources. Access to such online resources expands the choice of authentic material available and allows it to be found more easily. Internet-based materials have the potential to bring experts in relevant fields directly into the EAP classroom, an option which would otherwise be unavailable to the majority of students. The challenge, however, is to choose appropriate content, not only in terms of subject matter, but also in terms of genre and features of academic discourse (see Chapter 7 for a discussion of these aspects). For example, a TED talk (https://www.ted.com/talks) may be suitable in topic and engaging in delivery but is likely to differ significantly from an academic lecture or conference presentation. As with traditional materials, content should be chosen to fit student needs, and tasks should be constructed that contribute to achieving the learning objectives of the course.

In terms of a framework for language learning, the opportunity for students to create, share and respond to content has become more widespread through the use of virtual learning environments (VLEs), email, social media, blogs and other forms of computer-mediated communication (CMC). It is now easier for students to collaborate, upload their work and share it more widely, as well as to respond to others' content more immediately. For example, social media sites such as Facebook can be used to organize group work and provide the opportunity for peer-to-peer feedback, while text messaging and Twitter can enable students to comment on a classmate's presentation in real time (Bloch, 2013). However, in addition to facilitating human interaction *via* the computer, CMC also promotes interaction *with* the computer, for example, in language-learning tasks. Computer-assisted language learning (CALL) materials can provide immediate feedback on how well a student performs and can offer individualized, targeted practice to address weaknesses.

CALL materials also offer specific affordances that distinguish them from traditional materials (Reinders & White, 2010). First, they have a multimedia capability, that is, the ability to integrate text, video, images, animation and sound and to allow users to interact with the material. This enriches the learning environment and offers scope for accommodating students' different learning styles by enabling users to select their preferred media. Second, CALL materials are available for use anywhere and at any time, an attribute becoming increasingly important, given the spread of hand-held devices such as smartphones and tablets. Mobile-assisted language learning (MALL) exploits the prevalence of such devices; for example, students can access websites in class and evaluate them for their suitability as academic sources. A useful checklist for developing this aspect of digital literacy is provided by Stapleton and Helms-Park (2006). A third affordance of CALL materials is that information can be presented and accessed in a non-linear way, which allows users to determine their own pathways through the material. In order to support this process, student activity can be tracked and the program can offer suggestions to enhance learning; the use of e-portfolios, which help students reflect on their learning and plan for future study, can also be effective, although the system has to be carefully designed to maximize student engagement (Tuksinvarajarn & Watson Todd, 2009). CALL materials, then, can enable students to exercise greater control over their learning and help them to become more reflective and autonomous learners. As with all new approaches, however, decisions on adopting new technologies should be driven by the pedagogical advantages they offer within the individual teaching context.

TASK 5 Evaluating CALL materials

Access some CALL EAP materials (e.g. through the **BALEAP** website: https://www.baleap.org//resources/eap-related-websites). Do one of the tasks and evaluate the material by answering the following questions.

1   To what extent does the material exploit the affordances of CALL? That is, what does it do that could not be done without CALL? For example, does it provide students with a multimedia experience, or can it be used in a non-linear way?
2   Would your students find the material more user friendly or more effective than traditional types of material?
3   Would you use this material in your own teaching context? Why or why not? Can you suggest any improvements that would make it more useful?

Profiles of practice

Here are some views of teachers on using and developing EAP materials. Read them and answer the questions below.

Saeed

My college isn't well resourced in terms of technology, but almost all my students have smartphones. I used to ask them not to use their phones in class, but then I realized that Internet access was an advantage. Sometimes I divide the class into groups and get each group to choose a different website on the same topic. They have to introduce their website to the other groups and explain why they chose it. Then the class chooses the best one. This helps them think about what makes a website suitable for academic work.

Mitsuko

I have just finished my PhD using corpus analysis to investigate disciplinary differences in master's **dissertations**. I've got a job as an EAP instructor at a university where I have the opportunity to turn my research results into materials for my class. It does take time, but the students really appreciate the authentic texts and corpus results I give them and I can re-use the materials next year.

Felicia

I teach at a university where I have a large group of undergraduate engineering students (about 80). They are lower intermediate level and not at all interested in English. As I don't know much about engineering, I follow the textbook. The students seem to like this, because they know what to expect. I am not confident enough to create my own materials and I don't think it should be the job of the teacher. Authors and publishers are specialists in that.

Patrice

I've taught EFL at a private school for about 10 years, but for the last two years I have also had to teach in a presessional EAP course. To be honest, I can't see what all the fuss is about. For grammar, I just use the general language materials that I've always used, although for reading I sometimes take a scientific report from the newspaper. There's no point in looking for authentic materials; they'll get that from the subject specialists when they join their courses.

1   How relevant to your own situation are the teaching circumstances described above?
2   To what extent do you agree with the teachers' views?
3   Do you use materials in a similar way, and if not, how does your use differ and why?

REFLECTION

Think about the issues we have dealt with in this chapter: the authenticity of materials, the value of textbooks, the development of your own materials and the impact of technology on materials. What is your position with regard to each of these issues? Have your views changed since reading the chapter? What effect will your views have on your future use of materials in EAP?

Further reading and resources

Cowie, N., & Sakui, K. (2013). It's never too late: An overview of e-learning. *ELT Journal, 67*, 459–467.
This paper provides an easy-to-read description of some current uses of e-learning.
Harwood, N. (Ed.). (2010). *English language teaching materials: Theory and practice*. Cambridge: Cambridge University Press.
This volume contains a useful section of chapters on EAP.
Harwood, N. (Ed.). (2014). *English language teaching textbooks: Content, consumption, production*. Basingstoke: Palgrave Macmillan.
The introduction gives a good overview of research on textbooks. Several chapters concern EAP.
Materials Development Association (MATSDA)
You have to pay to join MATSDA, but the website has useful sample articles available free at http://www.matsda.org/
Mol, H., & Tan, B.T. (2008). EAP materials in New Zealand and Australia. In B. Tomlinson (Ed.), *English language learning materials: A critical review* (pp. 74–99). London: Continuum.
This paper reviews three presessional course books at intermediate to early advanced level.
Tribble, C. (2009). Writing academic English: A survey review of current published resources, *ELT Journal, 63*, 400–417.
This article surveys approaches to writing as well as reviewing a wide range of books.

Section III

Teaching and assessing EAP

Chapter 7

Academic discourse

In Sections I and II of this book, we considered general issues regarding the position of EAP and the factors involved in planning an EAP course. Here we narrow our focus to specific aspects of EAP teaching and start by addressing the questions 'What is academic discourse like?' and 'How can I teach it?' After reading this chapter, you will know how academic discourse varies and will understand several key discoursal issues that may cause problems for EAP students. This knowledge will help you make decisions about selecting texts and choosing features of discourse to teach or practise in class.

REFLECTION

What are the main differences between a) and b) in each pair of examples? Think about aspects such as the purpose of the text, the producer and the audience.

1	a) essay	b) newspaper article
2	a) seminar discussion	b) conversation
3	a) lecture for undergraduates	b) textbook for undergraduates
4	a) **research article**	b) seminar discussion
5	a) conference presentation	b) undergraduate presentation
6	a) research article	b) essay

How do you think these differences affect the linguistic features that you would find in each example?

You probably noticed that there are several important ways in which we can distinguish these examples, including academic (1a, 2a) versus non-academic discourse (1b, 2b); spoken academic (3a, 4b) versus written academic discourse (3b, 4a); expert producer (5a, 6a) versus non-expert producer (5b, 6b); specialist audience (1a, 2a) versus non-specialist audience (1b, 2b); purpose of the communication: transmit new research knowledge (5a, 6a) versus display knowledge gained by the student (5b, 6b). The differences between these examples lead to differences in the linguistic features that typically occur. For example, a lecture is more likely to use contractions (*we've*) than a textbook, while a seminar discussion would use more second person pronouns (*you mentioned*) than a **research article (RA)**.

Variation in academic discourse

As you saw in the Reflection above, the notion of variation between texts is essential both for distinguishing academic from non-academic discourse and for making finer distinctions within academic discourse as a whole. Let us look, then, at some aspects of variation that are important in EAP.

Variation in register

When we approach a text, we can recognize that it arises out of a certain social context; in other words, it belongs to a certain **register**. For example, we recognize a student essay as belonging to an educational context because we make a connection between the characteristics of educational activity and the way in which language is used in that context. Here are three examples of texts that might arise in the context of academic life:

1   An examination question on the causes of World War I for an undergraduate course in history
2   A conversation between two undergraduates about the history examination question above
3   An undergraduate seminar on the causes of World War I

When we assign a text to a register, we rely on three aspects of the social context (Halliday, 1978):

- *Field* covers the subject matter of the text and the social activity of the participants.
- *Tenor* covers aspects of the relationship and roles of the participants, including the level of formality.
- *Mode* is the way language functions in the situation and includes whether the text is spoken or written.

Thus we can characterize the register of 1 above by saying that the field is specialized history, the tenor is formal and the mode is written. The use of these three aspects also allows us to differentiate between 1, 2 and 3. Although they share the same field, they differ in terms of tenor and mode: 2 is in spoken mode with an informal tenor, while 3 is in spoken mode with a formal tenor.

For students, the field is often specified, but learners may have difficulty achieving the expected tenor; for example, they may use features typical of spoken discourse in their written texts, or their spoken presentations may be too formal. Such problems lead to texts which are inconsistent in register. As EAP teachers, if we take into account the register aspects of field, tenor and mode, we can differentiate between texts that might otherwise seem similar, which helps us choose more appropriate texts for our students. This is especially important because different registers are associated with different sets of **lexicogrammatical** features. While it might be tempting to base a task on a text from a newspaper because it is more accessible, the language that learners encounter in such a text will not be typical of written academic discourse.

Variation between spoken and written academic discourse: Multidimensional analysis

One key aspect of variation in academic discourse is between written and spoken modes. In this section, we see how variation in mode can be investigated using multidimensional analysis (MDA) (Biber, 1988). MDA is an approach which uses statistical techniques to identify clusters of co-occurring linguistic features in large **corpora**. Texts which share patterns of linguistic co-occurrence are assumed to share common communicative functions and thus to belong to the same register or **genre**. MDA allows us to characterize the features of a set of texts and to compare it with any other set to determine how they vary.

Biber (2006) uses MDA to describe the characteristics of a range of discourse types that students encounter at university, including both academic genres like seminars and administrative ones like brochures. His findings show that there are consistent differences between spoken and written discourse, whatever its purpose. Thus all the written discourse is dense in information and uses elaborated reference, features often achieved through the use of noun phrases and nominalization (*detailed consideration of this example*) (see the section below for more detail on nominalization). Written language also uses an impersonal style, marked by the use of conjuncts (*however*), passive verb forms without *by* and subordinators (*because*). Spoken academic discourse tends to be characterized by features that show the personal involvement of the speaker, such as the use of contractions and first and second person pronouns (*I'm, you've*). It is also marked by situation-dependent references, which are those that can only be understood within the immediate context and include time and place adverbials like *next* and *earlier*.

These differences are found because the circumstances of production differ between spoken and written academic discourse. Written language is usually permanent and pre-planned, which enables the production of dense text and the use of elaborated reference; it is produced outside the presence of a relatively unspecified reader, which accounts for its impersonal style. Spoken language tends to be unrehearsed, short-lived and produced in real time, usually in the presence of listeners. This results in features of situation-dependent reference and a more personal, involved style. However, the distinction between spoken and written discourse is not absolute; we can view texts as situated along a continuum of oral to literate production. For example, spoken discourse that is monologic and pre-planned (e.g. lectures) is likely to show more features of written discourse than relatively unplanned discourse with more than one speaker (e.g. seminars).

Variation in disciplines

One of the most important variables that affects all aspects of academic discourse is the **discipline**. It is disciplines that structure both the work that academics perform and the courses that students follow. In their classic study of academic disciplines, Becher and Trowler (2001) describe them in terms of 'academic tribes' which have 'territories'. This metaphor vividly captures the nature of disciplines as groupings that consist of people and networks of communication (the tribal aspect) as well as typical subject matters and ways of constructing knowledge (the territorial aspect).

Individual disciplines can be categorized broadly according to subject matter as belonging to one of four **domains**: hard-pure (physics, chemistry), soft-pure (philosophy, sociology), hard-applied (clinical medicine, engineering) or soft-applied (business studies, education). Although the boundaries between the four domains cannot be precisely drawn and even within a single subject area there can be considerable diversity of approach, it is possible to identify certain features that characterize each domain.

- Hard-pure fields tend to deal with universals and be impersonal and value-free; they construct knowledge cumulatively, with one person's work building on that of another; work typically leads to outcomes of discovery and explanation.
- Soft-pure fields are more concerned with particular cases and are more personal and value-laden. The development of knowledge is predominantly recursive, i.e. the views of others are put forward in order to take up a position in relation to them; work tends to result in understanding and interpretation.
- Hard-applied disciplines are concerned with technological know-how and control over the physical environment. They have clear functional purposes; work tends to result in products and techniques.
- Soft-applied fields are also functional; they are concerned with improving professional practice and often take a case study approach; work tends to lead to the development of protocols and procedures.

These fundamental differences between disciplines lead to differences in discourse, as confirmed by many contrastive studies. The corpus-based work of Hyland has been particularly influential in providing linguistic data which support Becher and Trowler's analysis. For example, in a large study of 240 RAs, Hyland (2001) showed that first person pronoun use was much lower in hard than soft fields, a finding which underscores the description of hard fields as dealing with universals in an impersonal and objective way.

Disciplinary differences, then, are an important variable which we need to take into account. In multidisciplinary contexts, it may not be possible to provide material in all relevant disciplines and even in single-discipline classes there may be field-specific variation with accompanying differences in discoursal features. In both cases, however, we can avoid making over-generalizations and encourage students to examine the discourse of their own discipline individually.

Variation in genre

As we saw in Chapter 4, genres belong to discourse communities and arise to carry out the purposes of those communities. Thus in educational contexts we expect a textbook to be a long text divided into chapters which contain explanations and examples, while a handout is likely to be a short text consisting of several paragraphs with information in bullet points. In order to decide which genre these texts belong to, we activate our knowledge of the way in which teachers generally achieve two different purposes: the textbook gives extensive explanations, while the handout supplies a set of notes. Thus in very general terms, genre can be thought of as combining register with purpose. For a text to be successful, it needs to be consistent in both register and genre. It would be inappropriate if a textbook writer addressed the reader as 'darling', since this would be inconsistent in terms of register, specifically tenor. Nor would we expect it to include a chapter containing greetings to the reader, as this **move** belongs to conversational genres and would make the text inconsistent in terms of genre.

As genres carry out different purposes within their discourse communities, their language features differ as well. One important distinction is between expert and learner genres, which we can illustrate by contrasting the RA with the doctoral **thesis**. Although these two genres may seem similar, they have different purposes and audiences and it is these that drive the discoursal differences. As we saw in the Reflection, the RA is written by an expert to fellow experts and is designed to transmit new research knowledge. The doctoral thesis, however, has both fellow experts and examiners as readers and must therefore convey new research knowledge, while also displaying extensive mastery of the field. This leads to greater attention being paid to the literature review, since this is a key site for displaying the writer's in-depth disciplinary knowledge (Swales, 2004).

Variation according to genre has important implications for the choice of texts and their use in the EAP class. Thus an expert genre like the RA is not necessarily suitable for teaching writing to undergraduates, since students at this level are not normally required to present new knowledge to the **disciplinary community** as experts. However, to the extent that undergraduates are expected to read RAs, the genre could provide appropriate material for teaching reading. The choice of suitable texts depends upon the results of the **needs analysis** and the individual teaching circumstances of the teacher, but an understanding of variation in academic discourse is important to inform this choice.

TASK I Variation in EAP

1   Choose two short texts/extracts (about 200 words each) of academic discourse which vary in mode (spoken/written), discipline and genre. Use **MICASE** for spoken texts and **MICUSP** for written texts. See Chapter 4 for access details.
2   Compare the two texts and identify at least five features that characterize the variation in mode, discipline and genre.
3   Do your two texts show the differences in usage that you would expect? Explain what you find.
4   Would a similar task be useful for your students? Why or why not?

Key features of academic discourse

In this section we are particularly concerned with features that affect the construction of discourse beyond the sentence level, rather than with sentence-level grammar points. We do not provide a full account of all important features; instead we focus on those aspects that are likely to cause students problems, particularly when they try to produce texts themselves.

Among the criticisms that are often voiced by content lecturers is that student texts are 'disjointed'; they fail to make a point or develop arguments logically. We begin by considering how information is presented in English and what makes a text flow.

Theme and information structure

In order to explain why such problems occur, we can analyze clauses as thematic units and information units (Halliday, 1994). The 'theme' of a clause is the first element; it establishes what you are talking about; the remaining part of the clause is called the 'rheme'; it establishes what you are saying about your theme and any associated circumstances. As illustration, we take the extract in Table 7.1.

Table 7.1 Theme and rheme

Theme	Rheme
Written language	is usually **permanent and pre-planned**
which	enables **the production of dense text and the use of elaborated reference;**
it	is produced **outside the presence of a relatively unspecified reader...**
Spoken language	tends...

The theme is often the subject of a clause and is chosen so that it fits in with what has gone before, thereby enabling the reader to understand how the information in the present clause relates to previous information. Thus, maintaining the same theme will ensure that a text keeps its focus on the topic discussed; in the example in Table 7.1, *it* refers back to *written language*, while *which* refers back to the whole of the previous clause. A change in theme (*Spoken language*) signals a textual boundary and alerts the reader to a shift in focus.

In terms of information structure, the English clause tends to begin with 'given information', i.e. information which is known to both producer and receiver, and to end with 'new information', which is the point of the clause, the reason for writing or speaking. Thus it is the rheme that generally carries the new information that the writer wants to convey, seen in bold in Table 7.1. Texts often progress by using an element of new information from the rheme as the given element in the thematic position of the next clause. In the following example, the new information of the first sentence is in bold; it becomes the given information of the second sentence (underlined). We understand *This research* as given information because it refers to *a study*, the new information of the previous sentence.

> *These findings are corroborated by **a study of textbook use in Saudi Arabia**. This research confirms the existence of both guidance and constraint metaphors.*

Information and thematic structure are essential to the development of texts, and problems in this area can cause difficulties for readers, who may not be able to establish how one statement relates to another or to identify the point of the message. An understanding of these elements of discourse structure can help students create texts that flow more smoothly and in which the new information is readily distinguishable.

Cohesion

In addition to difficulties with theme and information structure, students may also struggle to produce texts that are cohesive. Cohesion refers to the way in which text is created through lexical and grammatical ties which connect one part of the text to another in meaning (Halliday & Hasan, 1976).

Many EAP materials provide guidance and practice on cohesive ties, but the teaching of conjunction (*however, as a result*) is often given more weight than other options, leading to a situation in which students attempt to use conjunctive ties as a substitute for adequate management of theme and information structure. This approach leads to texts that have a sort of spurious surface cohesion but are fundamentally not coherent, as seen in the student example below, where *at the same time* does not succeed in establishing cohesion between the sentences.

> *Stone is one of the most widely applicable materials in building.* **At the same time** *stone decay has become a commonly used term in scientific journals (Viles, 1994).*

Thematic choice, information structure and cohesion, then, are important aspects of discourse that students need to be able to handle if they are to produce effective academic texts. As shown in the example, problems in this area can lead to texts that are difficult to follow or where readers cannot distinguish the point that the writer is trying to make.

Noun phrases and nominalization

A high use of noun phrases is a key characteristic of written academic discourse, as shown by Biber and Gray (2010), who find that academic writing is predominantly constructed around the use of nouns, while conversation tends to privilege verbs. In particular, academic writing is characterized by its use of noun phrases, which are often premodified by adjectives (*economic weakness*) and nouns (*an absorption spectrometer*) and/or postmodified by prepositional phrases (*areas of concern*).

One effect of this nominal/phrasal style is to make the text structurally compressed; but while concision is highly prized in academic writing, a very compressed text is likely to be more difficult for students to read and write. In the following example, we can see a typically complex noun phrase (in bold) and contrast it with its much lengthier and rather clumsy clausal equivalent.

> **The erosion rate of 0v.126 mg/g for this air plasma sprayed thermal barrier coating** *is low. . .*

> *The coating, which is designed to form a barrier to heat and which is fabricated by being sprayed with plasma while it is exposed to the air, eroded at the rate of 0.126 mg/g, which is low . . .* (clausal equivalent)

Noun phrases contribute to the construction of **terminology** and act as a sort of shorthand for specialists, but the relations between the elements are not clearly specified, making them difficult for learners and non-specialists to understand. It may not be obvious, for example, what *air plasma sprayed* means. Is *air plasma* a type of plasma? Is the coating sprayed with air or with plasma? Similarly, noun phrases are difficult for students to produce. They might write *thermal coating barrier* or *erosion rate with 0.126 mg/g*. Thus learners need plenty of exposure to and practice with authentic academic texts that are characterized by the use of this nominal style.

Nominalization is the use of a noun or noun phrase to express the meaning of a process or property; for example, the process of *explaining* can be nominalized as *explanation*. Nominalization has several important effects on the text. First, it makes texts more abstract. For example, when we use the clause *writers use nouns*, we need a subject and verb, but when we nominalize it, these elements disappear: *the use of nouns*. Nominalization also allows us to re-present material in a reduced form, which can create cohesion by functioning as given information. For example, in the two sentences below, *this position* is a nominalization of the clause *EAP textbooks do not represent authentic academic discourse* and is given information.

> *It has been argued that EAP textbooks do not represent authentic academic discourse. **This position** is supported by several corpus-based studies.*

The nominalization labels the whole of the previous statement in a way that shows the reader how the information is to be understood (it is a *position*) and may indicate the writer's **stance** (see the next section for an explanation of stance). For example, if the writer wanted to accept the criticism of textbooks, the nominalization *this problem* could be used. The choice of nominalization also indicates to the reader how the text will proceed. We expect a *problem* to be followed by potential solutions, but a *position* to be supported or challenged.

Thus the effects of nominalization are far-reaching; not only does it contribute to the construction of terminology, making texts more concise and abstract, but it can also create cohesion, indicate the writer's stance and help the reader follow the text. It is thus essential for students to understand the multifunctionality of nominalization and to practise both reading and writing texts that have a high density of such nominal expressions.

Stance and evaluation

Although you may think of academic discourse as being objective and neutral, its key purpose is to persuade the audience that the work reported is valid and reliable. In support of this claim, a large body of research has shown the widespread use of evaluative language in academic texts. **Stance** or evaluation can be defined as the expression of the writer/speaker's attitudes, opinions, judgements or feelings. Students may be most concerned about whether to use *I, we* or a passive form, but stance is expressed through many lexical and grammatical means, including adverbials (*unfortunately*), clauses (*it is surprising that*), modal verb forms (*should*) and noun-preposition phrases (*the evidence of*).

In earlier sections, we saw that stance varies according to mode (Biber, 2006) and discipline (Hyland, 2001); it also varies according to genre, as Harwood (2005b) shows in computer science. He found that the use of *I* was rare in RAs but widespread in master's **dissertations,** where its purpose was to impress the examiner by portraying the writer as a careful researcher. Indeed, when students underuse personal pronouns, especially for important functions such as making claims, their texts can lack credibility and authority (Hyland, 2002). Thus in making decisions on personal pronoun use, students need to consider not just disciplinary and genre usage, but also the function of the pronoun in the text.

Another stance feature that may cause difficulty for learners is **hedging**. A hedge is a word or phrase that lessens the impact of a statement. Its use allows authors to modify their commitment to what they say, as seen in the example below (hedge in bold).

> *The reason for this is not clear. It **could** result from local variations . . .*

Hedging allows authors to present information even under conditions of uncertainty and offers some protection from being attacked. In the example above, the hedge *could* makes it more difficult to criticize the explanation because the author has not signalled full commitment to its truth. Hedging is also used for politeness reasons because the reduction in commitment has the effect of softening the author's statement. Making a new claim is always potentially threatening to others in the field, since it may run counter to other work or established views. In these circumstances, hedging not only shows modesty regarding the author's own work but also makes criticisms of other researchers more acceptable within the field. This is particularly important for learners, who may be urged to be critical but may feel uncertain about challenging more experienced researchers. The following example shows the use of the hedge *may well* to soften criticism of a measure suggested by an earlier researcher. The criticism (*too strict*) would be much stronger without the hedge.

> *Russell (2009) suggests a measure for important cases. . . . It **may well** be that this measure is too strict . . .*

Hedging is only interpretable within its disciplinary and generic contexts, and achieving the appropriate level of hedging is part of what students learn as they become familiar with disciplinary norms and expectations. However, work on recognizing, understanding and incorporating hedges will sensitize students to the importance of this area and help them deal with it more competently.

Intertextuality and source use

Another key characteristic of academic discourse is its intertextuality. In other words, academic texts constantly refer to the work of earlier researchers, making use of it in the construction of the author's own arguments. The use of sources can pose significant problems for EAP students, ranging from the mechanics of **citation** conventions to issues surrounding plagiarism (see Chapter 12).

Different citation conventions are followed in different fields and students must be aware of and use the appropriate conventions. However, good source use is much more complex than simply following conventions; citation is a key tool for achieving the purpose of the text. Varying the form of citation allows the writer to create different rhetorical effects, and there are several different aspects that deserve students' attention. First, citations can be categorized into two types according to the way in which they are incorporated into the text (Swales, 1990). In **integral citation**, the name of the cited author has a role in the grammar of the reporting sentence; in **non-integral citation**, the name of the cited author appears in parentheses or a number refers to the name, which is given in the list of references.

Integral citation

1 Baudrillard argues that representations of reality are really constructions of reality.[8]
2 I will refer to aspects of Swales's (2004) model where relevant in this thesis.

Non-integral citation

3 This material is found to be relatively electron-beam sensitive [66].
4 This finding echoes those of other researchers (e.g. Boulton, 2010; Yoon, 2011).

Both integral and non-integral citation can be used with any type of citation convention, although there is a tendency for numerical conventions to employ more non-integral forms. The choice of citation type has been associated with the prominence assigned to the elements of the citation: integral citation places emphasis on the cited author, whereas non-integral citation gives emphasis to the finding. For this reason, very frequent integral citations can create an impression of a less confident writer. Non-integral citation also allows the citation of multiple sources for a single statement, as in example 4, thus creating a more compressed and less explicit style of referencing.

It is also valuable for learners to study the grammar that is often used for citation, in particular, the use of a reporting clause followed by a *that*-clause complement, as seen in example 1 above. Here, the reporting clause (*Baudrillard argues*) introduces the cited work, while the complement clause contains the cited finding. Reporting clauses are useful in citation because they allow the author to introduce the ideas and statements of others and at the same time to comment on them through the choice of reporting verb. Thus some reporting verbs, such as *show* and *demonstrate*, commit the writer to accepting the validity of the cited work; others (*underestimate*) show the writer's lack of acceptance of the cited work; the majority, however, (*argue, state*) are neutral in terms of commitment. Hence reporting clauses are one of the ways in which authors can show their stance in relation to the literature.

A third approach to citation focuses on the functions they perform. Work by Petrić (2007) on master's dissertations distinguished seven different functions and identified those that were more likely to occur in assignments that gained high grades. She found that the more successful writing tended to include citation types that incorporated some element of writer comment or stance with regard to the source. These included evaluating the cited work, comparing the cited work with the writer's work and establishing links between two or more cited sources. By contrast, the lower rated assignments tended to use citation simply to attribute language or content to another source, without incorporating any comment on it.

Students in EAP classes, then, need practice not just in referring to the sources of ideas and content, but also in making clear how these sources contribute to the construction of their own argument. They may need help to convey the purpose of the citation in relation to their own work and to create their own research story out of the disciplinary literature.

TASK 2 Selecting texts for teaching features of academic discourse

1   Find a text (written or spoken) that would be suitable for teaching one or more of the features of academic discourse described above (information structure, nominalization, stance, source use) to an EAP group you are familiar with.
2   What feature(s) of academic discourse would you teach and why?
3   What makes this text suitable for these students?

Teaching and learning features of academic discourse

In the previous section, we examined some discoursal issues that may cause problems for learners; next we consider some approaches that have been used to deal with such issues in EAP contexts.

If you are an experienced general English teacher, you may have used an approach which is based on teaching a set of grammar points using the deductive procedure of Presentation–Practice–Production (PPP). PPP is based on a view of language as divisible into discrete items that can be taught separately, and is thus often implemented at the level of the individual sentence. While needs analysis may show that your students require practice in sentence-level grammatical features, they will also have to handle discoursal features, which span whole texts. It is these features that we have particularly highlighted in the section above. Thus even where we can distinguish an individual instance, for example of a hedge, it does not operate in isolation, but rather in conjunction with the statement it modifies, situating that information in relation to the entire argument. Working at sentence level, then, is limited in its applicability, since it does not allow us to take account of this wider context and the discoursal and interpersonal implications of the feature we are teaching.

Approaches to teaching academic discourse contrast with PPP in that the starting point is typically the text; as Swales (2002) points out, EAP is characterized by its top-down approach. Genre-based work (see Chapter 4) is of this type, since it begins by analyzing an example of a genre, considering its audience, purpose and the social context in which it occurs and identifying its constituent moves and **steps** in order to understand how its structure fulfils its purpose. The linguistic features of the text are studied to ascertain how they are used to realize this generic structure, and while individual features are practised, such work is performed in relation to the genre being taught and with an understanding of why the feature is used and how it functions to achieve its purpose.

When teaching a genre, students' attention can be drawn to important linguistic features by means of questions which instruct them to identify certain forms and link them to their functions or vice versa. Learners can also be asked to compare different versions of the text or to modify the text themselves so that they can observe the way in which changes in the text lead to changes in its effect. The aim is to increase students' conscious awareness of a given feature, a procedure which draws on the hypothesis that learners must first notice language features before they can be learned (Schmidt, 1990). Building on their increased awareness, students can then be asked to incorporate the studied feature into their own example of the genre.

In contrast to a genre-based approach, corpus-based work is a bottom-up procedure. Corpora (see Chapter 4) offer a useful supplement to work on texts and are especially relevant in the case of a register- or genre-specific corpus. However, their most important benefit is that they provide multiple authentic examples of the feature studied. This allows the implementation of an inductive approach such as that proposed by Carter and McCarthy (1995): Illustration–Interaction–Induction. Illustration exposes students to authentic data in the form of concordances. At the Interaction stage students discuss the data, with the teacher retaining the option of intervention to help them notice features and come to conclusions. Finally, at the Induction stage, students formulate their own rules or generalizations derived from the data. This procedure also promotes noticing and encourages students to make and test hypotheses.

How, then, can features of academic discourse be taught? We have outlined some possible options above and clearly your work must fit within your own context and meet the needs of your learners. However, it is important to adopt an approach that allows for the teaching of discoursal features to be integrated into work on texts and for students to focus on the construction of meanings that are appropriate and relevant within their academic context. Finally, we would encourage you to experiment where possible and reflect on what works. Teaching and learning are such complex activities that there can be no one-size-fits-all formula and a combination of approaches is most likely to prove effective.

TASK 3 Texts and contexts for teaching academic discourse

Here are some types of texts that have been used to teach written academic discourse.

- A report from a newspaper on the discovery of a new cancer drug
- An essay that gained a good grade, written by an undergraduate for a geography course
- A set of research article abstracts in economics
- A text on university life, specially written by the teacher to illustrate stance features

1   In each case, can you think of a teaching context in which this type of material would be suitable? Consider the type of students who could use it and the features it could be used to teach.
2   If you do not think the text could be used successfully, explain why it would be unsuitable.

Profiles of Practice

Read the following descriptions by four EAP teachers who use either top-down or bottom-up approaches for teaching features of academic discourse and then respond to the questions below.

Karin

My students know a lot about academic discourse in theory, but they often don't link it to their own practice, so I try to use their writing as the basis for work. After they've done an essay, I collect examples of the feature I want them to focus on, for example nominalization, and compile them on a handout. I choose short extracts which are either successful or unsuccessful. I give this out and the students have to work in groups to discuss the examples and, if necessary, improve them. We then discuss their ideas in the whole class; students have to choose the best version and explain why it works well. It's not enough for them to say, 'It sounds better!'

Igor

All my students share the same first language, so they tend to have the same problems. They take a test at the beginning of the term and I use the results as the basis for prioritizing what to teach. Each week, we focus on one grammar point, for example conjunction, and I ask the students to read the relevant section in the grammar book. In class, I go over the explanation and we do the practice sentences from the book. For homework I ask them to write a paragraph using the point they have been practising and we have a test on it in class the next week. This way I can keep a good check on what they've done and we manage to cover all the material for the end-of-term exam. The students also know where they are and what they are supposed to have learned.

Jaemin

I like using MICUSP. So at the beginning of the term I show students how to access it and use the examples to help with their writing. They really like this because it's something new and they can do it by themselves. When I want to teach a specific feature, say the use of first person pronouns in written reports, I take some relevant examples from the corpus, get them to look at the data in groups and come up with some generalizations. We discuss their ideas and they have to use what they've learned in writing their own report.

Pilar

I want my students to see how certain linguistic features are linked to genre moves and steps. Sometimes they seem to think that choosing, for example, a modal verb is quite arbitrary. If they can understand the reason behind the language choices, I think that helps them later when they write on their own. For example, when we focus on writing a discussion section, I revise the use of modal expressions. I get them to underline all the examples they can find in the text we're using and we discuss why they're used, linking their function to the moves of the discussion. Then they have to write a discussion section for homework and again I get them to underline all the modal expressions they've used.

1 Have you used any of these methods?
2 If so, were they successful? Why or why not?
3 Are there any new approaches that could be useful or any that would not be suitable in your teaching context? Why or why not?

TASK 4 Debate on the place of grammar in EAP

Think about your experience of teaching grammar so far, in both general and EAP contexts and discuss the following questions. Explain the reasons for your opinions and give examples to support them.

1 Compared with general English students, do you think EAP students need more grammar, less grammar or the same amount?
2 What about the content of grammar teaching? Do EAP students need to focus on the same grammar points as general English students or different ones? What are the main differences and similarities?
3 Would EAP students benefit from using the same approaches to learning grammar as general English students or should EAP courses approach grammar differently? What are the main differences and similarities?

REFLECTION

In this chapter we have seen some of the sources of variation in academic discourse. What implications does this have for your own teaching practice? To what extent do you already deal with the features of academic discourse described above, i.e. theme and information structure; cohesion; nominalization; stance; source use? If you do not deal with them all, which features are you most likely to incorporate into your teaching in future? Is what you have read likely to change any aspects of the way you teach academic discourse?

Further reading and resources

Biber, D. (2006). *University language: A corpus-based study of spoken and written registers*. Amsterdam: Benjamins.
This book provides an in-depth account of spoken and written university registers. Chapter 1 gives an overview of university language, while Chapters 4 and 5 deal with grammatical variation and stance respectively.
Biber, D., Johansson, S., Leech, G., Conrad, S., & Finegan, E. (1999). *Longman grammar of spoken and written English*. Harlow: Pearson Education.

This is an excellent corpus-based reference grammar, which distinguishes between academic writing and other registers like conversation.

Biber, D., Leech, G., & Conrad, S. (2002). *Longman student grammar of spoken and written English*. Harlow: Pearson Education.

This is the more concise student version of the grammar above.

Musgrave, J., & Parkinson, J. (2014). Getting to grips with noun groups. *ELT Journal, 68*, 145–154.

This article describes and illustrates tasks for teaching noun phrases in EAP.

Swales, J.M. (1998). *Other floors, other voices: A textography of a small university building*. Mahwah, NJ: Erlbaum.

In this book, Swales presents a number of engaging case studies of the textual practices of scholars in several different academic disciplines.

Chapter 8

Academic vocabulary

Vocabulary is a key area of language learning, but EAP teachers frequently find it difficult to know what vocabulary their students need, while students cite vocabulary as one of their key areas of concern. They may find reading difficult because academic texts contain many words that they do not know, or feel uncertain about using **academic vocabulary** appropriately.

The broad aims of this chapter are to examine the nature of the vocabulary that EAP students need and to highlight the learning and teaching processes which underpin successful vocabulary acquisition. By the end of the chapter you will know how various types of vocabulary items are distinguished and be able to make informed decisions about which vocabulary should be taught in your particular context, and about the approaches which can be used. Before you read this chapter, consider what you already know about vocabulary and use this knowledge to help you carry out the task below.

REFLECTION

Place the words and phrases below into one of the following categories:

1   words and phrases which are useful to anybody;
2   words and phrases which are useful to EAP students, regardless of their subject;
3   technical terminology which only people in certain subject areas need to know.

What did you base your decisions on?

a)   ashamed
b)   catachresis
c)   chiton
d)   consult
e)   demonstrate
f)   executable

g)   express
h)   if we look at
i)   investment
j)   job
k)   labour
l)   of course
m)   section
n)   show
o)   statistically significant
p)   stochastic
q)   straightforward
r)   supply chain
s)   these
t)   unless

What kinds of vocabulary are there?

The task above reflected a division which is commonly made among three types of vocabulary: **general, academic,** and **technical terminology.** These types of vocabulary have different roles in EAP teaching. The category of general vocabulary is made up of words such as *job, show* and *these*, which occur frequently and are used in a range of contexts. While EAP learners may need to develop their knowledge of general vocabulary, these words are not usually the focus of EAP instruction, precisely because they come under the heading of general English, and because learners typically have a solid foundation in general English before embarking upon EAP studies.

Various efforts have been made to define the body of English words which should be considered general vocabulary. An early and influential attempt was West's (1953) General Service List of English Words (GSL), which was compiled for pedagogic purposes and consists of around 2,000 of the most frequent word families in English (word families are groups of closely related words, such as *adopt, adopted* and *adoption*). Chosen according to criteria including frequency, range, necessity and ease of learning, the GSL is estimated to cover about 80 per cent of most written texts. Although still widely used, it is recognized that the GSL has several limitations, including its age, coverage and the subjectivity of its criteria. Recently there have been two attempts to create new General Service Lists, using **corpus** methods on a very large scale: Browne (2013) draws on corpora of a quarter of a billion words to obtain a list of nearly 3,000 items, while Brezina and Gablasova (2013) derive a list of over 2,000 items from corpora totalling 12 billion words.

Another category of vocabulary, technical terms, are restricted to a given **domain** and require specialist knowledge to understand their meaning. They rarely have exact synonyms, are resistant to semantic change and have a narrow range of occurrence. Learning technical terminology often happens within subject-area classes, because in order to understand the meaning of a technical term, it is necessary to understand the subject-specific concept which it represents. For example, the word *chiton* from the task at the beginning of the chapter is a term for a form of marine life; understanding its meaning entails understanding the nature of this species, and so knowledge of the word entails knowledge of the subject of marine biology.

Several different methods have been used to distinguish technical terminology, including: rating scales (Chung & Nation 2004); computer-based techniques such as keyword analysis (keywords are words that are unusually frequent in one corpus when compared with a reference corpus); and systematic classification, which establishes a taxonomy of field-specific terms. Kwary (2011) reviews these methods and recommends combining keyword analysis with systematic classification in order to obtain a comprehensive list of technical terms. There are also lists of terms from specific subject areas such as engineering (Mudraya, 2006; Ward, 2009), applied linguistics (Khani & Tazik, 2013) and medicine (Wang, Liang & Ge, 2008).

Between a core of words for general use and a vocabulary of technical terms, we can distinguish an academic vocabulary. This category comprises items which are widespread in academic discourse, but not very frequent in general English (*establish*, *evidence*). This area of vocabulary is particularly important for EAP students. Because these words occur frequently in academic contexts, it is necessary to have a good knowledge of them in order to have the best chance of understanding lectures, textbooks, etc. However, since these words occur less frequently than general vocabulary, learners are less likely to have encountered them and learned them. In addition, unlike technical terminology, academic vocabulary is not the focus of instruction in the subject classroom. Ensuring that students learn academic vocabulary is therefore an important objective of EAP instruction.

Attempts to identify the core academic vocabulary in English were limited in scope and *ad hoc* until Coxhead (2000) produced the groundbreaking Academic Word List (AWL). The AWL was created from a corpus of 3.5 million words of academic text in four **discipline** areas and consists of 570 word families divided into 10 sublists by frequency, with each sublist containing roughly 60 families; sublist 1, for example, contains headwords *analyze*, *concept* and *research*. Coxhead's analysis showed that, together with the GSL, the AWL covers 80–90 per cent of the corpus.

The AWL filled a pressing need and quickly became widely used in teaching and materials development. However, as a prototype for a corpus-based, principled word list, one of its accomplishments was to serve as a springboard for further development. Weaknesses in the AWL have been identified. For example, a procedural starting point was to eliminate words on West's General Service List, but since that list is now outdated, many of its problems were passed on to the AWL. Since then, other lists have been developed which avoid some of the problematic aspects of the AWL. One of these is the Academic Keyword List (AKL) (Paquot, 2010), which includes both general and academic vocabulary. Another is the Academic Vocabulary List (AVL) (Gardner & Davies, 2014), which was created from a corpus of 120 million words of written academic discourse from nine disciplinary areas. They used frequency of occurrence to distinguish academic vocabulary from general vocabulary, and in order to separate the academic core from subject-specific terminology, words had to occur in several academic disciplines to be placed on the academic list.

TASK 1 Using academic word lists

1   Choose a short text of the type that you would use in class (about 200 words) and underline the words that you consider to be 'academic'.
2   Open the *Compleat Lexical Tutor* (Cobb, 2014) (see 'Further reading and resources' for access details) and upload your text into VocabProfiler so that you can see the AWL words. If you cannot do this online, consult the list of AWL words from Coxhead (2000) and mark the words manually.
3   Compare the words you identified with those in the AWL. Are these the words that you expected? Can you explain any differences you see?
4   Now either upload your text to the AVL online (see 'Further reading and resources' for access details) or check the AVL list in Gardner and Davies (2014) and look at the words that are identified.
5   Compare words identified by the AVL with those you found and those in the AWL.
6   To what extent do the three sets of words overlap and how do they differ?
7   Which list would be more useful in your own teaching situation?
8   Using information from your preferred list, what sort of tasks could you construct for your class?

Multi-word units

So far we have looked at vocabulary as though it consisted of individual words alone, but words do not exist in isolation; rather they form preferred associations with other words. These associations run the spectrum from **collocation** – for example, in academic text, *paper* collocates with *this* (*this paper*) and *statistically* collocates with *significant* (*statistically significant*) – to more fixed expressions.

There is much evidence to suggest that language users know large numbers of semi-prefabricated phrases which constitute single choices. Thus a phrase such as *on the other hand* is stored and retrieved as a whole, using what Sinclair termed the **idiom principle**. He contrasted this with the open-choice principle, which sees language use as deriving from a complex series of individual word-by-word choices (Sinclair, 1991, pp. 109–110). Although both principles are necessary for explaining language use, fixed and semi-fixed phrases have been estimated to account for between 50 per cent and 80 per cent of all text, and indeed it is often a lack of competence with them that makes learners' EAP production sound 'unnatural'. Several different cover terms are used to refer to these units, including formulaic sequences, conventionalized language and prefabricated utterances (prefabs); here we will use the term **multi-word unit** (**MWU**).

A number of different characteristics are associated with MWUs; two which are key for learners and teachers are transparency and fixity. First, MWUs may be situated on a cline from transparent to opaque in meaning. At the transparent end of this cline, the meaning of the whole MWU can be worked out from the meaning of the individual items (*it should be noted that, in more detail*), while at the opaque end, the meaning of the MWU is distinct from the meanings of the individual elements (*of course, come up with a*).

MWUs may also consist of a series of fixed elements, or they may allow lexical or grammatical variation in one or more slots. In the examples above, *of course* is completely fixed, but there are two variable slots in *it should be noted that*; that is, both the modal verb *should* and the lexical verb *noted* could be replaced, giving forms such as *it must be stressed that* or *it can be concluded that*. Fixed MWUs are also known as clusters, chunks, *n*-grams (sequences of *n* words, e.g. 2-grams, 3-grams), or lexical bundles.

Most work in EAP has so far centred on identifying this type of MWU, in particular lexical bundles (Biber et al., 1999), which consist of sequences of three or more consecutive words that occur frequently enough to be noteworthy (in the case of three-word bundles, at least 10 per million words). Those identified in academic prose include: *part of the, the fact that, in the case of*. As seen in the examples, most lexical bundles are not complete structural units, and in academic prose they tend to form part of noun phrases or prepositional phrases. Lexical bundles perform a wide range of functions and in EAP include **stance** expressions (*I think it was*), discourse organizers (*if we look at*) and referential expressions (*at the end of*).

By now you may be wondering whether it is worth teaching and learning MWUs. After all, students have enough to do just learning individual words and why make it harder for them? There are, however, several important reasons for focusing on MWUs. First, they are processed more quickly than non-formulaic sequences; thus teaching the most frequently encountered phrases offers students some preconstructed building blocks to improve the fluency of their production and increase the efficiency of communication. L2 speakers tend to employ fewer MWUs than **L1** speakers and overuse a small number of favourite phrases, which are not the same as those in proficient L1 production. Explicit teaching of MWUs can also raise learners' awareness of the importance of **phraseology** and lead to increased and more appropriate use. In academic writing, certain MWUs act as 'triggers' which initiate a **move** or **step**. For example, in the **CARS model** (see Chapter 4), *little is known about the* introduces the 'indicating a gap' step, while *the purpose of the present study* initiates 'announcing present research' (Cortes, 2013). Such MWUs are clearly useful for EAP students to master, as they are characteristic of proficient and fluent writing.

An academic phrase list

Like words, some MWUs are associated with specific disciplines. For example, Hyland (2008) reports different usage of MWUs in four disciplines: electrical engineering, applied linguistics, biology and business studies, and suggests that this corresponds to characteristic disciplinary patterns of argumentation. Other MWUs can be considered part of a common academic core.

Despite the attention given to MWUs in academic discourse, there are fewer pedagogical lists of phrases than of words. The most comprehensive list of MWUs is the Academic Formulas List (AFL) compiled by Simpson-Vlach and Ellis (2010). This list is based on two corpora of British and American academic speech and academic writing, each containing 2.1 million words. The most frequent 3-, 4- and 5-grams were identified, and MWUs were selected for inclusion if they were significantly more frequent in academic than in non-academic text and if they occurred frequently across a range of disciplinary areas. The utility of the phrase for pedagogic purposes was also assessed using a measure called 'formula teaching worth'. In order to gauge this, 20 experienced EAP practitioners were asked to rate the MWUs according to whether they considered the phrase to be fixed, to have a meaning or function in itself and to be worth teaching. This measure was then used to provide a rank order of the most useful MWUs for pedagogical purposes. Three lists are provided, a core AFL, consisting of formulas present in both spoken and written language, and two lists of the 200 most frequent phrases, one for spoken and one for written language. The formulas are presented in the three functional categories mentioned above: stance expressions, discourse organizers and referential expressions and are further classified within each category. For example, the largest category of formulas, referential expressions, includes subcategories of 'identification and focus' (*as an example*) and 'contrast and comparison' (*the relationship between*); stance expressions include subcategories of 'ability and possibility' (*you can see*) and evaluation (*the importance of*); and discourse organizers include subcategories of 'cause and effect' (*in order to*) and textual reference (*in the next section*). The authors stress, however, that the AFL is designed as a resource for materials production rather than for direct teaching use and that the formulas need further contextualization for pedagogical purposes.

TASK 2 Using the AFL

1   Using the same text as in Task 2, underline the MWUs that you consider to be 'academic'.
2   Now consult the AFL in Simpson-Vlach and Ellis (2010) and mark any MWUs that occur in your text.
3   Compare your MWUs with those identified by the AFL. To what extent do the two sets of phrases overlap and in what ways do they differ?
4   Do you agree that the formulas identified are worth teaching? Would the AFL be useful in your own teaching situation?
5   Using information from the AFL, what sort of tasks could you construct for your class?

Teaching and learning vocabulary

The previous section provided an orientation to academic words and phrases. This section puts that knowledge into practice by applying it to two fundamental questions: how are words and phrases learned; and how can teachers facilitate that process? However, another question must be addressed first: what does it mean to 'know' a vocabulary item?

TASK 3 What is 'vocabulary knowledge'?

1   Look up *investment* and *consult* in a learner dictionary.
2   Apart from the definition, what sort of information is given about the two words?

Vocabulary knowledge: What does it mean?

When you looked up the words in Task 3, it is likely that you found, in addition to a definition, information about how the words are pronounced and facts about their grammar, for example, that *investment* is a countable noun, the implication of which is that it needs to be used with a determiner, and that *consult* is a monotransitive verb (although that may not be the term used in your learner dictionary), so that it requires a direct object. If either of them had particular morphological distinctions (e.g. an irregular plural or past tense form), or if they were highly formal or likely to be offensive to people, that would be indicated as well. These features illustrate that knowing the meaning of a vocabulary item in the fullest sense entails knowing quite a lot more about it than what it means. (This is also true for multi-word units, but in the discussion which follows we will refer to 'words' for the sake of convenience.)

A first important distinction can be made between **receptive knowledge,** which is the ability to understand a word when it is encountered in speech or writing, and **productive knowledge,** which is the ability to use it. At its most basic, knowledge of a word implies an association between a concept and the form which represents it; that is, knowing that *fly* signifies a particular kind of insect. Beyond that, though, as the task above illustrated, there is a great deal to be known about a word, including:

- both its orthographic form (how it is written) and its phonetic form (how it is pronounced)
- variations on its form: inflections (e.g., fly→flies, think→thought) and derivations (fly→flight, think→unthinkable)
- features with implications for grammatical choices, such as whether a noun is countable or an adjective is gradable
- frequent collocations
- **register** associations

Thus a more relevant question than whether a learner knows a word is often how well the learner knows the word. This is the distinction between breadth of knowledge (how large an individual's vocabulary is) and depth of knowledge (how well an individual knows a given word).

What vocabulary do EAP learners need?

Vocabulary is of critical importance to EAP learners. The largest body of research on vocabulary needs has dealt with reading and has demonstrated that in order to attain comprehension to an acceptably high level, a reader must know the vast majority of words in the text: somewhere between 95 per cent and 98 per cent (Hu & Nation, 2000; Laufer & Ravenhorst-Kalovski, 2010). In Coxhead's (2000) study, 71 per cent of the corpus was covered by the first thousand words in the original version of the GSL and 76 per cent was covered by the first two thousand words. The AWL itself accounted for 10 per cent of the corpus overall. The remaining 14 per cent which was not covered by either of these lists presumably consists to a large extent of terminology which is too tied to a specific subject to be represented in the AWL. Gardner and Davies (2014) found a not entirely dissimilar figure for their AVL: it covers 14 per cent of their academic corpus. Thus it is clear that knowledge of general vocabulary, academic vocabulary and technical terminology are all important. Without all three, students will not reach the level of vocabulary coverage needed to be able to read academic texts, understand them and have good prospects for learning the unknown words.

In deciding which words to teach in an EAP class, all three of these types of words must be considered. The case for teaching general vocabulary is easy to make in the sense that because it is more common than academic vocabulary or terminology, there are significant benefits to knowing it. However, because EAP classes are aimed at students who have already attained a high enough level of proficiency that studying in English is a realistic objective, many of them already have a strong general vocabulary. The decision to teach general vocabulary, then, should only be made if information from a diagnostic test or some other source indicates that this is an area of need.

Terminology is arguably of greatest relevance to EAP students, since their objective is to use English in order to learn about their subject areas, and terminology cannot be separated from subject knowledge. However, three factors can make it difficult or less appropriate to teach terminology. The first is that terminology is explicitly taught in subject area courses, together with the concepts that the terms represent. It may therefore be unnecessary to teach it in the EAP classroom as well. An exception, though, is the case of learners who have begun to study the subject area in the L1 before moving to **English-medium instruction** and may as a result not have learned important, basic terminology in English. A second barrier to teaching terminology is that the EAP teacher may not have the necessary specialist knowledge in the subject in question. Finally, teaching terminology is only appropriate in an **ESAP** course which is sufficiently specialized to make the terms relevant to all students.

Academic vocabulary, by contrast, is the area which is always relevant to EAP learners because it is, by definition, what they will encounter in academic discourse, regardless of the academic disciplines in which they work. Thus, in deciding what vocabulary to teach, a first question is whether a course permits attention to vocabulary at all; in a course with a very specific remit, for example, writing a **thesis**, and very limited time resources, there may not be scope to address vocabulary in any meaningful way. However, if vocabulary is to be taught, then a core academic vocabulary is the natural starting point, and the remaining question is whether it is appropriate and feasible to address general or technical words as well.

How is vocabulary taught and learned?

All aspects of language, vocabulary included, can be learned in two ways. The first is as the result of explicit, form-focused instruction either in the classroom or in assigned tasks completed outside the classroom. To the extent that the scope of a course permits explicit teaching of vocabulary, there are good EAP resource materials, a selection of which are listed at the end of this chapter.

Language is also learned incidentally. Incidental language learning is the result of exposure to a language when it is being used for communicative purposes. For example, a student who is able to understand most of the words in the textbook will be able to understand what the new ones mean from context, and after encountering them repeatedly, will learn them.

Because depth of knowledge involves knowing about how words are used in context, an effective way of helping students to expand their vocabulary is to create tasks which expose them to new words in context, and enable them to make the best use of those opportunities. The former can be accomplished by finding (or encouraging learners to find) texts which are at an appropriate level of difficulty and of relevance to them as EAP students.

Enabling students to learn new words as they encounter them involves to a great extent raising their awareness about the many aspects of word knowledge. Many students believe that knowing a word consists of knowing its translation in their L1, and while this is important, there is much more to depth of vocabulary knowledge than that. Effective vocabulary teaching includes encouraging students to gain the habit of investigating many aspects of form, meaning, associations and patterns when they come across a new word.

Learners should also be encouraged to find ways of recording what they learn somewhere: in a vocabulary notebook, a spreadsheet, on flashcards, etc. There is no single best form for recording vocabulary knowledge; of greatest importance is that students are personally comfortable with the form, so that they will use it.

Finally, a very useful resource for EAP students is the learner dictionary. There are several competing, well-established publishers of learner dictionaries, and their products are all of very high quality. Both the paper volumes and the accompanying CDs offer rich and valuable information. Of particular interest to EAP students is the new *Oxford Learner's Dictionary of Academic English* (2014). However, to get best use out of any dictionary, most students need an introduction, particularly if they are accustomed to using bilingual dictionaries which contain as little as a one-word translation in some entries. Assigning a learner dictionary to students is therefore often a good idea, but spending lesson time exploring its features and using the resources which the major publishers make available for the purpose is also important.

Testing vocabulary

Vocabulary testing can be done for diagnostic purposes or as a form of assessment in a course in which vocabulary knowledge is a learning objective. Testing among other forms of examination is the topic of Chapter 12, but in this section we look at aspects of testing with particular relevance for vocabulary.

In assessing vocabulary, it is important to be clear about the objective, and specifically about what degree of depth the test aims to measure. This can be illustrated with a question like the one below:

1   Translate *investment* into your first language.

This asks the learner to produce a translation equivalent of a word. If the learner is able to do so, it demonstrates the most basic sort of word knowledge, the relationship between form and meaning. A correct answer to this question suggests that the item is part of the learner's receptive vocabulary, but not necessarily his or her productive vocabulary. Reversing the question – giving a prompt in the learner's L1 and asking for a translation in English – would show that the learner can use the word productively, if the question is answered correctly. However, if it is answered incorrectly, it is not possible to tell whether this is because the learner does not know the word at all or only knows it receptively. The format used in the Vocabulary Levels Test, shown in Figure 8.1, is a test of receptive vocabulary knowledge.

This format is multiple choice with three possible answers corresponding to a group of six words, three of which are target items and three of which are distractors. Because each target item is a distractor for the other two in each group, it is possible for test-takers to respond quickly compared with other formats, and thus it is possible to test enough items to get a good measure of vocabulary breadth.

A very different approach is shown in Figure 8.2. The Vocabulary Knowledge Scale (VKS; Wesche & Paribakht, 1996) asks for one of five responses,

---

1   concrete
2   era   _____ circular shape
3   fiber   _____ top of a mountain
4   hip   _____ a long period of time
5   loop
6   summit

(Adapted from Schmitt, Schmitt & Clapham, 2001)

Figure 8.1 The Vocabulary Levels Test

I.   I don't remember having seen this word before.
II.   I have seen this word before, but I don't know what it means.
III. I have seen this word before, and I think it means _____ (synonym or translation).
IV.   I know this word; it means _____ (synonym or translation).
V.   I can use this word in a sentence: _____. (Write a sentence.)

(If you do this section, please also do Section IV) (p. 180)

(Adapted from Wesche & Paribakht, 1996)

Figure 8.2 The Vocabulary Knowledge Scale

each indicating increasingly deeper knowledge about the target word. This format therefore gives good information about depth of vocabulary. However, relatively more time is needed to respond to each item, limiting the number of items which can be tested. In addition, marking items III.–V. entails some subjectivity.

In some contexts teachers need to test a specific set of vocabulary. These examples illustrate the variety of formats which can be used and show that each gives rather different sorts of information. If the purpose of a vocabulary test is to diagnose breadth of vocabulary, there are two freely available tests which can be useful. The Vocabulary Levels Test, developed by Paul Nation and validated and refined by Schmitt, Schmitt and Clapham (2001), is a test primarily of general vocabulary, although some items from the AWL are tested as well. The Academic Vocabulary Test was developed by Pecorari, Shaw and Malmström (in preparation) and is based on the Gardner and Davies (2014) vocabulary list.

Profiles of practice

Several EAP teachers were asked how they work with their students' vocabulary learning. Read their answers, consider them from the perspective of your own teaching context and answer the questions below.

Elisabeth

At the beginning of the term, I explain what the Academic Word List is. I show students where to find a copy of it, and I tell them that there will be a test on the AWL at the end of the term. Each week in class we look at twenty items from the AWL. Students do exercises using them, and can ask questions. However, they have to do most of the work of learning the AWL on their own.

John

I teach English to students of physics, and my own first degree was in physics. I have a list of terms which I think are important for all students of physics, regardless of level or specialization. Students in my class have to pick one of the terms and give a short presentation on it. That helps them understand what it means to feel as though you understand a term thoroughly, and I think it motivates them to learn the other terms on the list as well.

Miguel

I ask my students to keep a vocabulary log and enter new words into it. At the beginning of the class I teach them what things they can write in the log: the meaning of the word; the translation in Spanish; whether it has any irregular forms. I encourage them to write down whole sentences where they see the word being used so that they can notice patterns in collocation, etc.

Sarah

Every week we read an article from the *Economist*. The articles there are well written and there are a lot of words which students don't know but find useful. They have to mark the words they don't know when they read the article at home and then look up the meaning of ten of them in the dictionary. In class everyone has to present one or two words they didn't know but have learned from the article. I note down the words they present. Every two weeks we have a vocabulary quiz based on those words.

1   Have you used any of these approaches?
2   Which one(s) would work best for your students?
3   Are there any which are unsuitable in your context? Why or why not?

TASK 4 Dealing with terminology needs

Ward (2009) reports the results of an attempt to create an engineering word list which can serve as a sort of middle stage between the AWL and tightly subject-specific terminology, in that it is intended to be equally applicable to all engineering disciplines.

1   Read Ward's article and then reflect on an EAP context with which you are familiar.
2   How broad or narrow are the terminology needs of the students?
3   If you were going to replicate Ward's work to produce a word list relevant for an EAP group with which you are familiar, how would you select your corpus?

REFLECTION

Reflect on what you have read about academic vocabulary in this chapter. What implications does it have for your own teaching practice? To what extent do you already take account of the aspects of academic vocabulary dealt with in this chapter? How might you change the way you teach vocabulary to incorporate those aspects of EAP vocabulary that were new to you?

Further reading and resources

Academic Vocabulary List (AVL)

    This site gives access to the AVL and allows you to input your own text to see frequency information and compare it with the **COCA** academic component. It is available here: http://www.academicvocabulary.info/

Academic Word List (AWL)

    This is Coxhead's AWL site, where you can find the word list and many useful links to sites that offer ideas and materials for working with the list.

    It is available here: http://www.victoria.ac.nz/lals/resources/academicwordlist/

Cobb, T. (2014). *The compleat lexical tutor* (version 8). Montreal, Canada: University of Quebec.

    This site gives access to the GSL and AWL and has many vocabulary tasks and tests. It is available here: http://www.lextutor.ca/

McCarthy, M., & O'Dell, F. (2008) *Academic vocabulary in use*. Cambridge: Cambridge University Press.

    This student practice book deals with general academic vocabulary, including both words and phrases.

Milton, J. (2009). *Measuring second language vocabulary acquisition*. Bristol: Multilingual Matters.

    This is an accessible but in-depth account of the issues covered in the section on teaching and learning vocabulary.

Schmitt, D., & Schmitt, N. (2005). *Focus on vocabulary: Mastering the Academic Word List*. New York: Longman.

    This is a student book for practice on the AWL.

Vocabulary Resources

    A selection of vocabulary-teaching and vocabulary-testing resources are available on Paul Nation's website at http://www.victoria.ac.nz/lals/about/staff/paul-nation

Chapter 9

Written expert genres

Writing is a pervasive feature of academic life, but it is noteworthy that there is only partial overlap (in terms both of **genres** and of specific linguistic and rhetorical features) among the texts students write (the subject of the next chapter), the texts they are expected to read and the texts which are produced by more established members of the academic community. This chapter provides an orientation to what we will call 'expert genres', genres produced primarily for and by established academics. We will then look at the descriptive work which has been done on them, and the ways they differ across academic **disciplines**. The chapter concludes with the pedagogical implications for the EAP classroom. By the end of this chapter you will know what the key expert genres are, what characterizes them and their use across disciplines, and how you can help your students approach them for reading purposes. The reflection below will help you begin to think about these expert genres.

REFLECTION

Make a list of the written academic genres which you have asked your students to produce, or which you have produced. Now make a list of the kinds of texts which you have read as a student, or encouraged your students to read. How much overlap is there between the two lists? What accounts for the differences and similarities in the two lists?

The lists you produced in the reflection above probably had more points of difference than similarity. This is because most student writing is done to facilitate and/or to assess their learning, while the works they read have been produced for the purpose of communicating knowledge about the subject. We can thus distinguish (although the categories are not absolute) between pedagogical process genres (e.g. essays, examination answers) and research process genres, which are written to report research findings and are primarily intended to be read by other researchers.

The research genres are important for a number of reasons. Many of them have been extensively researched and thus are part of the fabric of the EAP research tradition. In addition, even if EAP students are not called upon to produce them, they need to be able to read many of them. Finally, some EAP learners are junior or established academics who need to perform the full range of professional communication in English, and have to produce as well as understand research genres. They are also important because, for a number of reasons, they are perceived by many learners as problematic.

TASK 1 Why is academic language hard?

A common perception of academic language is that it is often heavy, dry and difficult to read. Reflect on your own experiences and your memory of your early encounters with **research articles** and other research genres to answer these questions.

1 Which features of academic discourse contribute to the perception that it is dry?

2 What if anything makes or made the research genres difficult for you?

Now look at a research article and try to identify things which might make it difficult for an EAP learner to read and understand. The features we mentioned in Chapter 7 will help you here.

Your answer to Task 1 may have included the fact that some degree of subject knowledge is generally required to be able to understand the content of a research article easily. However, you very likely mentioned some aspects of language as well. As we saw in Chapter 8, both specialist **terminology**, such as *atrioventricular* or *tensile strength* and general **academic vocabulary** like *replete, mitigating* and *obsolescence* are common in academic writing, as are grammatical features, such as **nominalization**, which we saw in Chapter 7. These features, which can be both difficult and intimidating for students, are not the exclusive property of written research genres, but both spoken academic genres and the academic writing produced by novices make less use of them.

What are the research genres?

The genres produced primarily by and for researchers include the following:

- The **monograph** is a book which presents an in-depth treatment of a specific topic, the whole of which is written by a single author or a team of authors.

- An **edited volume** or anthology is also a book-length work, but it consists of chapters written by different individuals, all of which address a given topic.
- An **academic journal** is a form of periodical; that is, several issues per year are published, consisting of research articles and possibly other features, such as book reviews, short notes about ongoing research, or opinion pieces.
- A survey article or state-of-the-art article describes the research to date on a given topic, providing references to the relevant studies on that topic and usually identifying significant themes and areas in which further research is needed.

Although a significant body of research has provided descriptive accounts of the writing done by established academics, it has not been even-handed. Two genres in particular have received a great deal of attention: the research article and the abstract.

The research article

Research articles (**RAs**) are relatively short works (ranging from a few pages in the hard disciplines to 20–30 in the soft areas) and they occupy a special status in EAP as the most thoroughly researched expert genre. This is in part because of their importance for academic writers. The peer-reviewed RA, particularly if it appears in a top-ranked journal, triggers the academic reward system at all levels. It is an extremely prestigious form of publication across the university and the one which is most likely to be used as a measure of research productivity, since the monograph, while highly valued, occurs only infrequently in some disciplines.

The research article has been described as having a canonical structure consisting of four main parts, the introduction, methods, results and discussion, as well as additional features such as the title, abstract and reference list. This prototypical structure – known as **IMRD**, after the four principal components – is subject to variation. It is most likely to occur in pure form in the scientific, technical, engineering and mathematics (STEM) disciplines. By contrast in literary studies it is very difficult to separate the methodological approach from the findings, and subject headings are more likely to be thematic rather than generic. Even in those fields in which conformity to the IMRD model is more prevalent, variations are found in terms of its precise realization or in terms of how the sections are labelled. For instance, the introduction can be broken down into a shorter introduction and a separate literature review, or the findings and conclusions can be merged. Instead of 'introduction', the initial section could be called 'background'; the 'methods' section can be called 'methods and materials'; 'conclusions' can be used instead of 'discussion', and so forth.

The sections of a research article have fundamentally different functions. The purpose of the introduction is to present the background to the work, in order to situate the new work in relation to it. The methods section describes the research procedures, in part (at least in some subject areas) so that they can be repeated by other researchers and in part because it is not possible to assess the value of findings without understanding how they were produced. The results section is an account of the significant findings, and the discussion puts the findings in context, indicating what their implications are, whether they signal the need for further research, etc. Because the sections of an RA serve different purposes, they also are characterized to some extent by different features, and much descriptive research has dealt with individual sections of the RA.

Most intensively studied is the introduction, which was the subject of John Swales's landmark **Create a Research Space (CARS) model,** which was initially presented in 1981 and has subsequently been revised (e.g. 1990, 2004). As seen in Chapter 4, the CARS model demonstrates that authors typically use a series of **moves** aimed at identifying the area in which the current RA is located and showing why it is an appropriate area of inquiry. These moves are accomplished by various **steps:** for example, the act of establishing the area which the RA inhabits can be accomplished by saying that it is an addition to an existing research tradition or by claiming that there is *not* sufficient research to illuminate an area.

Significantly for the EAP teacher, these generic moves and steps are sensitive to forms of expression, and EAP learners can benefit greatly from seeing the link between form and function. For example, the function of asserting that too little research has been done in a research area can be accomplished by fairly standard multi-word units such as *No previous study has investigated . . .* or *no systematic investigation,* both of which generate thousands of hits on Google Scholar. The descriptive research on RAs thus allows valuable connections to be made between common rhetorical forms and what they accomplish, and this connection between form and function is a powerful tool for EAP learners.

The RA introduction is a fairly stable and formulaic section in relative terms. Although there is scope for variation, most novice academic writers can benefit from learning its typical form. Less standardized in structural terms are the other IMRD sections, and it is probably for that reason that far fewer studies of them have been done and that those studies which have been carried out have produced more heterogeneous results.

TASK 2 Design a teaching activity

1   Find a research article which has an IMRD structure.
2   From each IMRD section, select sentences which have a clear relationship to that section. For example, 'A survey was sent to the head teachers of

100 primary schools' describes a research procedure and thus has a clear association with the methods section.

3   Turn the sentences into a worksheet activity asking students to identify the section from which each sentence comes, and to explain how they know.

4   Write a key for the worksheet in which you comment on the features which learners should notice and reinforce the idea that certain formal features, such as **MWUs**, are likely to appear in certain sections because they advance the rhetorical purpose of that section.

Abstracts

Abstracts exist in several forms, although not all studies have distinguished strictly among them. Abstracts are generally a high-stakes genre, although that is to some extent a function of the different purposes which are served by the various types.

Research articles typically have abstracts which appear at the beginning of the full paper and are also usually freely available in the database(s) in which the journal appears, even when full-text access is restricted. Abstracts therefore help a potential reader determine whether the article is of sufficient relevance to invest time and energy (and indeed possibly financial resources) into reading it. The impact of a research article, most frequently measured by **citations**, is a key indicator of research quality, and contributes to decisions such as hiring, promotion and salary increase. RA abstracts, then, are important because they can help an article to be read widely, which is a precondition to its being cited widely. The conference abstract performs a similar type of persuasive role towards the end of its life cycle: it is printed in the conference programme, and its purpose there is to help conference participants make choices about which sessions they wish to attend. Another, earlier function is to allow evaluators to decide whether or not the paper will be accepted.

After the RA, the abstract is perhaps the most researched expert genre (e.g. Bondi & Lorés Sanz, 2014) and it has often been described in terms of its rhetorical structure. Two principal approaches have been taken to this description. To the extent that the abstract presents a condensed version of the entire article or conference paper, it can be analyzed using the IMRD structure. However, the abstract typically puts disproportionate emphasis on the background to the research, including arguing for its necessity, and for that reason the CARS model has been used as a descriptive tool. In fact, each of these analytical perspectives can identify some but not all of the features of the abstract, demonstrating that it is a hybrid genre.

Less researched expert genres

The research article introduction and abstract have received a great deal of attention, in part because they both have relatively regular rhetorical structures, and that permits the results of these genre analyses to be transformed into guidelines for writers, an end use which is very much in line with the pedagogical focus of EAP work. Other features or genres which have been investigated to a lesser extent include sections other than the introduction in RAs (Bruce, 2009); the titles of RAs (Anthony, 2001); and referees' comments (Gosden, 2003).

A group of genres which are clearly underresearched are those which Swales (1996) called **occluded**, or hidden from view. Strictly speaking, these genres are highly visible to senior academics; they are occluded primarily to early-career academics, as they are the genres which are read primarily by established professionals. A typical example of the occluded genre is the grant proposal. This is a crucial text, and indeed can be particularly vital for PhD students and younger academics who are trying to finance study or research in order to establish an academic career. However, the people who read and evaluate them (and typically have a voice in the decision to allocate money) are quite senior. This means that the people who most need to learn about how the genre is typically and successfully realized are not the ones who have the opportunity to read it.

The limited research which has been done on grant proposals has shown that they, like RA introductions, can be said to have a fairly stable rhetorical structure, including many of the same moves as in an RA introduction, such as indicating a gap in the existing research, while other moves, such as indicating compliance with ethical research guidelines, are unique to the funding application (Connor & Mauranen, 1999). Because the specific demands of any given funding body dictate the form of the application, more research would help clarify which characteristics are generalizable to most good applications and which are specific to a particular funding body.

Other occluded genres include job application letters, external examiners' reports on **theses** and **dissertations**, and email correspondence to editors. An important selection of these genres are given treatment in the EAP textbooks produced by Swales and Feak (e.g. 2009). but there is scope for more teaching materials in this area. A further set of relatively unresearched academic genres are the 'everyday' expert genres described by Hyon and Chen (2004) in an account of the sort of workplace discourse they needed to use and produce, including memos to colleagues, reports, test instruments, conference papers, correspondence with students, minutes of meetings and feedback to students. Although many of these are not what are typically thought of as 'academic genres', they are an integral part of the life of most academics, and although they do not trigger academic rewards in the same way that a research article or a book does, without the ability to engage in them, academics would find it difficult to pursue their careers.

Compared with the research article and the abstract, these genres have received very little research attention, and in order to provide EAP support to individuals planning for or actually embarked upon an academic career, descriptive research on which to base materials and teaching approaches could be useful.

Disciplinary differences

Many of the differences among academic disciplines in terms of academic discourse have been commented on in this book, particularly in Chapter 7. One noteworthy area of difference lies in which forms of publication are common and prestigious. In the humanities and social sciences, the book (either monograph or anthology) is very influential, with the research article prestigious but more common in the social sciences or those branches of the humanities (like linguistics) which are influenced by them. There is a trend towards single authorship as well, which is most pronounced among the canonical humanities subjects such as philosophy and literature.

The research article is also common in the STEM disciplines, but the conference proceedings paper has a prestige and importance which it generally lacks in the humanities. Technical reports, research letters and short communications are extremely uncommon in the humanities but are found in the STEM disciplines; the opposite is broadly true of research monographs and anthologies. Importantly, these trends are not arbitrary. Research findings remain relevant in a field like archaeology longer than they do in molecular biology. Conference papers and RAs are relatively quicker means of disseminating research findings than a book, and thus are more suitable for the hot-off-the-presses results of research in molecular biology. Books take longer to produce but are expected to have a longer useful life span than RAs, and so are well suited for publishing results which will not become outdated in a short period of time. This point serves as an additional illustration of a theme that has come up repeatedly in this book: differences in how texts are constructed across disciplinary cultures are not arbitrary but are closely related to the practices and forms of knowledge construction valued by those disciplines.

Teaching the expert genres

Since English is the **lingua franca** of academic life, there are many academics, from PhD students to professors, who are second language users of English but must use English for professional purposes. For these individuals, the descriptive accounts of professional genres mentioned above can provide a useful foundation for understanding the conventional characteristics of important genres which they must learn to produce. There is also a long-standing tradition of basing research into features such as evaluative language and citation on **corpora** consisting of published expert texts. The reasoning underlying this approach (and it is a reasoning which can be subjected to criticism) is that published research writing has gone through a quality control process. Therefore, if descriptions of textual features are to be turned into prescriptions for novice writers to follow, the descriptions should be based on texts of high quality. Research into the expert genres can thus inform the teaching of academic writing to a certain extent.

However, the majority of EAP learners are engaged in coursework rather than research writing, and their most pressing need with regard to the expert genres is learning to read them. In teaching second language reading, the customary approach is to break the skill down into subskills such as skimming (reading quickly to get a sense of the overall content of a text), scanning (searching through a text for specific information), and predicting what direction a text may take next. Most general EAP textbooks include activities for addressing these subskills. However, not all of these subskills are equally relevant to the EAP expert genres. This section describes three areas where attention in the classroom can create particular value for the learner.

Understanding the nature of the expert genres

It is widely accepted that good reading is critical and active reading, and one element in being an active reader is the ability to understand and engage with the author's purpose. This can be challenging in the case of the expert genres because they are often new and unfamiliar. Learners come into contact with the expert genres only when they have progressed far enough in their education that they are expected to engage with specialist, research-based knowledge about their subjects. The expert genres, then, are not only linguistically challenging, they are potentially intimidating because they are unfamiliar.

Learners can benefit from an orientation to the types of professional genres which exist, how they differ from each other and why they have the features which characterize them. For instance, learners can be shown the differences between research monographs, anthologies or edited volumes and research articles and can be encouraged to make connections between the form of publication and the sort of contribution it makes to the literature. There is nothing particularly difficult to understand about the fact that monographs are larger than journal articles and journal articles are typically published more quickly than monographs, but those facts may still be new to EAP learners, in the sense that they have not previously reflected on them. Those facts also explain, however, why fields in which research moves on very quickly, such as many areas of the natural sciences, have a preference for publishing journal articles, and why monographs are especially common in subject areas in which the pace is more leisurely, such as the humanities.

Drawing attention to the different forms of publication helps learners understand where to look for different types of information (i.e. if the learner needs a general orientation to a topic, a monograph is more likely to provide that sort of background than a research article, but a recent research article is a good place to look for references on a specific topic). It also helps learners understand authorship practices. It is common for EAP writers to make mistakes in referencing, such as citing the editor of a volume as the source of a quotation which should actually be attributed to the author of the chapter from which it was taken. One consequence of this is that the referencing is not technically accurate, but more importantly, such a mistake indicates that the learner does not understand where responsibility for the statement in question actually rests. Without understanding the difference between an author and an editor, it would be possible to read two entirely opposite positions in two chapters in the same volume and believe they are attributable to the same person.

In short, then, an understanding of the forms of academic publication is key to being able to read and use them, and EAP learners cannot be assumed to have this understanding; it is often something which should be taught in the EAP class.

Understanding the purposes for reading expert genres

As learners arrive at a point at which they need to read the expert genres, their purposes for reading begin to change. Textbooks are read in order to understand the content which is the purpose of the course and the object of assessment. The other expert genres are read with a broader range of objectives in mind, and an overarching purpose is often that the information they contain is needed in order to perform some sort of writing task. In other words, it is likely that learners will need to work actively in some way with these genres.

Learners should be encouraged to be aware of and consciously articulate that purpose, and to understand what it suggests about their reading. For example, the same research article could be read by a student who is trying to identify a dissertation topic; a student who has been assigned to write a literature review; and a student who is working on a topic in a different but related area and wants to know if a particular problem has been treated within another subject area. In the first case, the purpose for reading would be to look for a gap in the existing literature which would justify a new project; in the second it would be to map connections between that article and others on the same topic; and in the last case, the purpose for reading would be to understand whether there is a relationship between the article and a different body of literature.

In fact, one common purpose for engaging with one of the expert genres is to read a small portion of the text, just enough to make a decision about whether it would be relevant to read more. RA abstracts exist precisely for the purpose of enabling that decision, and in some areas it is common to skim the methods section to see whether the method used justifies attention. Reading parts of texts only is good EAP reading practice, and learners who are accustomed to being encouraged to read entire textbooks in a linear fashion may require help to understand why this is the case.

Making the text accessible

A difference between EAP and general English teaching is that good teaching practice in the latter area requires a teacher to find reading texts which are at an appropriate level for the learner, sufficiently hard that there is a challenge for the learner but sufficiently easy that the challenge is reasonable. However, this is usually not an effective approach in EAP. If authentic genres such as research articles are excessively challenging for learners, giving them more accessible genres would result in exposure to discoursal and linguistic features which are not the ones needed. Learners who need to be able to read the expert genres therefore need scaffolding to make those genres accessible. Two areas for attention are their generic form and their linguistic features.

As we saw above, the expert genres are characterized by fairly stable generic structures, and none more so than the research article, in which the structure is closely related to its purpose of communicating new research findings. That makes it possible to show learners how to take specific questions to each part of an RA, as Figure 9.1 shows.

Introduction

In what area is the research presented here situated?
What do we already know about the topic?
What do we still need to know about the topic?
What are the questions which this article will answer?

Methods

How did the author gather the answers which are about to be presented?
What is the relationship between the questions guiding the investigation and
    the approach to answering them?

Results

What were the answers to the questions?

Discussion

What does it all mean?
Now that I know the answers, what can I do with them?

Figure 9.1 Interrogating the research article

Monographs and other expert genres have a less predictable structure but there are nonetheless regularities which can be connected to the sorts of information available in parts of the text. Survey review articles, for instance, are organized either chronologically or thematically (or sometimes both), and usually conclude by identifying future research directions. By observing the structure of a survey review article, the reader can identify specific questions which can be expected to be answered in each section of it. Encouraging EAP learners to be proactive in taking questions to specific parts of a text will help make difficult texts more accessible.

The linguistic features which make academic texts difficult to read include, as we saw in Chapter 7, long and complex nominal phrases which contain a great deal of information packaged densely. References to ideas from other sources is also characteristic of academic writing and can be off-putting to inexperienced academic readers, who may feel as though they are listening to a conversation about people they do not know. To a disciplinary insider a reference like *As Swales (1990) noted in his groundbreaking volume* . . . is informative, but to someone who has never heard of Swales, it can create an impression of being inadequately prepared for reading the newer, citing text.

To some extent the solution for this is practice – reading academic texts is not as challenging to experienced readers as it is to novices. But since a perception that the task is difficult is demotivating and may cause learners to avoid that practice, classroom attention to the characteristic linguistic features of academic discourse is beneficial. A particularly useful strategy is to identify difficult features and illustrate for learners that the difficulty is a side effect, not the intended purpose. For example, the language of referencing helps writers simultaneously transmit information and evaluate it: *As Swales noted* indicates that the writer agrees with what Swales said.

As we saw in Chapter 7, certain features of academic discourse, for example nominalization, make texts very difficult for students to understand and therefore require some unpacking, as illustrated in Figure 9.2.

In Figure 9.2, understanding the relatively compact expression in the original article would require the reader to understand which processes are implicit in nominalizations and to supply some information, such as who performs the agentless passive *attributed*. However, with specialist terminology largely replaced, nominalizations turned back into processes, and passive verbs made active, the text is 70 per cent longer than in its original form, and importantly, the longer text is not more readable; indeed, the greater length effectively separates ideas which are closely related, making it more difficult to see the relationships among them. The original says what it means with admirable economy. Drawing attention to features like these and showing learners how they work within the text will help them understand the reasons why academic texts look the way they do, and assist them as they come across similar features.

Typical features of academic writing:

   In particular, the norms of the speech community are reflected in the lexical choices. In the case of this phraseological formula, given the private and semi-vulgar nature attributed to bathroom functions, this is seen in the choice between euphemistic or dysphemistic alternatives.

(Adapted from Levin, 2014, p. 3)

Unpacking:

   In particular, the choice to use one wording or another reflects the norms of the people using a language. In the case of this phraseological formula, given that people consider bathroom functions to be of a private and semi-vulgar nature, the choice between saying things in a way which makes them seem more pleasant, or deliberately makes them seem less pleasant, shows this tendency for word choice to reflect norms.

Figure 9.2 Unpacking the features of academic discourse

TASK 3 Understanding a research article

1   Find a research article in a field which is relevant for your students.
2   Apply the questions in Figure 9.1 to the research article and note down your answers.
3   To what extent did this procedure help you to read and understand the article?
4   Which questions were particularly helpful?
5   Can you suggest any other questions which you think would help students to follow this article?

Profile of practice

Read the following description of one teacher's experience and answer the questions below. Shannon teaches EAP to multilingual groups of BA and MA students from a range of backgrounds, and one of her courses includes a unit on how to read a research article. In order to understand their difficulties with RAs, she spoke to some people who were likely to have a fresh memory of learning to read expert genres in English: current PhD students and some who had recently completed their studies. A feature which several identified as difficult was definitions.

   This seemed rather surprising to Shannon at first; after all, if the prevalence of technical terminology makes academic writing hard to read, then definitions should make it easier by explaining what some of the inaccessible terms mean. However, the two definitions in Figure 9.3 illustrate the nature of the difficulty. The lower one comes from a learner's dictionary and is direct and accessible in style, particularly compared to the upper one, which is taken from a research article. The stylistic differences in the two are explained by their different purposes: the dictionary definition was written for the purpose of explaining the meaning of the word *euphemism* to someone who does not know it; by contrast, definitions in research writing aim to establish how a term will be used in the work, setting forth its parameters, either because a term has been contested or used inconsistently in the literature, or to establish criteria which can be used to categorize things as falling under the definition or not. In other words, definitions in research writing are used to enhance technical accuracy rather than comprehensibility for an inexpert reader.

When Shannon realized this, she was able to change her approach to teaching the skill of reading a research article. She now encourages students to identify definitions in the articles they read. If the term defined is one which is unknown to them, she advises them to consult a dictionary for a more accessible definition and then compare the two, to understand what the more technical definition adds to the simpler one.

1 Would this approach work in your teaching context? Why or why not?
2 Do you think that Shannon's approach is likely to be successful with other aspects of reading?
3 Have you faced any similar problems in your teaching of reading, and if so, how did you deal with them?

According to Allen and Burridge (1991: 11) a euphemism 'is used as an alternative to a dispreferred expression, in order to avoid possible loss of face: either one's own face or, through giving offense, that of the audience, or of some third party.'

(Levin, 2014, p. 3)

euphemism (for something) an indirect word or phrase that people often use to refer to something embarrassing or unpleasant, sometimes to make it seem more acceptable than it really is.

(*Oxford Advanced Learner's Dictionary* online)

Figure 9.3 Definitions of *euphemism*

TASK 4 What expert genres do learners need?

1   Gather lists of assigned or recommended reading from several courses and from a range of academic disciplines. Tips for finding them: at many universities they are available online. If not, you could ask at department offices or ask friends or colleagues who are students or lecturers for the reading lists from their courses.
2   Try to classify the items on the lists as either research or pedagogical process genres.
3   Can you identify any trends? Are research process genres assigned more at certain levels, or in certain subjects?

REFLECTION

This chapter described genres which many students will no longer engage with once they leave university. Can you identify any transferable outcomes from learning about these expert genres? That is, will knowing about them make students better able to read or write different kinds of texts? Do some of the expert genres have more, or more important, transferable outcomes than others? Are the transferable outcomes greater for some students than others?

Further reading and resources

Academic Phrasebank
Created by John Morley at the University of Manchester, this resource contains a large selection of multi-word units for academic writing. Access it at http://www.phrasebank.manchester.ac.uk/
Becher, T., & Trowler, P.R. (2001). *Academic tribes and territories: Intellectual enquiry and the cultures of disciplines* (2nd ed.). Buckingham: The Society for Research into Higher Education & Open University Press.
This book takes an anthropological view of academic practice. Chapter 6, 'Patterns of communication', describes the characteristics of academic publications across disciplines, and the book as a whole demonstrates the ways in which the discipline-bound characteristics of academic discourse are linked to the forms of knowledge creation which are prized in the disciplines.
Curry, M.J., & Lillis, T. (2013). *A scholar's guide to getting published in English: Critical choices and practical strategies*. Bristol: Multilingual Matters.
This book provides guidance and practice for junior researchers and other academics on writing for publication.
Hyland, K., & Shaw, P. (2016). *The Routledge handbook of English for academic purposes*. London: Routledge.
Several chapters describe professional written genres, including research articles (Samraj), conference posters (D'Angelo), textbooks (Bondi) and 'outreach' genres such as research blogs (Kuteeva).

Kuteeva, M., & Mauranen, A. (Eds.). (2014). Writing for publication in multilingual contexts. *Journal of English for Academic Purposes, 13*, 1–4.

Many of the articles in this special issue speak to the demands placed on the EAP skills of established academics who are second language users of English.

Swales, J.M. (2004). *Research genres: Explorations and applications*. Cambridge: Cambridge University Press.

In this book, Swales presents a number of thoughtful considerations about academic genres. Of particular relevance for expert genres is Chapter 7, 'The research article revisited'.

Chapter 10

Written learner genres

In Chapter 4 we introduced the idea of **genre** and saw how genres in EAP carry out the communicative purposes of **disciplinary communities**. Chapter 9 focused on some of the expert genres that EAP students come into contact with; next we turn to the genres students have to write. First, we analyze and describe some major undergraduate and graduate genres, and then discuss the approaches that have been used in teaching and learning academic writing. By the end of the chapter you will be familiar with some key learner genres and be able to make informed decisions about which genres to teach and which teaching options would be suitable within your own context.

REFLECTION

Refer back to your list of genres in Chapter 9 or make a new list of genres you have written as a student. Were you taught how to write these genres? If not, how did you find out how to do so? Think about other **disciplines** that you are familiar with. Do they use the same learner genres or can you add to your list? Which genres would be appropriate for your own EAP students to learn and which would not? Explain why.

You may well have noted down quite a long list of different genres, including, for example, essay, literature review, examination answer, statistical exercise, notes etc., and if we include genres from a broad selection of disciplines, our list would be much longer, adding perhaps laboratory report, design specification, case study, etc. The sheer number and diversity of genres required presents students with a huge learning task, especially since they may be working in more than one discipline simultaneously. Moreover, there may be no explicit instruction in writing learner genres; students may lack exemplars to study and may simply be expected to know how to write them.

Learner genres

Written texts of all types are of central importance in academic work, as they provide one of the most important means by which knowledge is produced and communicated. As pedagogical process genres, learner genres have two key functions which distinguish them from expert genres. First, they constitute the means by which students carry out their learning. It is in completing their written assignments that students are expected to apply the material that has been presented and thus to develop their knowledge and understanding. Second, written texts are also the main means by which learning is assessed. Although there may be oral examinations as well, it is still written texts that dominate the means of evaluation throughout the university. Thus for students, written texts are high-stakes genres; they decide whether a student succeeds or fails.

From our list of genres above, it is clear that even within a single discipline, learner genres are so numerous that it would not be possible for a time-limited EAP writing course to teach them all. As we have already seen, genres have their own characteristic structures, deriving from the disciplinary context to which they belong and the purpose they serve. Thus it is necessary for the teacher to select from the huge diversity of learner genres those most needed by their own group of students.

Undergraduate genres

One of the ways in which we can obtain evidence for selecting target genres and describing them is to consult a **corpus** such as **BAWE**, introduced in Chapter 4 (Nesi & Gardner, 2012).

Essay

According to Nesi and Gardner's analysis, the essay is the most frequently occurring genre family, used across all four disciplinary areas and at undergraduate and master's levels. Its key purpose is to develop the student's powers of independent reasoning, which it seeks to achieve through the requirement to construct a sound and convincing argument. Essays consist of three stages, which vary according to the type of essay. Nesi and Gardner distinguish six different types: exposition, discussion, challenge, factorial, consequential and commentary.

Exposition, discussion and challenge essays all argue for a specific position which is stated at the end of the essay, but they have different starting points and development. The exposition essay begins with the student's position statement and presents evidence for it; the discussion essay starts with a description of the issue under consideration and then gives alternative views on it; the challenge essay begins by countering an accepted view and then brings evidence to support the student's position. All three of these essay types are used to respond to titles that require the student to develop a standpoint on an issue; they can be summarized as follows:

- exposition essay: position statement – evidence – restatement of position
- discussion essay: description of issue – alternative arguments – final position
- challenge essay: challenge to accepted view – evidence – position statement.

Both factorial and consequential essays discuss the factors involved in a state of affairs; they begin by describing the situation and end with a summary of the student's position. The factorial essay discusses contributory factors to the situation, while the consequential essay presents its consequences. These essays are not purely descriptive but show the student's evaluation of the evidence in support of his or her own position; they can be summarized as follows:

- factorial essay: description of state of affairs – contributory factors – summary of student's position
- consequential essay: description of state of affairs – consequences – summary of student's position.

Commentary essays discuss texts rather than issues. They begin by introducing the text(s) under review, which are then commented on and analyzed; commentaries conclude with a summary, which may present the student's own position; this type of essay can be summarized as follows:

- commentary essay: introduction of text(s) – comments – summary.

TASK 1 Using Nesi and Gardner's essay genres

1   Obtain an essay title from a content lecturer, your students or an EAP book and decide which type(s) of essay would be a suitable response.
2   Does the title clearly suggest the type of essay required or could it be answered in more than one way?
3   Write an outline plan of the essay indicating its type and the content that would fit into each part.
4   If possible, ask a member of the relevant discipline or a classmate to evaluate your outline.
5   Did Nesi and Gardner's genre stages help you plan the essay?
6   Would this type of task be useful for your students? Why or why not?

Research report

Research reports are another genre that occurs across all four disciplinary areas; they may be written throughout undergraduate study or may constitute a final assignment in the form of a long essay or project report. The purpose of the research report is to demonstrate that students can conduct research using appropriate disciplinary methods and tools, and they are expected to develop their own research questions and situate them within the relevant literature. In the BAWE data, two types of research reports have been identified. *Topic-based reports* are often found in arts/humanities and have an introduction followed by three argument chapters, each with a heading relating to the report topic, and a conclusion. *Genre-based reports* are typical of experimental disciplines and have the **IMRD** structure. These structures are presented in Table 10.1.

When we compare the structure of research reports with that of theses, we can see a clear resemblance between topic-based research reports and topic-based theses, while genre-based research reports resemble simple/traditional theses (see Table 10.2).

Graduate genres: Thesis and dissertation

We saw in Chapter 9 that graduate writers need to produce expert genres like the **research article** or conference abstract and may also have to write learner genres such as the laboratory report or essay. However, in terms of degree success, the most important written genre is the **thesis** or **dissertation**. These are both high-stakes genres, because failure at this stage can mean failure in the course as a whole and the prospect of having no qualification to show for months or years of work. It is useful to begin, however, by clarifying what is meant by these two genre labels, since usage can vary according to country, university or even individual department. Thus in the US and institutions following the US pattern, the words 'dissertation' and 'thesis' are used interchangeably to indicate the work submitted to gain a PhD, while for a master's qualification, only 'thesis' is used. By contrast,

Table 10.1 Structure of research reports

Topic-based structure	Genre-based structure
Introduction	Introduction
Argument chapter	Method
Argument chapter	Results
Argument chapter	Discussion
Conclusion	

(Adapted from Nesi & Gardner, 2012)

in the UK and UK-influenced systems, 'thesis' is used for a doctoral degree and 'dissertation' for a master's. However, even within the same university there may be slight variations; for example, 'thesis' may be the term used in certain types of master's courses. Here we follow the UK terminology, referring to 'doctoral/PhD thesis' for the PhD qualification and 'dissertation' for the master's; we use the term 'thesis' alone when referring to both genres.

As we saw in Chapter 7, although there are parallels to be drawn between the generic structure of PhD theses and research articles, there are also differences due to their different audience and purpose. Research article writers are experts in their fields whose primary purpose is to present new information to the research community of fellow-experts. Doctoral writers, however, have a dual role: as (almost) experts, they have to present a new contribution, but at the same time, as students and examination candidates, they have to demonstrate a thorough knowledge of the field.

Thesis structure

Master's and doctoral texts vary significantly in word length, with dissertations ranging from about 10,000 to 35,000 words, while doctoral theses tend to have an upper limit of about 80,000 words. Humanities and social science PhD theses tend to be at the upper end of that limit and may be substantially longer than those in the natural sciences, which can be closer to about 60,000 words. However, whether students are writing a relatively short 10,000-word dissertation or a full 80,000-word PhD thesis, it is likely that this text will be the longest they have ever written, and length brings with it the need for detailed attention to structure.

There are three major ways of structuring the PhD thesis: simple/traditional, article compilation/complex and topic-based (Swales, 2004). They appear in Table 10.2.

Table 10.2 Three PhD thesis structures

Simple/traditional	Article compilation/complex	Topic-based
Introduction	Introduction	Introduction
Literature review	Literature review (sometimes included in Introduction)	Literature review (optional)
Methods	General methods (optional)	Theoretical framework (optional)
Results	IMRD	Method
Discussion	IMRD	Topic 1: Analysis – Discussion
Conclusions	IMRD etc.	Topic 2: Analysis – Discussion
	Conclusions	Topic 3: Analysis – Discussion etc.
		Conclusions

(Adapted from Swales, 2004)

The simple/traditional thesis follows the same type of structure (IMRD) as an empirical research article, although the thesis generally requires a longer literature review, and this is usually supplied as a separate chapter. The problem with this structure is that it is not always suitable for a doctoral text, which is many times longer than a research article. This may well lead to an unbalanced structure, with a results chapter that is much longer than the others. However, it is likely to be more appropriate for a dissertation, especially when a single piece of research is reported.

The second type of structure is suitable both for those submitting an article compilation and for those who report more than a single experiment. Here, writers use an outer shell of chapters (introduction, literature review, general methods and conclusions), which link the material together to form a single text, while each of the remaining chapters has its own individual IMRD structure. This structure lends itself particularly well to work which reports several experiments and to publication of the chapters as separate research articles. However, it may not be so useful for dissertations, due to their more limited scope.

The third type is more likely to be preferred by those carrying out non-empirical studies, especially in social science and humanities fields. Again there is an outer shell of chapters (introduction, literature review, theoretical framework, method and conclusions), which surround the body chapters and apply to the whole thesis. The nature of the individual body chapters varies widely according to the discipline and the subject matter of the individual study and may include analysis and interpretation of texts, description and evaluation of theories, approaches or models.

Overall, the number of simple/traditional doctoral theses seems to be decreasing, while the article compilation/complex structure is likely to be preferred in natural science and the topic-based structure in social science and humanities. However, there is no one-to-one correspondence between disciplinary area and thesis structure type.

TASK 2: Investigating thesis structure

1   Obtain a thesis either in your own discipline or in a discipline of your students. Universities usually make doctoral theses available in e-form through their libraries, and some countries have a national database where you can access them.

2   Look at the structure as shown by the table of contents and decide which type the thesis most resembles.

3   How closely does your example follow the structure you chose and how does it differ?

4   Can you explain why the thesis employs this structure and any differences you see between them?

5   Would this task be useful for your EAP students? Why or why not?

Introduction and literature review

As we can see from their structure, theses consist of a number of part-genres, each of which has its own generic structure. Thesis introductions and literature reviews both tend to follow a three-**move** pattern similar to Swales's (2004) **CARS model** for research article introductions: establishing a territory, establishing a niche and presenting the present research (see Chapter 4 for more details).

Body chapters

As evident from the generic structure of theses, the body chapters differ markedly according to discipline and individual study. Research has focused on empirical dissertations, which tend to have a relatively conventional structure and, being shorter, lend themselves more easily to analysis. The set of moves and **steps** given in Figure 10.1 draws particularly on analyses of discussion sections in plant biology (Dudley-Evans, 1986) and language teaching (Basturkmen, 2009).

The key element in this generic structure is the move sequence Result – Comment, which may be repeated as many times as necessary to discuss all the results. Within this sequence, the comment move is of great importance, since it enables writers to link their research to the literature and to make claims which show the significance of the results and what they mean for the development of knowledge in the field.

Conclusion

Theses typically have a final chapter entitled 'Conclusion', which carries out the task of reviewing the work performed, setting out the implications for

---

Move 1 Background information (optional)

Move 2 Summarizing results (optional)

Move 3 Reporting a single result

Move 4 Commenting on the result

    Step 1A Explaining the result and/or
    Step 1B Comparing the present result with a result in the literature and/or
    Step 1C Evaluating the result/making a claim or generalization from the result

(Adapted from Basturkmen, 2009; Dudley-Evans, 1986)

Figure 10.1 Moves and steps in thesis discussion sections

Move 1 Introductory restatement

    Step 1A Work carried out (ST)
    Step 1B Purpose, research questions or hypotheses (HSS)

Move 2 Consolidation of research space

    Step 1   Method
    Step 2   Findings/results
    Step 3   Claims
    Step 4   References to previous research
    Step 5   Product(s) (ST)

Move 3 Practical applications and recommendations (ST)
or practical implications and recommendations (HSS)

    Step 1A Applications or implications (ST)
    Step 1B Implications (HSS)
    Step 2   Recommendations

Move 4 Future research

    Step 1   Recommendations

Move 5 Concluding restatement (HSS)

    Step 1   Overall claims/findings

(Adapted from Bunton, 2005)

Figure 10.2 Moves and steps in thesis conclusions

the field and indicating directions for future research. The majority of conclusion chapters of PhD theses follow a pattern of four or five moves, with different choices made in science and technology (ST) versus humanities and social science (HSS) (Bunton, 2005). The most frequent moves and steps are presented in Figure 10.2, but not all moves and steps occur in all theses.

TASK 3 Analyzing a genre

1   Obtain an example of a learner genre or part-genre that we have dealt with here (essay, research report, discussion, conclusion) and analyze it according to the appropriate set of moves and steps.
2   How closely does your example follow the generic structure given here and how does it differ?
3   Would this task be useful in your own teaching situation? Why or why not?

Teaching and learning academic writing

So far we have looked at how some of the key learner genres have been analyzed, and asked you to try out this type of analysis and consider the extent to which it could be helpful in your own teaching situation. While genre analysis constitutes a powerful tool for teaching and learning EAP, it is by no means the only possible approach, and there are other goals that can be proposed for an academic writing course.

TASK 4 What are the goals of teaching academic writing?

Here are some possible answers to the question of what should be taught. Decide whether you think each one is vital (should always be taught), important (should sometimes be taught) or unimportant (should rarely/never be taught). Have any of them been goals of a writing course you have taught? If so, explain why.

We should teach students how to:

1   write grammatically correct sentences with accurate use of punctuation, spelling and lexis
2   express functions such as comparing and contrasting, defining
3   use study skills such as writing a bibliography, finding and selecting sources
4   carry out processes such as brainstorming ideas, planning, drafting and editing
5   write genres such as essays or thesis introductions
6   analyze and critique the institutional circumstances that give rise to their assignments
7   write texts that are appropriate within their own discipline
8   use corpora to edit their writing

You may have thought that all of the above could potentially be goals of academic writing courses and indeed they have been. However, it is important to bear in mind that goals are set within a given educational context and are designed to respond to specific student needs. We have already made the point that academic writing is key to the student's success at university. It is therefore not surprising that issues concerning how writing can best be taught and learned are contested and that many different approaches have been and continue to be advocated. We highlight some of these approaches, many of which are extensively used in certain teaching contexts.

Structural approaches

Structural approaches arose in response to the perception that students had language deficits. They tend to have a primary focus on the accuracy of surface forms and on the text as a finished product. Courses aim to teach grammatical and lexical accuracy at the sentence level. Presentation of technical and semi-technical vocabulary is through specially written texts and grammar is practised through exercises and drills.

Composition and rhetorical/functional approaches

The need to help students write longer texts gave rise to composition and rhetorical/functional approaches. Here, texts are viewed as products belonging to one of several 'rhetorical modes', which carry out functions such as comparing and contrasting, explaining a process or defining. The task of the student is to learn these textual patterns together with their linguistic realizations and to reproduce them correctly. Course materials often present models for students to imitate, and tasks focus on the characteristic surface features of the texts. The rhetorical/functional approach tends to be used in **EGAP** contexts and is widespread in the US, where courses in composition aim to develop students' writing skills through teaching essay writing on general topics.

Process approaches

The advent of learner-centred pedagogical theories gave rise to process approaches. Writing is seen as a recursive process, in which students move through several iterative stages in the production of their texts, from generating ideas and planning through writing multiple drafts to revision, proofreading and final submission. Process-based materials often begin with pre-writing tasks designed to help students discover what they want to say, e.g. by presenting readings on a given topic to stimulate interest and engagement or by brainstorming to get ideas. When a student has written a first draft, it is read and commented on by the teacher and possibly other students; then the writer proceeds to redraft, gradually revising and editing the text until the final draft is completed. In putting the learner centre-stage, process approaches privilege the individual voice of the student, who is encouraged to express his/her identity in the text by taking a personal **stance** towards a general topic of interest. Process-based instruction is often combined with composition and rhetorical/functional approaches and used in EGAP contexts.

Study skills approaches

Another approach used to compensate for students' perceived linguistic deficits is the provision of study skills to support their writing. Study skills approaches focus specifically on the strategies that are necessary for the production of successful academic texts. In writing instruction, these include attention to both surface-level issues such as referencing conventions and text formatting, as well as global aspects of text construction such as selection of sources and construction of arguments. Study skills approaches tend to be implemented in EGAP courses using general academic content; they rest on the assumption that the general skills taught are relevant to all disciplinary contexts and can readily be transferred to the student's own field.

Genre-based approaches

Genre-based approaches can be seen as a reaction to the personal emphasis of process approaches and as a return to focusing on texts. However, consideration of texts as instances of a genre widens this focus from earlier sentence- or paragraph-level concerns to texts as instances of social practice. Since genres are embedded in the work of the discipline, teaching them also demands attention to disciplinary differences and leads to a tendency for genre-based approaches to be used in **ESAP** contexts.

Both the systemic functional linguistics (SFL) and move analysis approaches to genre described in Chapter 4 are widely used in academic writing. In move analysis, students follow a four-part process: analysis–awareness–acquisition–achievement (Swales & Feak, 2009). First, learners analyze and comment on individual instances of the genre, comparing them with examples from their own fields. The aim here is 'rhetorical consciousness-raising', with students encouraged to notice the moves and steps specific to the genre, along with their linguistic realizations. This procedure is followed by detailed study and tasks to promote acquisition, culminating in students' production of their own examples of the genre. Proficient use of the genres of a discipline is held to be fundamental to academic success, and the genre-based model remains one of the most widespread today.

Academic literacies and critical EAP approaches

As we saw in Chapter 4, both academic literacies and critical EAP take a critical stance towards prevalent forms of writing instruction and aim to have a transformative effect on institutions and individuals. Academic literacies draws particular attention to the gap between lecturer and student expectations and seeks to use dialogue around texts to bridge this divide. Critical EAP focuses particularly on the socio-political dimensions of EAP, using the academic writing class as a place where teachers can help students reflect on and ask questions about the external circumstances that affect their lives. However, a note of caution is sounded by Morgan (2009), who points out that being critical should be presented as an option, not a requirement.

Corpus-based approaches

Corpus-based **data-driven learning (DDL)** also focuses on textual issues and is often used in combination with other approaches to academic writing. As we saw in Chapter 4, DDL provides students with direct access to corpus data and asks them to notice recurring patterns of language and to make generalizations from the examples. Specialized corpora of academic writing are generally used, which allow numerous examples of authentic language in target disciplines and genres to be studied. These data can be used in several different ways. For example, the teacher can access a corpus, select some examples and construct a DDL task presented on paper or screen. Alternatively, a corpus can be consulted as need arises in class either by the teacher or by students themselves. DDL can play a role at all stages of the writing process, to provide key **phraseology** on a topic, to examine the preferred ways of signalling genre moves, to check student queries and to construct tasks on specific problem areas. Corpus consultation fosters student autonomy, as learners can access corpora independently without needing to rely on others for help with their writing. This claim is supported by work which shows that students carry on using corpora in the long term, after their academic writing course has ended (Charles, 2014).

Technological tools for writing

Many new possibilities are opened up by the use of technology in the teaching and learning of academic writing and it is certain that there will be further developments in this area. The use of corpora is likely to increase as new corpus tools and more user-friendly interfaces are developed, for example, the Word and Phrase (academic) interface of **COCA** (Davies, 2008), which supplies writers with information on any word or phrase in a text they submit (http://www.wordandphrase.info/academic/). Also based on corpus data, the WriteAhead system provides suggestions (e.g. **collocations** and word completions) automatically as students write their abstracts (Liou, Yang & Chang, 2012). Progress is also under way on tools that aim to help learners structure their texts appropriately. The SAFeSEA project (Supported Automated Feedback for Short Essay Answers) allows users to input drafts of their essays and receive formative feedback designed to encourage reflection and understanding of essay structure (Whitelock, Twiner, Richardson, Field & Pulman, 2015). The use of such tools could provide students with a valuable supplement to class-based teaching, facilitate wider access to academic writing expertise and promote greater student autonomy.

Choosing approaches to writing instruction

You can see, then, that academic writing has been taught in a number of different ways, each of which brings into focus a different aspect of the undertaking. At this point, you may feel that there are so many possibilities that it is difficult to decide on a suitable approach. To help you get an overview of the options, we summarize them in Table 10.3.

Table 10.3 Approaches to writing instruction

Approach to writing instruction	Teaching focus
Structural	Grammatical and lexical accuracy at sentence level
Composition, rhetorical/functional	Rhetorical/functional text patterns, e.g. defining, contrasting
Process	Processes of writing, e.g. pre-writing, drafting, revising
Study skills	Skills to support writing, e.g. referencing, using sources
Genre-based	Disciplinary genres, e.g. thesis, essay
Academic literacies and critical EAP	Transformation of writing practices, institutional change
Corpus-based	**Lexicogrammatical** issues and discourse signalling

Although we have presented these approaches as if they were separate, many academic writing courses are hybrids, combining aspects of different approaches. Thus a rhetorical/functional course may include process-based work; critical and corpus tasks may be integrated into a genre-based approach and so on. In planning or carrying out any writing instruction, you should, of course, analyze the needs of your own students. We have already suggested in Chapter 7 that work on features of academic discourse is best integrated into work on texts. You could start, then, by finding out which genres your students have to write and then consider how you can incorporate attention to the necessary grammatical, lexical and phraseological issues within a focus on these genres. In specifying your students' writing needs in detail, you will probably discover whether work on study skills is required, and this can be included where appropriate, while opportunities for carrying out the processes of drafting and revising will arise as students practise writing the genre. As with the teaching of discourse features, it is likely that a combination of approaches will be most effective.

Profiles of practice

The EAP teachers below teach academic writing in different contexts and using different approaches. Read their accounts and answer the questions that follow.

Kuang

My students are taking a master's degree in engineering and I teach a 10-hour insessional course to prepare them for writing their dissertation. The department has given me a set of successful dissertations and I also have to follow the departmental guidelines. I've done a genre analysis of the texts, and each session we focus on one part-genre, e.g. introduction, design specification. We look at several examples together and analyze them into moves and steps. I also get them to notice and write down the language that signals the moves.

Gabriella

I have a multidisciplinary group of students who are writing doctoral theses. I get them to construct their own corpora from RAs in their field and they use AntConc, a free **concordance** tool, to research the language of their own discipline. This helps them to see typical ways of expressing ideas in their own discipline. They also use the corpus to edit their own texts, which lets them become more independent of teachers and proofreaders. The downside is that there can be technical difficulties, but we can usually sort these out, and in the long term, students appreciate having a tailor-made resource like this.

Helen

My students are in a 6-month presessional course before starting undergraduate science degrees. They have already been accepted into their courses, so it's important for them to become familiar with departmental expectations. First, we get students to interview subject tutors and students in their department to find out about the type of writing they'll have to do. Then, in consultation with a subject tutor, they choose a suitable topic and write a report which is graded by both content and EAP tutors. Involving departments like this shows students that writing is essential to gaining a good science degree and helps smooth the transition to undergraduate work for both tutors and students.

Ramon

My students are taking a preparatory course for the IELTS examination, so they have to practise exam writing. First, we analyze a model exam answer and discuss what makes it successful. Then we work on writing a text of that type together in class. I introduce useful vocabulary and we discuss the content and structure of the text. Then we develop the text together on the board, with students suggesting alternatives and taking it in turns to write down the version we choose. Then they have to write a similar text for homework.

1   Have you used any of these approaches in your teaching?
2   Would they be suitable or unsuitable for your students? Why or why not?
3   What are the differences and similarities between the approach(es) you use and those described by these teachers?

TASK 5 Discussion on L2 writing and EAP writing

In 2013, the *Journal of Second Language Writing* invited several scholars to describe what L2 writing means to them. Read these short extracts from some of the contributions and discuss the following questions.

1 To what extent do you share these views?
2 How far do they reflect your concerns as an EAP writing teacher?
3 Can you illustrate these issues with examples from your own context?

Belcher (2013, p. 438)

[L2 writing] is becoming less about what exactly L2 writing teachers should do for their students and more about how to facilitate learner autonomy.

Ferris (2013, p. 429)

[I]t is important for me and for other L2 specialists to be fully aware of and realistic about the many, many variables that can facilitate, impede, or prevent L2 writers from accomplishing their communicative goals within academic or professional settings.

Lee (2013, p. 436)

Given the centrality of sociocultural contexts in L2 writing teachers' practices, we need to . . . explore pedagogical approaches that suit specific contexts, and study individual teachers and learners in their own contexts.

Silva (2013, p. 433)

[L2 writing] is now moving toward an eclectic view, employing elements from different approaches to address L2W instruction in particular contexts.

REFLECTION

As you have seen in this chapter, academic writing is a highly complex, multi-faceted phenomenon which has been addressed in many different ways. What are the implications of this chapter for your own teaching practice? Think about the approaches to teaching academic writing introduced here and those you regularly employ. What approach or mix of approaches is most suitable for your students? Are there any new approaches that you now intend to try out?

Further reading and resources

Anthony, L. (2014). AntConc (version 3.4.3) [Computer software]. Tokyo, Japan: Waseda University.
   This free concordance software is designed for student use, but you need to have your own corpus to use it. It is available from http://www.laurenceanthony.net/

Charles, M. (forthcoming). Corpus tools for writing students. In J.I. Liontas (Ed.), *The TESOL encyclopedia of English language teaching*. Hoboken, NJ: Wiley.
This article provides an account of the uses of corpora for writing purposes and gives an extensive list of freely available corpora, tools and websites.

Hyland, K. (2004). *Genre and second language writing*. Ann Arbor: University of Michigan Press.
Although not specifically about EAP, this book provides an excellent account of the genre-based approach.

Nesi, H., & Gardner, S. (2012). *Genres across the disciplines: Student writing in higher education*. Cambridge: Cambridge University Press.
Chapter 4 in this excellent volume is key to understanding the essay genre in more depth.

SAFeSEA Project (Supported Automated Feedback for Short Essay Answers)
A video about the project is available here: http://www.open.ac.uk/research-projects/safesea/

Chapter 11

Spoken genres

So far in this book we have emphasized the written **genres** which are so important to academic achievement, but of course control of spoken genres also plays a large part in students' success. In this chapter we first focus on listening; we look at lectures and deal with the teaching of listening comprehension and note-taking. We then investigate speaking with reference to giving presentations and seminar participation, and consider the teaching of speaking.

By the end of the chapter you will know how lectures are structured; you will understand the difficulties entailed in listening and note-taking and will have a good evidence base for teaching in these areas. In the context of speaking, you will know what makes a successful presentation and how to encourage active participation in seminars and discussions.

REFLECTION

What spoken genres have you participated in during your academic life (e.g. lecture, seminar)? What are the circumstances in which each genre takes place? Who are the speakers and listeners? Are there many or just one? How much speaking and listening does each participant do? What is the purpose of each of these genres?

There are many different spoken genres that students encounter at university and you may have focused particularly on those that contribute to instruction, for example, lectures and seminars. However, we should not forget that administrative procedures such as library registration and course enrolment form part of students' experience and must be dealt with in order for studies to proceed smoothly. As you probably realized from the reflection, spoken genres differ on a number of parameters; for example, they may take place in situations of one-to-one or one-to-many; they may be largely monologic or allow for multiple contributions; speakers and audience may be experts or students; and the purpose may be pedagogic, administrative or social.

Academic listening

The skill of listening involves activating several sources of knowledge, including the phonology, syntax, semantics and pragmatics of the language, along with body language such as eye contact and gesture. In order to understand speech, listeners must decode auditory and visual signals (often referred to as 'bottom-up processing') and must also construct meanings from the input (often called 'top-down processing'). Constructing meanings relies on conceptual knowledge derived from the listener's knowledge of the world, of information already presented and of the overall context in which the speech occurs. Thus conceptual knowledge supplements the information gained from decoding and may be vital in compensating for gaps in the understanding of less proficient learners.

Although effective listening depends upon using and integrating the two processes successfully, constructing meanings is particularly important for academic listening. Field (2011a) suggests that it consists of two operations. The first entails amplifying the decoded information by placing it in context, inferring connections between ideas, understanding reference and interpreting the speaker's intentions. The second operation refers to how the listener handles this information; for example, in listening to a lecture, the listener selects relevant content, integrates it into the ongoing development of the lecture and builds a representation of how the lecture is structured into major and minor points. Much research on listening to lectures focuses on the ways in which meanings are constructed, and teaching listening skills involves helping students to develop good meaning-making strategies.

Lectures

The lecture is one of the most important spoken genres in academic work. Like the written learner genres described in Chapter 10, it is a pedagogic process genre: its purpose is to facilitate learning. For students it is a high-stakes genre, because it is the source of much of the information they need to master in order to be successful in their courses. One of the ways students can cope with the demands of lectures is by becoming aware of how they are structured so that they can recognize the stages in their development.

The introduction is particularly important in this regard, because its purpose is to prepare the audience for what follows. Based on an analysis of introductions taken from a range of disciplines, Thompson (1994) identified two major functions: 'setting up a framework' orients the audience to the lecture's structure, and 'putting the topic in context' facilitates understanding of the content. Occurring before these two major **moves** is an initial 'warming up' move, which enables the audience to settle down (Lee, 2009). Each move consists of several **steps**, although not all steps are present in all lectures. The analysis of lecture introductions appears in Figure 11.1. Work on identifying the moves and steps of introductions will help students know how the lecture develops and what to expect.

Research has also provided information on the functions performed in lectures (Deroey & Taverniers, 2011). Drawing on lectures in several disciplines from the **British Academic Spoken English (BASE) corpus**, six major functions have been identified: informing, elaborating, evaluating, organizing discourse, interacting, and managing the class. These functions occur throughout the lecture, though certain functions may be particularly prevalent at certain stages. For example, the functions of informing, elaborating and evaluating are likely to occur frequently in the body of the lecture, while the function of organizing discourse tends to be concentrated at the beginning. Work on these functions is useful in helping students to identify the way a lecture is structured and thus to engage in more effective top-down processing.

Move 1 *Warming up*

Step 1 Making a digression
Step 2 Course management matters
Step 3 Looking ahead

Move 2 *Setting up lecture framework*

Step 1 Announcing topic (obligatory)
Step 2 Indicating scope
Step 3 Outlining structure
Step 4 Presenting aims

Move 3 *Putting topic in context*

Step 1 Showing importance/relevance of topic
Step 2 Relating new content to content already known
Step 3 Referring to earlier lectures (obligatory)

(Adapted from Lee, 2009; Thompson, 1994)

Figure 11.1 Moves and steps in lecture introductions

TASK 1 Analyzing a lecture introduction

1   Access **MICASE** online and choose the browse function. At 'speech event type' select lecture-small or lecture-large, whichever is most appropriate for your teaching situation, and submit the request to browse. Access details for MICASE are given in Chapter 4.

2   From the list of lecture transcripts available, select one that is in a discipline useful for your teaching.

3   Open the transcript and apply the genre framework in Figure 11.1 to the introduction.

4   Make a list of the words and phrases that signal the moves and steps of your introduction.

5   Do the moves and steps cover all the material in your introduction? If there is material not covered, try to determine its function and give it a suitable name.

6   Is it easy to apply the analysis? What problems, if any, did you encounter and how did you deal with them?

7   Would this type of task be useful for your students? Why or why not?

Factors affecting listening comprehension in lectures

There are several issues concerned with the content and delivery of lectures that can hinder comprehension for L2 users of English. While it is clearly necessary to teach students to cope with these difficulties, if you have the opportunity to provide input to lecturers, these are areas where you could help raise awareness of good practice.

In terms of delivery, students often have problems due to speech rate, accent and pronunciation, and it has been suggested that lecturers should slow their speech rate. However, speech rate is related to lexical and propositional density: a higher speech rate is associated with less dense material (e.g. examples) and a slower rate with increased propositional density (e.g. complex ideas) (Nesi, 2005). Exposing students to lectures which incorporate varying speech rates would enable them to practise distinguishing between speech rates and taking notes appropriately.

Another problem for students is to grasp the overall structure of a lecture and how it is organized into major and minor points. There are several ways of signalling the parts of a lecture, including linguistic markers that operate on the macro-level to give the general outline of the lecture and those that function on a more local or micro-level to divide the lecture into smaller segments. As already mentioned, speakers may give an outline of their talk in the introduction; then, as the lecture progresses, they may signal the content using previews (*I will talk a bit about*) and reviews (*so far we've seen*). Markers such as *OK, right* and *now* often function to indicate textual boundaries at the micro-level, while intonation also serves to divide the lecture into segments. High pitch occurs initially, gradually lowering to the end of the segment and is followed by renewed high pitch at the beginning of the next segment (Thompson, 2003). Finally, visuals such as slides may be used to mark boundaries between parts of the lecture.

Students may also struggle to recognize repetition and redundancy or to distinguish main points from less relevant detail. Using the BASE corpus, Deroey (2015) investigated markers of importance and found that most tend to occur before the important point. The two most frequent types were oriented towards the content or the listener:

- content-oriented: *the point is, that's the message*
- listener-oriented: *you should remember, notice that.*

The marking of less relevant detail was achieved by

- giving directives: *ignore, don't write this down*
- showing the status of the message: *incidentally, as an aside*
- indicating the treatment of the message: *briefly, in a few words* (Deroey & Taverniers, 2012).

Students need practice in recognizing the signals provided by linguistic markers, intonation and visuals and in differentiating between important and less important information.

Comprehension may also be reduced when students are not actively engaged in the lecture and certain linguistic features are important for promoting interactivity. For example, personal pronouns *we* and *you* can be used to activate students' prior knowledge and to build rapport by personalizing the lecture and involving students in the ongoing discourse. Interactive lectures are also characterized by the use of questions, which facilitate student engagement by eliciting responses to content and checking understanding. Basturkmen and Shackleford (2015) draw attention to another valuable interactive technique: reformulation. Lecturers can reformulate potentially problematic language, not only to facilitate comprehension, but also to model conventional forms of expression in the discipline, thereby initiating students into the discipline's ways of thinking and expressing ideas. Techniques like these prompt students to be more actively engaged and their comprehension is deepened by participating in the construction of meaning, rather than passively receiving the information transmitted.

Another barrier to understanding may be due to differences between students and lecturers in terms of their cultural conceptions of the genre. This involves not only awareness of cultural differences and potential difficulties, but the wider issue of students' and lecturers' views on the purpose of lectures. Thus students tend to see lectures as primarily a vehicle for knowledge transmission, while lecturers have a wider range of objectives, including providing an overall framework for knowledge, promoting analytical thinking and critical engagement, developing disciplinary values, and motivating students (Badger & Sutherland, 2004). It is possible that this discrepancy in attitudes has a negative effect not only upon students' comprehension, but more generally on their willingness to engage with the material and on their perception of its utility. Discussion of such issues is one way to raise awareness of this potential conflict in attitudes and could lead to a better understanding of the role of the lecture in the overall course.

TASK 2 Identifying difficulties with listening comprehension

1   Attend a live lecture in a field relevant to your teaching or watch one on the Internet.
2   As you do so, note down the difficulties your students might experience.
3   What would be most difficult for them, e.g. understanding speech on the phonological level, identifying the organization and main points or something else?
4   What features of the lecture would facilitate listening comprehension?
5   How could you help your students to understand the lecture?

Note-taking

Over the last two decades there have been huge changes in the way that lectures are delivered and received: in terms of delivery, the widespread use of slides, the provision of notes or slides online and the use of recorded lectures or podcasts; in terms of reception, the increasing use by students of laptops, tablets and smartphones to access content, take notes and make their own recordings. However, despite these technological advances, live lectures still maintain their place as an important teaching tool, and students still take notes and perceive note-taking as necessary and useful; thus they need effective note-taking skills.

Note-taking is an extremely complex and cognitively demanding task, requiring a high level of top-down processing skills. Students must pay attention to the lecture, hold the information in their memories, organize it and take notes before it is forgotten, while simultaneously following the further development of the material. In addition, EAP students may face difficulties with bottom-up processing skills: decoding the stream of speech, dealing with unfamiliar vocabulary, hesitations, false starts, accent and speed of delivery, among others. Despite these difficulties, note-taking has been shown to have considerable benefits for learning. First, there is a product benefit, in that note-taking enables storage of the information, providing a record for recall and subsequent study. Second, there is a process benefit: note-taking focuses students' attention on the lecture and facilitates deeper processing through the analysis, selection and organization of the information.

Consideration of the benefits of note-taking leads to questions concerning what students note, what type of information is most useful and what they do with the notes afterwards. The majority of students note the main points rather than attempting to write everything down (Badger, White, Sutherland & Haggis, 2001). This approach is supported by research in psychology, which suggests that organized notes with main and subsidiary points are better for promoting long-term learning. However, more recently students have begun to take notes using computers, which speeds up the process, thereby allowing more material to be captured. Since a faster transcription rate has been associated with a higher quality, as well as quantity, of notes (Bui, Myerson & Hale, 2013), computer-based note-taking is potentially of great help to EAP learners. The most frequent activity after note-taking is re-reading the notes either immediately after the lecture or in preparation for an examination or assignment, although some students also rewrite their notes (Badger et al., 2001). These procedures accord well with findings from educational psychology which show that the combination of note-taking and subsequent review of the material is associated with higher achievement in tests and examinations.

However, advances in technology and changes in the way that material is presented to students mean that other forms of support have become available. Thus provision of online notes by the lecturer has been shown to have a beneficial effect on examination results, with students typically using them during the lecture, either in print form or online. Some lecturers make recordings or podcasts of their lectures available, and L2 users in particular have been found to make substantial use of this facility (Leadbeater, Shuttleworth, Couperthwaite & Nightingale, 2013). The provision of recorded lectures allows students to repeat or pause the material and to make notes at their own pace, clearly a great help for L2 users.

Teaching listening and note-taking

Before considering how to teach listening and note-taking, we may ask whether EAP materials correspond to authentic lectures in offering appropriate practice for students. Flowerdew and Miller (1997) note four areas where EAP materials lack the characteristics of authentic lectures:

- features of spoken language, e.g. micro-level structuring, repetition, and body language
- interpersonal strategies, e.g. personalization, comprehension checks
- discourse structuring, e.g. use of questions and macro-level markers
- integration with other media, including the use of visuals and integration with reading and seminar work.

Thompson (2003) adds that EAP materials offer little or no practice in using intonation to identify sections of the lecture, while Nesi (2005) notes that EAP materials do not illustrate the range of speech variation and purpose that occurs within the lecture. Deroey (2015) makes the point that many EAP listening materials are not corpus based; they teach few markers and do not necessarily cover those that are most frequent.

Under these circumstances, what tasks and procedures can be recommended to EAP teachers who wish to prepare students for listening to lectures and taking notes on their courses? While it may be necessary to use simplified material at early stages of listening work, the most important suggestion is to draw on authentic lectures as much as possible, by recording material in-house or by using Internet sources. Where needs analysis has revealed problems with decoding, work on individual features such as phonology should be carried out. However, it is likely that much of the work will need to focus on constructing meaning, with tasks to encourage identification of macro-level and micro-level structuring, inferencing, predicting and questioning. To this end, authentic lectures can be broken up into short sections and students can work in groups, for example, to determine the most relevant points or establish how a given point relates to preceding information and the argument of the lecture as a whole. The lecture can be paused and learners can be encouraged to monitor their comprehension by summarizing the material so far or formulating questions which they expect to be answered. It would also be useful to work on the use of visual input, for example by analyzing body language or matching slides to speech in order to show the extent to which they complement each other.

Listening comprehension can also be aided by tasks to develop appropriate metacognitive strategies, that is, strategies which help students understand how they learn. These not only improve understanding, but can also compensate to a certain extent for difficulties in listening. For example, at the pre-listening stage students could be asked to recall markers of importance or the functions of lectures; during the lecture, they might mentally number the points made; post-listening, they could relate the main points to information obtained by reading or consider the **stance** of the speaker towards aspects of the content.

For note-taking, the provision of guided notes or skeletons of the lecture for students to expand can be a useful way of focusing attention on salient points and is a task which reflects the reality of many courses (Narjaikaew, Emarat & Cowie, 2009). Both teachers and students need to be clear about the purpose of each note-taking task: is it to capture information or to promote cognitive processing of the material? Students should be encouraged not only to note down the information in a lecture but also to use note-taking to contribute to their learning. Teachers can set tasks that practise recall and review strategies and integrate noted material into a related spoken or written task such as a written report or an oral presentation. Providing realistic contexts in which students make use of their notes achieves task authenticity and gives students a clear reason for their note-taking.

TASK 3 Evaluating a listening comprehension and note-taking task

1 Choose a listening comprehension and note-taking task you might use in your teaching context.
2 Consider the four areas that Flowerdew and Miller (1997) identified as lacking in authenticity in EAP materials: features of spoken language; inter-personal strategies; discourse structuring; integration with other media.
3 To what extent does your task incorporate these features?
4 Could you adapt the task to make it more useful? See Chapter 6 on adapting materials.

Academic speaking

Many academic contexts require not just listening, but also making a spoken contribution to the discourse. As we saw in Chapter 7, spoken discourse is produced in real time, which has an effect on the features of production and imposes time pressure on the speaker, who needs to maintain fluency in an event which is constantly evolving and whose course cannot be predicted accurately. Academic speech events fall into two types:

- monologue, in which the speaker takes an extended turn, for example conference presentations and undergraduate talks
- dialogue or multi-person speech, in which two or more participants listen to others and respond to their utterances, for example seminars, class discussions, poster presentations and oral examinations.

The requirements of multi-person speech are particularly demanding, since it involves not only attending to the current speaker, processing the speaker's message and planning a suitable response, but also recognizing when to take a turn, managing the turn-taking smoothly and making a relevant contribution. Thus, while monologue can be rehearsed and even scripted to some extent, it is much less easy to rehearse participation in a multi-person genre.

Conference presentations

While the lecture is probably the most important spoken genre for undergraduates, the conference presentation is of great concern for graduates. Its purpose is to present new findings to fellow-experts in the discipline, and as it helps build reputation, it is a high-stakes genre for the speaker.

Because it is important to make a good first impression, it can be difficult to get started, especially for L2 presenters, and it is useful to know how introductions are structured. Rowley-Jolivet and Carter-Thomas (2005) distinguish three moves of the introduction; speakers first establish rapport with their audience, announcing their topic and giving the audience an outline of the talk. The second move gives background information necessary to understand the talk, while move 3 justifies the research, for example by indicating gaps in previous research and putting forward new research questions. Figure 11.2 presents these moves and indicates their constituent steps.

Although the analysis is based on the conference presentation, certain elements are relevant for all presentations, especially the need to outline the talk clearly and to give adequate background to the research so that the talk can be readily understood by the audience.

Move 1 Setting up the framework

Move 1 establishes rapport with the audience in two ways.

1 *Interpersonal framework* consists of steps that orient the listeners and/ or make acknowledgements.
2 *Discourse framework* consists of steps which announce the topic and/or indicate the structure and scope of the talk.

Move 2 Contextualizing the topic

Move 2 puts the topic into context. It consists of steps referring to the context of the specific conference and/or the general research context.

Move 3 Research rationale

Move 3 justifies the study in two ways.

1 *Motivation* consists of steps that indicate gaps/problems in the research, establish the importance of the research or add to what is known.
2 *Response* consists of steps that raise questions or make hypotheses, give an indication of results and outline research goals.

(Adapted from Rowley-Jolivet & Carter-Thomas, 2005)

Figure 11.2 Moves and steps in conference presentation introductions

Multimodality

Presentations are 'multimodal', that is, they use different modes of communication: spoken, written, visual and body language. As the modes offer different affordances and can be combined and sequenced in various ways, speakers have to learn how to handle them to achieve their purposes (Morell, 2015). For example, use of the spoken mode can precede the presentation of a visual, as when the presenter makes a point, then illustrates it with a diagram, and may occur with eye contact and gesture to explain or draw attention to the visual.

In particular, the role of the visual dimension is vital to understanding and constructing meanings in spoken presentations. Rowley-Jolivet (2004) distinguishes four types of visual (scriptural, numerical, figurative and graphical) and shows that the way these resources are deployed differs according to the content and methods of disciplines. For example, geology uses high percentages of figurative and graphical visuals, especially photographs and maps, while physics privileges scriptural and graphical visuals, reflecting the importance of both language and diagrams in this discipline. Delivering a successful presentation, then, necessitates recognizing the specific contribution of the visuals, as well as understanding how all four modes work together in order to transmit meaning.

Teaching presentation skills

Before we consider how to teach presentation skills, we need to distinguish the features that are typical of successful presentations and ask whether L2 users employ them. In linguistic terms, presentations are characterized by the use of short clauses, active voice and a number of features for highlighting new information, including inversion of subject and verb (*on the right are the corresponding figures*). As in lectures, interpersonal markers, including personal pronouns (*we, you*), are often employed to engage the interest of the audience and involve them in the ongoing presentation, while varying pitch and speech rate also contribute to interesting and lively talks. However, L2 speakers are likely to focus more on the informational aspects of their talk rather than attending to interpersonal elements and tend to use more features typical of formal written discourse such as passives; thus their presentations may fail to engage their audience fully and may be more difficult for the listeners to process. The organization of the presentation may also lack signals to orient the audience to the message, outline its organization or show transitions between sections.

What approaches can be suggested to improve this situation? Work on the use of visuals may help compensate for linguistic difficulties, thereby freeing up attention for focusing on audience interaction. Students could analyze successful lectures and presentations in terms of audience engagement to raise their awareness of the importance of this factor. They could practise signalling the development of their presentations clearly and initiating exchanges and responding to their audience using a more conversational approach. It may also be useful to highlight the differences between spoken and written modes in terms of contextual and communicative factors and to practise transfer between written and spoken genres.

Teaching participation in multi-person spoken genres

Although giving presentations is an important skill, it is equally vital for students to be able to take part in speech events with two or more participants who are simultaneously speakers and listeners. McCarthy (2010) suggests that the ability to engage successfully in such multi-person speech events is an important aspect of fluency which places high demands on speakers, especially when, as in academic contexts, they must compete with each other in order to gain the speaking turn. He further argues that fluency in such settings is a feature of the interaction, constructed by both speaker and listener, and that establishing and maintaining the flow of talk depends significantly on the ability of both parties to manage turn-taking smoothly. He notes, for example, that turn-openings tend to provide continuity in the discourse, linking back to the previous speaker's turn in order to facilitate a smooth transition.

In the context of a seminar, a turn-opening is often constructed through questions to which the presenter must respond, so it is useful to see how this Question – Response exchange plays out in the academic context. Basturkmen's (1999) research on seminars provides a detailed corpus-based analysis of Question – Response sequences. She finds that there are two ways of initiating a turn in a discussion.

- Elicits of Information request information which the speaker does not have any assumptions about and are typically performed by *wh*-questions (*What was the result for . . .?*).
- Elicits for Confirmation request information or ideas which the questioner has certain assumptions about and wishes to confirm. They can be carried out by yes/no questions (*Are they . . . ? Aren't you . . .*) and statements with/without a tag question (*This would still be . . . wouldn't it?*). These can indicate a negative evaluation of the presenter's content.

Elicits for Confirmation allow listeners to contribute their own content and ideas to the ongoing discussion. They are normally accompanied by other material (e.g. extra information, examples, or reasons), which helps contributors to justify taking the turn and establishes a context for their contribution. Changes of topic are often signalled by referring to an earlier point made by the presenter (*You focused earlier on . . .*), or by stating the topic of the elicit (*The policy of...*). Such devices serve to smooth the transition to a new topic as well as making the turn-taking less abrupt and therefore more polite. Politeness is also important when making a negative comment, and **hedging** is often used to soften the impact of criticism on a presenter's work. For more on hedging, see Chapter 7.

In addition to managing turn-taking and criticizing politely, it is important for students to interact constructively with others when discussing ideas or participating in teamwork. Research by Basturkmen (2002) on student discussion groups identifies not just a simple pattern of organization in which there is an exchange of ideas that are already formed, but also a more complex structure in which ideas emerge and are co-constructed through the interaction of all contributors. In such cases responsibility for the success of the interaction is shared by all members of the group. This research suggests that students should be given instruction and practice so that they become skilled in establishing and maintaining this type of interaction.

EAP speaking courses could begin by teaching the process of turn-taking, starting with practice on the relatively undemanding elicits of information, before proceeding to elicits for confirmation and hedged negative comments. Along with turn-taking, presenters and audience members could practise responding to questions by accepting contributions and taking them further. In order to promote constructive interaction, speaking instruction could focus on responding to seminar/discussion partners by building on their contributions, modifying and refining ideas until a satisfactory outcome is achieved. Tasks could be assigned that require participants to cooperate in order to complete them successfully.

TASK 4 Teaching spoken genres

1   For speaking purposes, which genre is the most important for your students, the presentation, the seminar or another genre?

2   What makes this genre particularly important and what is the role of the student's spoken contribution?

3   What factors might make students reluctant to speak in this genre?

4   How could you encourage them to do so?

Profiles of practice

Some EAP teachers were asked how they teach listening, note-taking and speaking. Read their accounts and consider them from the perspective of your own teaching context.

Peter (listening and note-taking)

I believe in a structured approach, so I pre-teach any vocabulary my students might not know. Then we listen to the whole lecture and go over the main points together. After that we break the lecture into sections and listen bit by bit for complete comprehension. My students are uncomfortable if they don't understand everything. In each class, I focus on specific strategies for understanding or note-taking, for example, recognizing markers of importance or teaching abbreviations and symbols for quicker note-taking.

Marcela (speaking)

For speaking I like to use the free software Audacity. My students make their own podcasts and store them on the learning platform so that everyone in the class can listen to them and add their comments. Sometimes they even put them up on social media and get listeners from all over the world. Knowing they have a real audience is a huge motivating factor. The software is also good for work on pronunciation because students can record themselves and see the wave form of what they say.

Dorota (speaking)

My students are graduates and I use poster presentations because that's a genre my students will have to cope with. I divide the class into two. In the first half of the lesson one group has to stand by their posters while the others circulate and ask questions and then we reverse it, so that everyone gets the chance to present a poster and be a member of the audience. The students can prepare a bit what they're going to say, but they're not allowed any notes except for the poster itself. At the end we display the posters where everyone can see them.

Ting (listening and note-taking)

I sometimes 'flip' my listening classes by reversing the normal sequence of activities. This means that students do some listening at home and submit their notes or worksheets to me before class. Then I can see what difficulties they're having and focus on those areas in class; for example, they often need work on specific listening strategies such as recognizing changes of topic. I tend to use podcasts from university websites and I might assign just part of a lecture, but students like being able to listen as much as they want and often finish the whole thing.

1   Have you used any of the above approaches?
2   Would any of them work with your students, and if so, which ones?
3   Are there any which are unsuitable in your context? Why or why not?

TASK 5 Debate on new technologies in listening and note-taking

There has been a lot of discussion about the role of new technologies in relation to listening to lectures and taking notes. What are the advantages and disadvantages of the following developments for L2 students? What implications do they have for the teaching of EAP listening and note-taking? How might they affect what you do in class?

- Students' use of computers/laptops/tablets to take notes
- Students' use of smartphones to record lectures or photograph slides
- The provision of recordings/videos/podcasts of lectures for students to access on demand
- The online provision of full/outline notes or slides by the lecturer
- The 'flipped classroom'. This refers to the procedure whereby all lecture content is provided online and class time is reserved for tasks, discussions, individual work etc.

REFLECTION

In this chapter we have seen some of the factors that contribute to students' problems with listening, note-taking and speaking and have suggested ways in which these could be addressed. What implications does this information have for your own teaching practice? Think about how you teach listening and note-taking and the materials you use. How far do these techniques and materials reflect the procedures and genres of academic work? Consider how you generally teach speaking. To what extent does it prepare students for participating in the genres they need for academic work? After reading this chapter, what modifications, if any, would you make to the way you teach listening and speaking?

Further reading and resources

Audacity (2014). (version 2.0.6) [Computer software].
   Audacity is freeware for recording and editing sound and is very useful for both listening and speaking. It is available from http://audacity.sourceforge.net/
Bloch, J. Flipping the L2 composition classroom
   This website curated by Joel Bloch offers access to many articles on the use of the flipped classroom. You can access it here: http://www.scoop.it/t/flipping-the-l2-composition-classroom
Field, J. (Ed.). (2011b). Listening in EAP [Special issue]. *Journal of English for Academic Purposes*, 10(2).
   This is a special issue on listening comprehension with an excellent overview of the field.

Flowerdew, J. (Ed.). (1994). *Academic listening*. Cambridge: Cambridge University Press.

Although published in 1994, this is a classic work, with some very good papers.

Swales, J. M. (2004). *Research genres: Explorations and applications*. Cambridge: Cambridge University Press.

Chapter 6 in this excellent volume deals with spoken research genres.

Chapter 12

Assessment and feedback in EAP

Assessment is a pervasive feature of higher education, and it is a broad concept, including tests, written assignments, oral presentations, and any other form which allows information about the learner's attainments to be measured. By the end of this chapter you will understand the ways in which assessment is commonly used in EAP contexts, and the mechanisms behind the best known diagnostic measures. You will also know some common forms of assessment, the factors which lead to feedback having maximum impact, and how to structure feedback and assessment to address a particularly vexing issue, plagiarism. Before reading this chapter on assessment, reflect on what you know about the topic.

REFLECTION

Drawing on your experiences as a student, list as many forms of assessment as possible, such as written examinations, essays, etc. Was the outcome of each equally important to you, or were some more important than others? Did each serve the same purpose or did they have different purposes? What sort of response did you get to each one? Was it a letter grade, a numerical score, comments from the teacher or something else? Did some forms of assessment seem fairer than others?

Purposes of assessment

In EAP as in other areas of education, assessment is performed for one of three broad purposes. Diagnostic assessment is carried out in order to benchmark the learner's level of proficiency. This is usually done in order to be able to make informed choices about the subsequent educational process. For example, diagnostic testing can take place at the beginning of a course to be able to place students in groups which are appropriate to their level. Diagnostic testing can also be used as a basis for admission to an academic degree programme, to determine whether students' levels of proficiency are such that they have good preconditions for success on a programme taught through the medium of English.

Summative assessment is done at the end of a course for the purpose of measuring the students' learning attainments. Summative assessment is thus the mechanism which triggers academic rewards, such as course credit, permission to advance to the next level of study, or an academic degree. By contrast, formative assessment is conducted during a course and is intended to help learners and teachers understand how the learner is progressing towards the learning objectives, while the opportunity still exists to influence that trajectory.

Summative and formative assessments are more distinct in theory than they are in much current language pedagogy. For example, academic writing is often taught through a process approach which involves multiple drafts, with the early drafts constituting formative assessment, while the final draft is awarded a grade. The widely used portfolio approach is similar, as learners work on a number of individual tasks across an extended period of time, receiving feedback on them and then moving on to progressively more challenging tasks. At the end of the course, the entire portfolio is resubmitted to be evaluated summatively.

Quality criteria in assessment

The results of assessment are extremely important. Most obviously, they are critical to students who hope to realize the reward towards which they have worked or who wish to achieve admission to a course or academic programme. The results are also crucial, though, to teachers and their institutions. If the result of assessment is that students do not receive the academic reward they deserve, there is an unfair negative impact on the individuals concerned. If an assessment process is too generous and confers academic rewards on students who have not earned them, that causes a negative impact on all of the other students whose work is devalued as a result. In both cases, doubt is cast on the assessment system, so that even individuals whose work has in fact been fairly assessed lack confidence in their results. If that lack of confidence becomes widespread, then there is a real risk of reputational damage to the institution. Quality in assessment is therefore at least as important as quality in other aspects of education.

Robust forms of assessment have four characteristics: alignment, validity, reliability and predictability. The principle of **constructive alignment**, introduced in Chapter 5, states that the content included in a course and the ways of assessing mastery of the content should be aligned with the learning objectives. Simply put, the learning objectives determine what to teach and the assessment should measure whether it has been learned. One implication of constructive alignment is that the content of assessment should be reflected in the stated learning objectives; skills or areas of knowledge which are not found there should not be assessed. Another implication is that alignment should be the basis for decisions about how to benchmark learners' work, particularly in the case of summative assessment, when it is easy to get caught up in questions of detail such as how many points are needed for a simple pass as opposed to a pass with distinction. The decisive factor, though, should not be how many points the student earned, but the extent to which performance on the assessment demonstrated that the student has mastered the learning objectives.

In order to be able to serve this purpose – providing evidence about mastery of the learning objectives – assessment must be characterized by validity. Validity means that the assessment really measures the thing which it intends to measure, and importantly, some forms of assessment give more direct measures of areas of attainment than others. For example, there are a number of ways to find out about a learner's knowledge of vocabulary. One is to give the learner a test like the Vocabulary Levels Test (mentioned in Chapter 8). Another is to ask the learner to write an essay and to evaluate the vocabulary usage. If the relevant learning objective is to be able to produce academic writing with appropriate and idiomatic vocabulary choices, then the essay will provide more direct information than the test, because the test would at best only demonstrate **receptive knowledge** of the meaning of the words tested, and not the ability to use them productively. However, if the stated learning objective is to learn the meaning of a specific set of words, then a test of those words is a better indicator than an essay, because failure to use the words in the essay could indicate either that the student does not know them or that the student did not believe they were relevant to the essay.

Reliability implies consistency among results. If a test is reliable, every student who has demonstrated mastery of the learning objectives will pass and no student who has not done so will pass. Importantly, this consistency should ideally be achieved not only within a given group, but across groups. Two groups of students taking the same course but taught by different teachers should be assessed consistently, and this year's group should be held to the same standard as last year's, no more and no less. This is of course very much a counsel of perfection. One threat to reliability is that courses can be taught by different teachers, either over a period of time or, if there are multiple groups of students, at the same time. Communication among teachers to develop an awareness of a shared set of standards is the best way of preventing this. Another potential problem is that language teaching places more emphasis on learning skills than on acquiring facts, and subjectivity is therefore hard to avoid. With open and more subjective forms of assessment, such as writing tasks, it is easy to focus too much on one feature of the work to the exclusion of others. For example, it may be easy to make an impressionistic positive assessment of a text which uses a small range of vocabulary and grammatical structures but is free of lexico-syntactic errors and to spot the errors in another text without noticing that the writer used a more advanced range of structures and words. Having clearly articulated assessment criteria helps avoid blind spots like this.

Assessment criteria also make it easier to achieve the very important goal of predictability. Students who lack a clear sense of the kind of assessment they will be subjected to, and the criteria which will be applied to them, can feel anxiety and insecurity, and these are not helpful to learning. Students who know how they will be assessed will bend their efforts to succeed on the assessment, and provided the assessment is in alignment with the course objectives, this will help them learn the things which the course is supposed to teach them. Predictability can be achieved by providing students with information about the assessment from the very beginning of a course. Sample examinations, or examples from previous years' successful and unsuccessful students can help make the information specific and concrete. It is also useful to show students how the assessment relates to the learning objectives for the course. This enables them to see assessment as part of the learning process, and not just a hurdle to get over. It is also beneficial for the teacher, though, because the process of articulating the ways that constructive alignment is manifested in a course forces the teacher to ensure that it is indeed present.

TASK I Analyzing assessment

Select two different forms of assessment which you have assigned to your students, or have yourself been asked to do. For example, you may consider an examination you have sat, or the instructions for a writing assignment you were asked to do. Compare the two in terms of the following:

1   Alignment: to what extent were the forms of assessment aligned with the course objectives and course content?
2   Validity: what were the assessments intended to measure? Did they succeed?
3   Reliability: if all students in a group had precisely the same levels of skill and knowledge, would they be awarded the same grade based on these forms of assessment?
4   Predictability: before being given these assessments, to what extent were students able to predict what they would be like?

Giving and using diagnostic tests

In the **Inner Circle** countries it is routine for university admissions to be contingent on the applicant achieving a minimum score on one of three prominent commercial tests which are widely administered internationally. They are the Test of English as a Foreign Language (TOEFL), the International English Language Testing System (IELTS) and (a more recent entry into the market) the Pearson Test of English (PTE). The three are similar in their coverage, with each featuring sections testing reading, writing, speaking and listening.

All three are examples of what are called criterion-referenced tests. These are tests on which assessment is measured with respect to an external set of already established criteria (as opposed to norm-referenced assessment, which results in a grouping or rank-ordering of test-takers according to their relative abilities). Criterion-referenced tests cannot be passed or failed; rather, test-takers receive a score which describes their performance against the criteria. Rather unhelpfully, each of these three tests uses a different scoring system, so that PTE ranges from 10 to 90, the (Internet-based) TOEFL from 0 to 120, and IELTS from 1 to 9. In order to interpret what these scores mean, it is necessary to rely on descriptors of the ability level which the numbers indicate. So, for example, the IELTS numerical scores are associated with qualitative descriptors such as 'modest', 'good' and 'expert' user (see Figure 12.1) and a brief discussion of what those labels imply.

Band 9: Expert user: has fully operational command of the language; appropriate, accurate and fluent with complete understanding.

Band 8: Very good user: has fully operational command of the language with only occasional unsystematic inaccuracies and inappropriacies. Misunderstandings may occur in unfamiliar situations. Handles complex detailed argumentation well.

Band 7: Good user: has operational command of the language, though with occasional inaccuracies, inappropriacies and misunderstandings in some situations. Generally handles complex language well and understands detailed reasoning.

Band 6: Competent user: has generally effective command of the language despite some inaccuracies, inappropriacies and misunderstandings. Can use and understand fairly complex language, particularly in familiar situations.

Band 5: Modest user: has partial command of the language, coping with overall meaning in most situations, though is likely to make many mistakes. Should be able to handle basic communication in own field.

Band 4: Limited user: basic competence is limited to familiar situations. Has frequent problems in understanding and expression. Is not able to use complex language.

Band 3: Extremely limited user: conveys and understands only general meaning in very familiar situations. Frequent breakdowns in communication occur.

Band 2: Intermittent user: no real communication is possible except for the most basic information using isolated words or short formulae in familiar situations and to meet immediate needs. Has great difficulty understanding spoken and written English.

Band 1: Non-user: essentially has no ability to use the language beyond possibly a few isolated words.

Band 0: Did not attempt the test: No assessable information provided.

Figure 12.1 IELTS band descriptors

(http://www.ielts.org/institutions/test_format_and_results/ielts_band_scores.aspx)

Because there is no pass or fail level on these tests, universities themselves decide what score to require for admission. Threshold scores are typically lower in some subject areas (for example, technical subjects) than they are in subjects which place a high demand on communication and discoursal skills (for example, the language-intensive humanities and the high-stakes caring professions). In using test scores as the basis for admissions decisions, institutional experience can be guided by help in interpreting scores provided by the producers. So, for example, IELTS states that an overall score of 6.5 indicates that a candidate needs further study before embarking on an academic course which is linguistically challenging, but for a course which is less so, that score is 'probably acceptable', and for training courses, regardless of the linguistic demands they place on students, a score of 6.5 is 'acceptable' (IELTS, 2013, p. 13). The PTE cautiously suggests that scores of 51 to 61 are needed for undergraduate study and 57 to 67 for graduate study (Pearson Education, 2012, p. 39).

Benchmarks like these are important in the admissions process as a support in helping institutions decide whether students, if admitted to a course, will have good chances for success. The question that classroom teachers bring to test scores (if they have access to them) is a different one: what does the score say about what my students already know and need to be taught? The difficulty of answering this question is compounded by the fact that many institutions accept scores from more than one test, so that in order to understand the level of a group of students, the teacher needs to understand how scores compare with each other. Since these commercial tests compete with each other, the test producers have no incentive to facilitate comparisons with competitors, so the usual approach is to position a range of test scores against an accepted framework of proficiency levels.

Two proficiency frameworks are particularly influential. The American Council on the Teaching of Foreign Languages (ACTFL) first established proficiency guidelines in 1986, has updated them periodically, and released a fourth edition in 2012 (ACTFL, 2012). The ACTFL framework provides level descriptors for the four skills – reading, writing, speaking and listening – and categorizes language users in five major levels: distinguished, superior, advanced, intermediate and novice. The three lower levels are further subdivided into high, mid and low bands. Each level is framed as a series of statements about what an individual at that level can do. Thus, a low novice reader is 'able to recognize a limited number of letters, symbols or characters' (p. 24), while a distinguished reader can 'understand a wide variety of texts from many genres including professional, technical, academic, and literary' (p. 21).

A newer set of proficiency guidelines is the Common European Framework of Reference (CEFR). Like the ACTFL scale, the CEFR is intended to describe the proficiency levels of users of all languages, not just English. It groups learners into three levels (A, or basic user; B, or independent user;

Table 12.1 Comparison of proficiency frameworks and levels

TOEFL ibt[3]	0–31			32–45		45–93		94–114	114–120
IELTS[2]	0–4			4–5		5–6.5		7–8	8–9
PTE[1]	0–24		24–42	36–59		51–76		67–85	80–90
CEFR		A1	A2	B1		B2		C1	C2
ACTFL[4]	novice low	novice mid	novice high	intermediate low	intermediate mid	intermediate high	advanced low	advanced mid	advanced high	superior	distinguished

[1] PTE scores benchmarked against the CEFR taken from Pearson, n.d.
[2] IELTS scores benchmarked against the CEFR taken from http://www.ielts.org/researchers/common_european_framework.aspx
[3] TOEFL ibt scores benchmarked against IELTS taken from https://www.ets.org/toefl/institutions/scores/compare/
[4] ACTFL scores benchmarked against CEFR taken from http://www.languagetesting.com/wp-content/uploads/2014/02/opic-cefr-study-final-report.pdf

and C, or proficient user) and then further subdivides each level in two. The resulting six-level scale has as its lowest level A1, at which level a language user can (among other things) 'understand and use familiar everyday expressions and very basic phrases', and ranges up to C2, at which level the user can 'understand with ease virtually everything heard or read' (Council of Europe, n.d., p. 24).

Both the simpler CEFR scale and the more fine-grained ACTFL scale can then describe language proficiency levels ranging from very basic to extremely proficient and, importantly for the teacher, do so by means of can-do statements which are helpful in understanding where learners are and what they need next. An approximate correspondence among the scores on the three major proficiency tests and these two proficiency level guides appears in Table 12.1.

Despite the prominence of these three important tests, other commercial tests exist. There is also a long tradition of locally produced diagnostic tests. Although the efficacy of in-house tests is underresearched (Basturkmen & Elder, 2006), some available research points to cost as a key factor in driving the choice to use locally produced tests (Jamieson, Wang & Church, 2013).

TASK 2 Measuring proficiency

Use the IELTS descriptors above to benchmark your own proficiency in English, if it is your second language, or if English is your first language, some other language which you know, and answer the following questions.

1   Where would you place yourself on this scale taking your overall abilities into account?
2   Where would you place yourself for reading, writing, speaking and listening individually?
3   How easy or difficult was it to decide?

Forms of assessment

Beyond diagnostic purposes, both teachers and students need ways to form a sense of how students are progressing towards mastery of the learning outcomes (i.e. formative assessment), and ways of measuring the extent to which students have attained the learning outcomes by the end of the course (i.e. summative assessment). The overarching principle in designing forms of assessment is alignment (discussed in Chapter 5), so that assessment measures all the course objectives and only the course objectives. More specifically, whatever form of assessment is used, it must be able to measure attainment of a learning objective; all the forms of assessment taken together must measure attainment of all of the course's learning objectives;

and assessment should not require students to possess knowledge or skills which were neither part of the course objectives nor the prerequisites for admission to the course.

Many EAP course objectives, like those of language courses more generally, are related to the performance of skills. Thus, some courses deal with academic speaking, and so the assessment would need to be based on one or more speaking tasks. These can be impromptu or planned, shorter or longer, and components of assessment can include higher-level skills, such as the ability to structure a talk effectively and use discourse markers to signal the structure to the listener, or local features such as pronunciation and intonation. Chapter 11 gives an overview of the features of spoken academic discourse.

Academic listening is important and ways of assessing listening include asking students to listen to a lecture and answer questions about its content. If you plan your teaching and assessment around the use of authentic texts, then adapting listening assessment for learners at lower levels involves adapting the scope of the task. So, for example, writing complete notes or a summary of the content of a ten-minute extract from a lecture is quite challenging. Being provided with key points and terms which come up in the lecture and organizing them in the order in which the lecturer presented them is less challenging. Multiple-choice or true-false questions about the content of the lecture or specific words or phrases used by the lecturer can, if carefully designed, be extremely accessible even to less proficient students.

Academic reading is another important **domain** in which EAP students can be asked to demonstrate proficiency. The same principles of adapting the task to the text in order to grade the level of difficulty apply. In addition, time is a very important factor in reading. Very proficient L2 users of English have been shown to perform as well as native speakers of English on tests of academic reading comprehension, but only provided they have more time to read than the native speakers (Shaw & McMillion, 2008). For learners at lower proficiency levels, the time available to read has a greater impact still on comprehension.

Writing is a prominent and important academic communication skill, and many EAP courses give particular attention to writing skills. Producing academic writing for assessment requires mastery of very many subskills, including the ability to read academic texts, to relate ideas from one text to another and to the new text being produced, to structure and support a coherent argument, to quote or paraphrase material from sources appropriately and much else. A common approach to teaching these complex and interlocking skills is to use portfolio assessment, a process which involves learners writing individual assignments, often through a multi-draft process, and then presenting them in a portfolio, which gives the teacher the opportunity to judge not only the quality of the finished work but the extent to which learners' performance has improved during the course.

Some of the content of EAP courses, like other language courses, is declarative rather than skill based. Knowledge of grammatical forms and academic words and phrases is part of producing and understanding academic discourse, and this sort of content can be tested by means of a written examination. An important choice to make in constructing examination questions is whether they will be open or closed. Generally speaking, an open question (such as asking students to complete a sentence with an appropriate word) is more challenging than a closed one (for instance, a multiple-choice or true-false question). This is another example of the way in which the degree of difficulty of the content can be mitigated by the degree of difficulty involved in the assessment task.

As this overview suggests, there are many forms of assessment which can be used in EAP teaching. Teachers do not always have a free hand to select the form of assessment for a course, and even when they do, it can be comfortable and efficient to stick with familiar forms. However, the use of a varied range of forms maximizes the chances of achieving the very important goal of matching assessment and learning objectives.

TASK 3 Aligning assessment

The task at the end of Chapter 5 asked you to write (among other things) learning objectives and forms of assessment for EAP provision in a specified setting. Using your answers to that task or some other course with which you are familiar, give a rationale for why the forms of assessment are valid, reliable, consistent and in alignment with course objectives.

Response and feedback

The purpose of formative assessment is to shape future work, and even summative assessment has the potential to play that role, since students can take what they learn from feedback in one course and apply it to the next one. Feedback, then, is a potentially important part of the learning process (and one which is often popular with students).

On measures of declarative knowledge, such as tests of receptive vocabulary, feedback can take the form of simply indicating whether the answer was correct or incorrect. However, since much EAP teaching is skill based, feedback often needs to be more detailed to be valuable. Most often, feedback on written or spoken assignments should address both local features, such as grammatical accuracy, and global features, like structure and coherence. When oral assignments involve high stakes, they may be recorded, because otherwise it is difficult to gather enough information to be sure of making a balanced assessment. The recording can then be reviewed with the learner. On written assignments a common approach to commenting on local features is to provide learners with enough information to identify and diagnose their own errors. Thus, instead of changing an incorrect irregular verb, a teacher might write *verb form?* (or an abbreviation indicating that) to encourage the learner to check.

However, this practice along with most others related to written corrective feedback (WCF) has been the subject of a certain degree of debate, as considerable doubt has been cast on whether or to what extent it improves future student performance. Reviewing the literature then available, Truscott (1996) pointed out that not only had a number of studies failed to find that corrective feedback produced a positive result, in some studies groups with feedback performed worse than those without. This led him to conclude that 'no valid reasons have been offered for continuing the practice in spite of these overwhelming problems. The conclusion is clear: Grammar correction should be abandoned' (p. 360).

Other studies have found beneficial effects for feedback but less support for an approach based on the idea that more is better. For example, Ferris and Roberts (2001) found that writers who received feedback were better able to edit their own texts than writers who did not, but that more explicit feedback did not produce any better results than less explicit. Bitchener (2008) also found positive results for feedback, but his study was designed to give students feedback about one point of grammar only, the use of articles. It is possible that sharply targeted feedback is effective where comments covering a wider range of areas might not be. More research is needed to inform this question, but given the time and energy that providing feedback requires, teachers are well advised not to assume that resources that go to feedback are well spent.

Cheating and plagiarism

Since assessment is the final hurdle in the way of some form of academic reward, such as course credits or a degree, it is inevitable that some students will try to obtain the reward through illegitimate means. Cheating is an attempt to try to circumvent the assessment process, and it is wrong for the same reasons that poorly planned and executed assessment is wrong: it results in rewards being given unfairly, and it diminishes the confidence of all parties in the assessment process, ultimately with negative impact on the value of the qualification students receive and on the institution's reputation.

While some cheating may be inevitable, there are things which teachers can do to prevent it. The causes of cheating are varied, but they include uncertainty about what practices are acceptable (Sutton & Taylor, 2011; Yeo, 2007) and views which are unlikely to agree with those of teachers (Ashworth, Bannister & Thorne, 1997). This suggests that being explicit about what is and is not permitted in assessment, and the rationale for those rules, could minimize cheating. When cheating is detected, it is important to respond to it. Many educational institutions stipulate detailed procedures; if yours does not, and if you discover or suspect cheating, it is a good idea to consult an experienced member of staff about how to respond.

Plagiarism is the use of an existing source text in a misleading way by a writer who wishes to portray that text as being his or her own. Plagiarism is most easily identified by resemblances between a text and its sources, and when it is identified, it is generally regarded as a form of cheating. However, a sizeable body of research (e.g. Abasi, Akbari & Graves, 2006; Pecorari, 2008) has demonstrated that some students produce texts which appear to be plagiarized because they lack the linguistic sophistication to perform academic writing tasks in a fluent and fully competent way, and adopt a strategy of using more proficient voices as models to copy.

Plagiarism is a difficult problem for the EAP teacher to address. Even if it does not constitute deliberate deception, if some students are allowed to copy assessment texts from sources, this is unfair for other students who do not. Plagiarism can also trigger harsh punishments, so it is important that learners emerge from their EAP instruction with the knowledge that it should be avoided, and the skills in academic writing for doing so.

The most effective way to help learners avoid plagiarizing unintentionally is to equip them with such good writing skills that they do not need to depend on the language of sources to get their message across. Because virtually all academic writing involves reading other people's work, and allowing the earlier works to influence the new one, it is not possible for academic writers simply to avoid using sources. They need to develop the skills to use them effectively. These include (among others) the ability to read academic texts and understand them thoroughly; to summarize and paraphrase; to select appropriate quotations and insert them into the new text smoothly; and to make effective use of reporting forms (e.g. *Smith argues, Jones reports*).

However, there is also considerable variation across academic **disciplines** and among individuals both in terms of conventional forms of source use and **citation** and in terms of how much recycling of texts is viewed as acceptable. Quite problematically for learners, then, practices in the EAP classroom may not reflect those which students have encountered, or will encounter elsewhere in the university. Plagiarism, then, is not only a problem for the EAP teacher, it is one which requires sensitive and nuanced handling, with pedagogical objectives front of mind (Pecorari, 2013).

Profile of practice

Read the following description of assessment practice and answer the questions below. At a university in the **Expanding Circle**, the English department offers a course in academic reading and writing for students who will be studying through the medium of English. One component in the assessment for the course is an essay written under examination conditions. Large numbers of students go through the course every year, so multiple teachers are involved. Frequently they are inexperienced and employed on a casual basis, so there is significant turnover in the teaching staff, and this posed a threat to the consistency of assessment: there was a risk that the changing pool of teachers would use idiosyncratic criteria in scoring the exams and that the results would not be comparable from one term to another.

To solve this problem, a process of team assessment was developed. When the essay exams had been written, the members of the teaching staff with involvement in the course, present or past, met for a full working day. They started the day by reading two or three of the essays and discussing what score they would give to them. Disagreements were resolved by discussion, drawing out the criteria which individuals were attending to, with permanent staff members sharing their experience by benchmarking the essays against scores given in earlier terms.

When the markers' standards and criteria were in alignment, they began reading the essays individually. Two markers read each essay independently. If an essay received two very close scores, the final mark was the average. If there was a significant spread between the two markers' scores, it went to a third reader. On the few occasions when this procedure did not produce a confident result, individual essays could be taken back for group discussion.

This process was successful in its intended objective of creating consistency within the course each term but also across terms. In addition, it had several significant benefits. Students were reassured that the assessment was not entirely subjective and arbitrary, and had more confidence in the process. The teaching staff felt that the exposure to other perspectives on student writing contributed to their professional development.

1   Have you ever been part of an assessment process in which you were required to align your judgements about students with those of your colleagues?
2   Do you think that taking part in a process like this would make you more or less confident about your ability to assess student work?
3   Would an approach like this work in your teaching context? Why or why not?

TASK 4 Read and report

Read the descriptors for two of the proficiency measures and frameworks described above (references appear in the section above). Now think about a group of students you have taught or been part of.

1   Consider the extent to which the two scales you have selected would help you describe the ability of individual students in the group in relation to each other.

2   Consider the extent to which the two scales would let you describe members of the group in terms of their readiness for academic study in English.

3   Present your findings about the relative usefulness of these scales.

REFLECTION

Many students find that they are more comfortable with some forms of assessment than others. Some people do well on written examinations, while others become nervous and freeze. Some students like writing assignments because they can be done at their own pace, while others complain of writer's block and are intimidated by a blank page or computer screen. Think about a form of assessment which you disliked as a student. Could it have been replaced by something better? Or are there reasons why, despite the fact that it was uncomfortable, it was good for its purpose?

Further reading and resources

Assessing Writing
   This journal publishes research articles and other content on approaches to assessing student writing in academic contexts at all levels. It is available at http://www.journals.elsevier.com/assessing-writing/

Bitchener, J., & Ferris, D. (2012). *Written corrective feedback in second language acquisition and writing*. New York: Routledge.
   This book-length treatment of the topic of feedback includes a section with especial relevance for teachers.

Ferris, D. (2010). Second language writing research and written corrective feedback in SLA. *Studies in Second Language Acquisition, 32*, 181–201.
   This literature review weighs up the research evidence on the effectiveness of feedback.

Fulcher, G., & Davidson, F. (Eds.). (2012). *The Routledge handbook of language testing*. New York: Routledge.
   This handbook surveys topics in language testing with relevance for EAP from a broader perspective.

Read, J. (2015). *Assessing English proficiency for university study*. Basingstoke, UK: Palgrave Macmillan.
   This recent book covers both theoretical and practical aspects of assessment, focusing particularly on post-entry language assessment in Australia and New Zealand.

Moving forward into practice

This book has given you an introduction to English for Academic Purposes. In this brief concluding section we turn to some themes which have informed the book throughout, and should inform your teaching practice going forward.

EAP exists to serve the learner

Pure areas of study require no justification. Topics can be researched and areas of content taught simply because they are there. As an area of applied linguistics, all EAP activity has a very practical focus: it exists to support people who need to use English in academic settings. This means that the needs of the learner should drive EAP, from course development to materials design, and that EAP research should answer questions which feed into these core activities.

Discourse and the disciplinary conversation

Academic discourse has been shown in this book to have distinct, characteristic features, many of which are unfamiliar to students and are complex to learn. In attempting to master this complexity, learners often look for rules which can be followed much in the same way that following steps in a recipe can lead to a good result. However, questions couched in yes-or-no terms ('Can I use "I"'? or 'Do I have to give a citation if I had an idea and then read it somewhere else?') can rarely be answered in the same simple terms.

This is because the choices which writers and speakers make are not the outcomes of obeying fixed rules; they are shaped by tendencies and a view of what is conventional in the discourse community. Those tendencies and conventions, in turn, are shaped by the needs and values of the discipline. An extremely powerful tool to give learners is an understanding of academic discourse within the context of a broader set of disciplinary practices and values. Working at deepening that understanding is therefore a good objective for in-service EAP teachers.

Professional development

Closely related to the above, another theme running throughout this book has been the idea that EAP teachers require a body of knowledge which is both broad and deep, and includes general English, the characteristic features of general academic English, and an awareness of the ways individual disciplines differ from each other. The scope of this body of knowledge may seem daunting, but in fact it does not all need to be in place before beginning to teach EAP. However, a career teaching EAP will be more rewarding if teachers make a commitment to in-service professional development to learn more about these areas along the way.

This book has given an indication of the areas in which you can continue your professional development. Because EAP provides fascinating insights into the ways language and knowledge work together to form understanding, and opportunities to be of service to colleagues across the academic community, working your way into the field is an exciting and deeply rewarding enterprise.

Glossary

Academic journal   An academic journal is a periodical publication; that is, it is published in issues which come out at regular intervals, for example every three months. The core content of a journal is typically several **research articles** reporting original findings. In addition, journals may contain other features such as book reviews, position papers on topics of current interest, conference listings, or bibliographies of recently published titles which might be of interest to readers of the journal.

Academic vocabulary   Academic vocabulary refers to a core of words which occur in academic texts much more frequently than they occur in everyday language, and therefore cannot be considered **general vocabulary**, but which are used across a range of fields and subject areas, and therefore cannot be considered specialist **terminology**.

Affect   Used as a noun, affect refers to emotions. Affective factors are important in language learning, as they play a role in determining the learner's openness to the target language, engagement with teaching and learning activities, etc.

BALEAP   BALEAP is a UK-based organization formerly known as the British Association of Lecturers in English for Academic Purposes. Its activities include a professional accreditation scheme and biennial conferences.

BASE (British Academic Spoken English)   BASE is a **corpus** of 1.2 million words, consisting of transcripts of lectures and seminars in the arts/humanities, life sciences, physical sciences and social sciences from a British university setting.

BAWE (British Academic Written English)   BAWE is a 6.5-million-word **corpus** of highly rated writing assignments done by undergraduate and master's students at UK universities. The assignments which make up the corpus were written in thirty subjects in the arts/humanities, life sciences, physical sciences and social sciences.

BNC (British National Corpus)   The BNC consists of 100 million words and contains texts from the late twentieth century. It has an academic component.

CARS (Create a Research Space)   The CARS model describes a set of moves and steps which the writers of introductions to research articles use to identify the area of work in which the article is located and to justify the need for the article.

Citation   A citation is a reference to another person's work; citation is the process of making that reference.

COCA (Corpus of Contemporary American English)   This corpus contains 450 million words of texts from the period 1990–2012 and includes an academic component.

Collocation   Collocation refers to the fact that words have preferred associations with other words. A collocation is a combination of words that is relatively fixed and occurs more often than we would expect by chance.

Concordance   A concordance is a set of lines retrieved automatically from a corpus. It shows the search word along with a few words of context on either side and is used to see the collocations and phraseology of the search word.

Constructive alignment   Constructive alignment is the principle that the content of a course, the learning objectives and the assessment should be aligned with each other. In other words, learning objectives are used to decide the course content, and the assessment should measure attainment of the learning objectives.

Corpus   A corpus is a collection of texts, usually in electronic form, that has been compiled for a specific purpose and according to specific criteria. The plural form is corpora. There are large general corpora like COCA and academic corpora like BAWE.

Data-driven learning (DDL)   Data-driven learning is an inductive teaching approach in which students work directly with corpus data to make hypotheses and verify generalizations about language use.

Disciplinary community   A disciplinary community is a discourse community that is based around disciplinary goals and purposes.

Discipline   Discipline is one of a number of terms used for areas of academic study. It frequently is used to refer to a single subject area, e.g. physics; however, it can be used for very broad subject groupings, such as the humanities or the natural sciences, or for more specific groupings, such as the life sciences and the physical sciences.

Discourse community   A discourse community is a group of people who share a set of goals and purposes which they achieve by means of conventional forms of communication with shared linguistic and discoursal features.

Dissertation   A dissertation is a written report of a research project used as a (partial) qualification for an academic degree. Like other academic terminology such as thesis, this term is used differently in different geographic areas. For example, in the US, dissertation refers to work written at the doctoral level, while in the UK it refers to work written at the master's level.

Domain   Domain refers to a social situation characterized by typical forms of behaviour which give rise to typical ways of communicating. In EAP, university study is one domain, contrasted with family life, but on a more specific level, each **discipline** can also be seen as a domain; hence we can refer to the domain of medicine.

Edited volume   An edited volume, also called an anthology, is a book-length publication composed of a number of chapters written by different individuals and gathered into a volume with a coherent theme and focus by one or more editors. The contributions to edited volumes frequently report research findings but may also present a survey of the field or some other content relevant to the theme of the work.

EGAP (English for General Academic Purposes)   EGAP refers to EAP courses which cover general academic discourse, not that of a specific **discipline** or group of disciplines. It contrasts with **ESAP** (English for Specific Academic Purposes).

ELF (English as a lingua franca)   ELF refers to the use of English as a means of communication among people who do not have a common first language, that is, in interactions where some or all of the participants have other first languages. Since the end of the Second World War, English has grown to achieve global lingua franca status in many **domains**.

EMI (English-medium instruction)   EMI is the umbrella term applied to instruction at any educational level and in any setting in which English is used for teaching purposes. Usually the term is used to describe settings in which English is not the first language of the community in which the educational institution is set.

ESAP (English for Specific Academic Purposes)   ESAP refers to courses which cover academic content that is specific to a certain **discipline** or a narrow range of disciplines. It contrasts with **EGAP** (English for General Academic Purposes).

Expanding Circle   In Kachru's **Circles model**, the Expanding Circle is made up of countries where English does not have status either as an official, dominant language or as a predominant second language, but where it is nonetheless widely used for some purposes, such as international contact. Because of the strong status of English as a global **lingua franca**, the Expanding Circle consists to all practical purposes of those places which are not part of the **Inner** or **Outer** Circles.

General vocabulary   General vocabulary consists of the words used in everyday life. It is not marked as being either technical **terminology** or part of the core **academic vocabulary**.

Genre   A genre is a kind of text, written or spoken, such as a PhD **thesis, research article** or lecture. Genres arise out of specific social contexts in order to carry out purposes that are characteristic of that context; for example, the lecture is an academic genre that communicates disciplinary information, usually to students. Genres have certain regularities of linguistic structure which are identified by means of genre analysis.

Hedging   Hedging is the practice of using language to limit the writer's commitment to an idea. A hedge is a word or phrase used for this purpose. For example, if a writer states *Black may be responsible*, the modal verb *may* is a hedge to indicate uncertainty about whether Black is responsible or not.

Idiom principle   The idiom principle describes one way in which utterances are produced, in contrast to the **open-choice principle**. The idiom principle refers to the fact that many utterances consist of groups of words produced as a single unit, rather than being put together word by word. Examples of such **multi-word units** include *what I mean to say is* and *I'll start by*.

IMRD structure   IMRD refers to a typical **research article** structure, consisting of four main sections which present the Introduction, Methods, Results and Discussion. It is used particularly in the natural sciences and technical fields.

Inner Circle   In **Kachru's Circles model**, the Inner Circle refers to those countries which use English as an official or dominant language. Inner Circle countries include the UK, the US, Australia and New Zealand. Because the circles refer to areas of language use, they do not map perfectly onto national borders. Thus, most of Canada is considered to be part of the Inner Circle, but French-speaking Quebec is not.

Integral citation   Integral citation is a form of **citation** in which the cited writer's name has a grammatical role in the text, e.g. *Brown (2008) stated that* . . . It is contrasted with **non-integral citation**.

Kachru's Circles model   Sociolinguist Braj Kachru developed the Circles model to describe the different statuses of English. He divided the parts of the world where English is used into an **Inner,** an **Outer** and an **Expanding Circle**. Although it has been subject to criticism, the model is still widely used.

L1   L1 refers to the first language of a speaker or writer. For example, an L1 speaker of English has English as a first language, in contrast to an L2 speaker of English, who does not.

L2   L2 refers to the second language of a speaker or writer. An L2 speaker of English has English as a second language.

Lingua franca   A lingua franca is a language that is used as a common means of communication by speakers of different languages.

Lexicogrammatical   Lexicogrammatical information or features are those that combine vocabulary and grammar. The use of this term implies that lexis and grammar are seen as interdependent rather than discrete. For example, the use of the noun *argument* is a lexical choice, but this noun is associated with certain grammatical patterns (e.g. *the argument that...*) and not normally with others (e.g. *the argument to ...*). In order to use the noun correctly, it is necessary to know its lexicogrammar.

MICASE (Michigan Corpus of Academic Spoken English) MICASE is a corpus that contains almost 1.8 million words of transcribed spoken academic genres, including seminars and lectures. It was gathered in a university setting in the US.

MICUSP (Michigan Corpus of Upper-level Student Papers) MICUSP is a corpus that contains 2.6 million words of university student writing which gained high grades, including, for example, reports and essays. It was collected in the US.

Monograph A monograph is a book on a closely defined theme or topic, the contents of which are authored by one or more individuals from cover to cover, as opposed to an edited volume, in which individual chapters are authored by different people.

Move A move is the name for a stage in a text that carries out a specific communicative function. Moves can be made up of smaller units called steps. An example of a move in the research article introduction is 'establishing a territory'. The idea of moves was first introduced in the CARS model.

Multi-word unit (MWU) A multi-word unit is a fixed or semi-fixed phrase.

Needs analysis Needs analysis is a procedure carried out when a course in English for specific purposes is planned. The aim is to determine which skills and knowledge the students need in order to carry out the specific purposes, but currently lack. The results of a needs analysis are used to inform the content of the course.

Nominalization Nominalization is the use of a noun or noun phrase to express the meaning of a process or property; for example, the process of *explaining* can be nominalized as *explanation*.

Non-integral citation Non-integral citation is a form of citation in which the cited writer's name does not have a grammatical role in the text. The name may appear in parentheses, e.g. *Many researchers have shown (Brown, 2008; Green, 2010)*, or a number is used, e.g. *It was shown [6]* and the full citation details appear in an endnote or footnote. It is contrasted with integral citation.

Open-choice principle The open-choice principle sees text as resulting from a complex set of individual choices. At the end of each linguistic unit (e.g. a word), the speaker/writer can choose from a wide range of options, restricted only by the need to obey grammatical rules. The open-choice principle contrasts with the idiom principle.

Outer Circle In Kachru's Circles model, the Outer Circle refers to those countries where English has a history of extensive usage alongside other languages. Colonization is a common source of English influence in the Outer Circle, which includes places such as India, Pakistan and Malaysia.

Phraseology Phraseology refers to the patterns of words which occur predictably together, in **multi-word units** or more open sequences.

Productive knowledge/skills/abilities Language skills are traditionally divided into those that are **productive**, involving the ability to produce the language (i.e. to speak or write it) and those that are **receptive**, involving being able to hear and understand. Many learners have a gap between the strength of their receptive and their productive abilities.

Progression Progression in curriculum planning is the principle that the objectives of one course should flow coherently from the previous courses in the curriculum. In other words, when a curriculum is characterized by progression, students who pass the first term of study have the necessary knowledge and skills to succeed in the courses in the second term of study, and so on.

RA (research article) RAs are published in **academic journals** and report the findings of a research study. RAs vary in length; in some areas in the natural sciences they can be only a few pages long, while in a few more discursive fields, such as comparative literature, they can be as long as 25–30 pages.

Receptive knowledge/skills/abilities Language skills are traditionally divided into those that are receptive, involving the ability to understand what one reads or hears, and those that are **productive**.

Register A register is a variety of language which is used within a given social setting and for a given purpose. For example, EAP is a register that is used within educational institutions to carry out educational purposes.

Stance Stance is the expression of the writer/speaker's attitudes, opinions, judgements or feelings. It can be carried out using many different linguistic features, including adverbs (*surprisingly*), adjectives (*groundbreaking*) and verbs (*suggest*).

Step A step is a unit which performs a specific communicative function in a text. There may be several steps in a **move**; e.g. 'making a topic generalization' is a step belonging to the move 'establishing a territory' in the **genre** analysis of **research article** introductions. The use of the terms 'step' and 'move' to describe textual strategies was first introduced in the **CARS model**.

Terminology Terminology is the set of words (called technical or specialist terms) which are used in a specific subject or **discipline** area, such as *atrioventricular* (medicine) or *polyphony* (musicology). Some technical terms also occur in general English but have specialist meanings which are distinct from their general meanings. For example, *counterpoint* has a precise meaning in music theory but is often used in general English as an approximate synonym of 'contrast'.

Thesis Like a **dissertation**, a thesis is the written report of a research study carried out as a (partial) qualification for an academic degree. In the UK, 'thesis' refers to work written for a doctoral degree, while in the US it refers to work written for a master's degree.

References

Abasi, A. R., Akbari, N., & Graves, B. (2006). Discourse appropriation, construction of identities, and the complex issue of plagiarism: ESL students writing in graduate school. *Journal of Second Language Writing, 15*, 102–117.

ACTFL. (2012). *ACTFL proficiency guidelines 2012.* Alexandria, VA: American Council on the Teaching of Foreign Languages.

Ädel, A. (2014). Selecting quantitative data for qualitative analysis: A case study connecting a lexicogrammatical pattern to rhetorical moves. *Journal of English for Academic Purposes, 16*, 68–80.

Ädel, A., & Swales, J. M. (2013). Narratives of nature in English and Swedish: Butterfly books and the case of *Argynnis paphia.* In N.-L. Johannesson, G. Melchers & B. Björkman (Eds.), *Of butterflies and birds, of dialects and genres: Essays in honour of Philip Shaw* (Vol. 104, pp. 17–34). Stockholm: Acta Universitatis Stockholmiensis.

Anthony, L. (2001). Characteristic features of research article titles in computer science. *IEEE Transactions on Professional Communication, 44*, 187–194.

Anthony, L. (2014). AntConc (version 3.4.3) [Computer software]. Tokyo, Japan: Waseda University. Retrieved from http://www.laurenceanthony.net/

Ashworth, P., Bannister, P., & Thorne, P. (1997). Guilty in whose eyes? University students' perceptions of cheating and plagiarism in academic work and assessment. *Studies in Higher Education, 22*, 187–203.

Audacity. (2014). (version 2.0.6) [Computer software]. Retrieved from http://audacity.sourceforge.net/

Badger, R., & Sutherland, P. (2004). Lecturers' perceptions of lectures. *Journal of Further and Higher Education, 28*, 277–289.

Badger, R., White, G., Sutherland, P., & Haggis, T. (2001). Note perfect: An investigation of how students view taking notes in lectures. *System, 29*, 405–417.

BASE. (n.d.). *British academic spoken English corpus.* [Electronic corpus]. Retrieved from http://www.coventry.ac.uk/research-bank/research-archive/art-design/british-academic-spoken-english-corpus-base/

Basturkmen, H. (1999). Discourse in MBA seminars: Towards a description for pedagogical purposes. *English for Specific Purposes, 18*, 63–80.

Basturkmen, H. (2002). Negotiating meaning in seminar-type discussion and EAP. *English for Specific Purposes, 21*, 233–242.

Basturkmen, H. (2009). Commenting on results in published research articles and masters dissertations in language teaching. *Journal of English for Academic Purposes, 8*, 241–251.

Basturkmen, H., & Elder, C. (2006). The practice of LSP. In A. Davies & C. Elder (Eds.), *The handbook of applied linguistics* (pp. 672–694). Oxford: Blackwell.

Basturkmen, H., & Shackleford, N. (2015). How content lecturers help students with language: An observational study of language-related episodes in interaction in first year accounting classrooms. *English for Specific Purposes, 37,* 87–97.

Bawarshi, A., & Reiff, M. J. (2010). *Genre: An introduction to history, theory, research and pedagogy.* West Lafayette, IN: Parlor Press.

BAWE. (n.d.). *British academic written English corpus.* [Electronic corpus]. Retrieved from http://www.coventry.ac.uk/research-bank/research-archive/art-design/british-academic-written-english-corpus-bawe/

Becher, T., & Trowler, P. R. (2001). *Academic tribes and territories: Intellectual enquiry and the cultures of disciplines* (2nd ed.). Buckingham, UK: The Society for Research into Higher Education & Open University Press.

Belcher, D. (2013). The scope of L2 writing: Why we need a wider lens. *Journal of Second Language Writing, 22,* 438–439.

Benesch, S. (1996). Needs analysis and curriculum development in EAP: An example of a critical approach. *TESOL Quarterly, 30,* 723–738.

Benesch, S. (2001). *Critical English for academic purposes.* Mahwah, NJ: Erlbaum.

Berkenkotter, C., & Huckin, T. (1995). *Genre knowledge in disciplinary communication: Cognition/culture/power.* Hillsdale, NJ: Erlbaum.

Biber, D. (1988). *Variation across speech and writing.* Cambridge: Cambridge University Press.

Biber, D. (2006). *University language: A corpus-based study of spoken and written registers.* Amsterdam: Benjamins.

Biber, D., & Gray, B. (2010). Challenging stereotypes about academic writing: Complexity, elaboration, explicitness. *Journal of English for Academic Purposes, 9,* 2–20.

Biber, D., Johansson, S., Leech, G., Conrad, S., & Finegan, E. (1999). *Longman grammar of spoken and written English.* Harlow, UK: Pearson Education.

Biber, D., Leech, G., & Conrad, S. (2002). *Longman student grammar of spoken and written English.* Harlow, UK: Pearson Education.

Biggs, J. (1996). Enhancing teaching through constructive alignment. *Higher Education, 32,* 347–363.

Biggs, J., & Collis, K. (1982). *Evaluating the quality of learning: The SOLO taxonomy.* New York: Academic Press.

Bitchener, J. (2008). Evidence in support of written corrective feedback. *Journal of Second Language Writing, 17,* 102–118.

Bitchener, J., & Ferris, D. (2012). *Written corrective feedback in second language acquisition and writing.* New York: Routledge.

Bloch, J. (n.d.). Flipping the L2 composition classroom. Retrieved from http://www.scoop.it/t/flipping-the-l2-composition-classroom

Bloch, J. (2013). Technology and materials. In B. Paltridge & S. Starfield (Eds.), *The handbook of English for specific purposes* (pp. 385–401). Oxford: Wiley-Blackwell.

BNC. (n.d.). *The British national corpus.* [Electronic corpus]. Retrieved from http://corpus.byu.edu/bnc/

Bondi, M. (2016). Textbooks. In K. Hyland & P. Shaw (Eds.), *The Routledge handbook of English for academic purposes.* London: Routledge.

Bondi, M., & Lorés Sanz, R. (Eds.). (2014). *Abstracts in academic discourse: Variation and change.* Bern: Peter Lang.

Boz, C. (forthcoming). Transforming dialogic spaces in an 'elite' institution: Academic literacies, the tutorial and high-achieving students. In T. Lillis, K. Harrington, M. Lea & S. Mitchell (Eds.), *Working with academic literacies: Research, theory, design*. West Lafayette, IN: Parlor Press.

Braine, G. (2001). Twenty years of needs analysis: Reflections on a personal journey. In J. Flowerdew & M. Peacock (Eds.), *Research perspectives on English for academic purposes* (pp. 195–207). Cambridge: Cambridge University Press.

Brenn-White, M., & Faethe, E. (2013). *English-taught master's programs in Europe: A 2013 update*. New York: Institute of International Education.

Brezina, V., & Gablasova, D. (2013). Is there a core general vocabulary? Introducing the New General Service List. *Applied Linguistics, 36*, 1–22.

Browne, C. (2013). The New General Service List: Celebrating 60 years of vocabulary learning. *The Language Teacher, JALT2013 Special Issue*, 13–16.

Bruce, I. (2009). Results sections in sociology and organic chemistry articles: A genre analysis. *English for Specific Purposes, 28*, 105–124.

Bui, D. C., Myerson, J., & Hale, S. (2013). Note-taking with computers: Exploring alternative strategies for improved recall. *Journal of Educational Psychology, 105*, 299–309.

Bunton, D. (2005). The structure of PhD conclusion chapters. *Journal of English for Academic Purposes, 4*, 207–224.

Carter, R., & McCarthy, M. (1995). Grammar and the spoken language. *Applied Linguistics, 16*, 141–158.

Carter, R., & McCarthy, M. (2006). *Cambridge grammar of English: A comprehensive guide*. Cambridge: Cambridge University Press.

Charles, M. (2014). Getting the corpus habit: EAP students' long-term use of personal corpora. *English for Specific Purposes, 35*, 30–40.

Charles, M. (forthcoming). Corpus tools for writing students. In J. I. Liontas (Ed.), *The TESOL encyclopedia of English language teaching*. Hoboken, NJ: Wiley.

Cheng, A. (2016). EAP at the tertiary level in China: Challenges and possibilities. In K. Hyland & P. Shaw (Eds.), *The Routledge handbook of English for academic purposes*. London: Routledge.

Cheng, L., & Wang, H. (2004). Understanding professional challenges faced by Chinese teachers of English. *TESL-EJ, 7*(4). Retrieved from http://www.tesl-ej.org/wordpress/issues/volume7/ej28/ej28a2/?wscr

Chun, C. W. (2009). Contesting neoliberal discourses in EAP: Critical praxis in an IEP classroom. *Journal of English for Academic Purposes, 8*, 111–120.

Chun, C. W. (2015). *Power and meaning making in an EAP classroom: Engaging with the everyday*. Bristol, UK: Multilingual Matters.

Chung, T. M., & Nation, P. (2004). Identifying technical vocabulary. *System, 32*, 251–263.

Cobb, T. (2014). *The compleat lexical tutor* (version 8). Montreal, Canada: University of Quebec. Retrieved from http://www.lextutor.ca/

Connor, U., & Mauranen, A. (1999). Linguistic analysis of grant proposals: European Union research grants. *English for Specific Purposes, 18*, 47–62.

Cortes, V. (2013). 'The purpose of this study is to': Connecting lexical bundles and moves in research article introductions. *Journal of English for Academic Purposes, 12*, 33–43.

Council of Europe. (n.d.). *Common European framework of reference for languages: Learning, teaching, assessment*. Language Policy Unit. Strasbourg: Council of Europe. Retrieved from www.coe.int/lang-CEFR

Cowie, N., & Sakui, K. (2013). It's never too late: An overview of e-learning. *ELT Journal, 67,* 459–467.

Coxhead, A. (2000). A new academic word list. *TESOL Quarterly, 34,* 213–238.

Creese, A., & Blackledge A. (2010). Translanguaging in the bilingual classroom: A pedagogy for learning and teaching. *Modern Language Journal, 94,* 103–115.

Crookes, G. (1997). What influences what and how second and foreign language teachers teach? *Modern Language Journal, 81,* 67–79.

Curry, M. J., & Lillis, T. (2004). Multilingual scholars and the imperative to publish in English: Negotiating interests, demands, and rewards. *TESOL Quarterly, 38,* 663–688.

Curry, M. J., & Lillis, T. (2013). *A scholar's guide to getting published in English: Critical choices and practical strategies.* Bristol, UK: Multilingual Matters.

D'Angelo, L. (2016). Conference posters. In K. Hyland & P. Shaw (Eds.), *The Routledge handbook of English for academic purposes.* London: Routledge.

Davies, M. (2008). *The Corpus of Contemporary American English: 450 million words, 1990–2012.* Retrieved from http://corpus.byu.edu/coca/

Deroey, K.L.B. (2015). Marking importance in lectures: Interactive and textual orientation. *Applied Linguistics, 36,* 51–72.

Deroey, K.L.B., & Taverniers, M. (2011). A corpus-based study of lecture functions. *Moderna Språk, 105*(2), 1–22.

Deroey, K.L.B., & Taverniers, M. (2012). 'Ignore that 'cause it's totally irrelevant': Marking lesser relevance in lectures. *Journal of Pragmatics, 44,* 2085–2099.

Dudley-Evans, T. (1986). Genre analysis: An investigation of the introduction and discussion sections of MSc dissertations. In M. Coulthard (Ed.), *Talking about text* (pp. 128–145). Birmingham, UK: University of Birmingham English Language Research.

ELFA. (2008). *The corpus of English as a lingua franca in academic settings.* [Electronic corpus]. Retrieved from http://www.helsinki.fi/elfa/elfacorpus

Eslami, Z. R. (2010). Teachers' voice vs. students' voice: A needs analysis approach to English for Academic Purposes (EAP) in Iran. *English Language Teaching, 3,* 3–11.

Evans, S. (2010). Business as usual: The use of English in the professional world in Hong Kong. *English for Specific Purposes, 29,* 153–167.

Ferris, D. (1998). Students' views of academic aural/oral skills: A comparative needs analysis. *TESOL Quarterly, 32,* 289–318.

Ferris, D. (2010). Second language writing research and written corrective feedback in SLA. *Studies in Second Language Acquisition, 32,* 181–201.

Ferris, D. (2013). What L2 writing means to me: Texts, writers, contexts. *Journal of Second Language Writing, 22,* 428–429.

Ferris, D., & Roberts, B. (2001). Error feedback in L2 writing classes: How explicit does it need to be? *Journal of Second Language Writing, 10,* 161–184.

Field, J. (2011a). Into the mind of the academic listener. *Journal of English for Academic Purposes, 10,* 102–112.

Field, J. (Ed.). (2011b). Listening in EAP [Special issue]. *Journal of English for Academic Purposes, 10*(2).

Flowerdew, J. (Ed.). (1994). *Academic listening.* Cambridge: Cambridge University Press.

Flowerdew, J., & Miller, L. (1997). The teaching of academic listening comprehension and the question of authenticity. *English for Specific Purposes, 16,* 27–46.

Flowerdew, L. (2012). *Corpora and language education*. Basingstoke, UK: Palgrave Macmillan.

Fulcher, G., & Davidson, F. (Eds.). (2012). *The Routledge handbook of language testing*. New York: Routledge.

Gardner, D., & Davies, M. (2014). A new academic vocabulary list. *Applied Linguistics, 35,* 305–327.

Gosden, H. (2003). 'Why not give us the full story?': Functions of referees' comments in peer reviews of scientific research papers. *Journal of English for Academic Purposes, 2,* 87–101.

Granger, S., Dagneaux, E., Meunier, F., & Paquot, M. (Eds.). (2009). *International corpus of learner English*. Louvain-la-Neuve: Presses Universitaires de Louvain.

Halliday, M.A.K. (1978). *Language as social semiotic*. London: Edward Arnold.

Halliday, M.A.K. (1994). *An introduction to functional grammar* (2nd ed.). London: Edward Arnold.

Halliday, M.A.K., & Hasan, R. (1976). *Cohesion in English*. London: Longman.

Haque, E., & Cray, E. (2007). Constraining teachers: Adult ESL settlement language training policy and implementation. *TESOL Quarterly, 41,* 634–642.

Harwood, N. (2005a). What do we want EAP teaching materials for? *Journal of English for Academic Purposes, 4,* 149–161.

Harwood, N. (2005b). 'I hoped to counteract the memory problem, but I made no impact whatsoever': Discussing methods in computing science using I. *English for Specific Purposes, 24,* 243–267.

Harwood, N. (Ed.). (2010). *English language teaching materials: Theory and practice*. Cambridge: Cambridge University Press.

Harwood, N. (Ed.). (2014). *English language teaching textbooks: Content, consumption, production*. Basingstoke, UK: Palgrave Macmillan.

Hewings, M., Thaine, C., & McCarthy, M. (2012). *Cambridge academic English*. Cambridge: Cambridge University Press.

Hu, H. M., & Nation, P. (2000). Unknown vocabulary density and reading comprehension. *Reading in a Foreign Language, 13,* 403–430.

Huhta, M., Vogt, K., Johnson, E., & Tulkki, H. (Eds.). (2013). *Needs analysis for language course design: A holistic approach to ESP*. Cambridge: Cambridge University Press.

Hutchinson, T., & Waters, A. (1987). *English for specific purposes: A learning-centred approach*. Cambridge: Cambridge University Press.

Hyland, K. (2000). *Disciplinary discourses: Social interactions in academic writing*. Harlow, UK: Longman.

Hyland, K. (2001). Humble servants of the discipline? Self-mention in research articles. *English for Specific Purposes, 20,* 207–226.

Hyland, K. (2002). Authority and invisibility: Authorial identity in academic writing. *Journal of Pragmatics, 34,* 1091–1112.

Hyland, K. (2004). *Genre and second language writing*. Ann Arbor: University of Michigan Press.

Hyland, K. (2005). *Metadiscourse*. London: Continuum.

Hyland, K. (2006). *English for academic purposes: An advanced resource book*. London: Routledge.

Hyland, K. (2008). As can be seen: Lexical bundles and disciplinary variation. *English for Specific Purposes, 27,* 4–21.

Hyland, K. (2015). *Academic publishing: Issues and challenges in the construction of knowledge*. Oxford: Oxford University Press.

Hyland, K., & Shaw, P. (Eds.), (2016). *The Routledge handbook of English for academic purposes*. London: Routledge.

Hyon, S., & Chen, R. (2004). Beyond the research article: University faculty genres and EAP graduate preparation. *English for Specific Purposes, 23*, 233–263.

IELTS. (n.d.). Test takers: My score. Retrieved from http://www.ielts.org/test_takers_information/getting_my_results/my_test_score.aspx

IELTS. (2013). *IELTS guide for educational institutions, governments, professional bodies and commercial organisations*. Retrieved from http://www.ielts.org/PDF/Guide_Edu-%20Inst_Gov_2013.pdf

Jamieson, J., Wang, L., & Church, J. (2013). In-house or commercial speaking tests: Evaluating strengths for EAP placement. *Journal of English for Academic Purposes, 12*, 288–298.

Jenkins, J. (2014). *English as a lingua franca in the international university: The politics of academic English language policy*. London: Routledge.

Johns, A. M. (2011). The future of genre in L2 writing: Fundamental, but contested, instructional decisions. *Journal of Second Language Writing, 20*, 56–68.

Johns, T. (1991). Should you be persuaded: Two samples of data-driven learning materials. In T. Johns & P. King (Eds.), *Classroom concordancing* (pp. 1–16). Birmingham, UK: University of Birmingham English Language Research.

Kachru, B. B. (1985). Standards, codification, and sociolinguistic realm: The English language in the outer circle. In R. Quirk & H. Widdowson (Eds.), *English in the world* (pp. 11–30). Cambridge: Cambridge University Press.

Khani, R., & Tazik, K. (2013). Towards the development of an academic word list for applied linguistics. *RELC Journal, 44*, 209–232.

Kuteeva, M. (2016). Research blogs, wikis and tweets. In K. Hyland & P. Shaw (Eds.), *The Routledge handbook of English for academic purposes*. London: Routledge.

Kuteeva, M., & Mauranen, A. (Eds.). (2014). Writing for publication in multilingual contexts. *Journal of English for Academic Purposes, 13*, 1–4.

Kwary, D. A. (2011). A hybrid method for determining technical vocabulary. *System, 39*, 175–185.

Laufer, B., & Ravenhorst-Kalovski, G. C. (2010). Lexical threshold revisited: Lexical text coverage, learners' vocabulary size and reading comprehension. *Reading in a Foreign Language, 22*, 15–30.

Lea, M., & Street, B. (2006). The 'academic literacies' model: Theory and application. *Theory into Practice, 45*, 368–377.

Leadbeater, W., Shuttleworth, T., Couperthwaite, J., & Nightingale, K. P. (2013). Evaluating the use and impact of lecture recording in undergraduates: Evidence for distinct approaches by different groups of students. *Computers & Education, 61*, 185–192.

Lee, I. (2013). Second language writing: Perspectives of a teacher educator-researcher. *Journal of Second Language Writing, 22*, 435–437.

Lee, J. J. (2009). Size matters: An exploratory comparison of small- and large-class university lecture introductions. *English for Specific Purposes, 28*, 42–57.

Levin, M. (2014). The bathroom formula: A corpus-based study of a speech act in American and British English. *Journal of Pragmatics, 64*, 1–16.

Li, Y., & Flowerdew, J. (2007). Shaping Chinese novice scientists' manuscripts for publication. *Journal of Second Language Writing, 16*, 100–117.

Lillis, T., & Curry, M. J. (2010). *Academic writing in a global context*. London: Routledge.

Liou, H.-C., Yang, P.-C., & Chang, J. S. (2012). Language supports for journal abstract writing across disciplines. *Journal of Computer Assisted Learning*, 28(4), 322–335.

Liu, J.-Y., Chang, Y.-J., Yang, F.-Y., & Sun, Y.-C. (2011). Is what I need what I want? Reconceptualising college students' needs in English courses for general and specific/academic purposes. *Journal of English for Academic Purposes*, 10, 271–280.

Louhiala-Salminen, L., Charles, M., & Kankaanranta, A. (2005). English as a lingua franca in Nordic corporate mergers: Two case companies. *English for Specific Purposes*, 24, 401–421.

Martin, J. R., & Rose, D. (2008). *Genre relations: Mapping culture*. London: Equinox.

Mauranen, A. (2012). *Exploring ELF: Academic English shaped by non-native speakers*. Cambridge: Cambridge University Press.

Mauranen, A., Hynninen, N., & Ranta, E. (2016). English as the academic lingua franca. In K. Hyland & P. Shaw (Eds.), *The Routledge handbook of English for academic purposes*. London: Routledge.

McCarthy, M. (2010). Spoken fluency revisited. *English Profile Journal*, 1, 1–15.

McCarthy, M., & O'Dell, F. (2008). *Academic vocabulary in use*. Cambridge: Cambridge University Press.

McDonough, J., Shaw, C., & Masuhara, H. (2013). *Materials and methods in ELT: A teacher's guide*. Chichester, UK: Wiley-Blackwell.

McGrath, I. (2006). Teachers' and learners' images for coursebooks. *ELT Journal*, 60, 171–180.

Menkabu, A., & Harwood, N. (2014). Teachers' conceptualization and use of the textbook on a medical English course. In N. Harwood (Ed.), *English language teaching textbooks: Content, consumption, production* (pp. 145–177). Basingstoke, UK: Palgrave Macmillan.

MICASE. (n.d.). *Michigan corpus of academic spoken English*. [Electronic corpus]. Retrieved from http://quod.lib.umich.edu/m/micase/

MICUSP. (2009). *Michigan corpus of upper-level student papers*. [Electronic corpus]. Retrieved from http://micusp.elicorpora.info/

Milton, J. (2009). *Measuring second language vocabulary acquisition*. Bristol, UK: Multilingual Matters.

Mol, H., & Tan, B. T. (2008). EAP materials in New Zealand and Australia. In B. Tomlinson (Ed.), *English language learning materials: A critical review* (pp. 74–99). London: Continuum.

Morell, T. (2015). International conference paper presentations: A multimodal analysis to determine effectiveness. *English for Specific Purposes*, 37, 137–150.

Morgan, B. (2009). Fostering transformative practitioners for critical EAP: Possibilities and challenges. *Journal of English for Academic Purposes*, 8, 86–99.

Morrow, K. (1977). Authentic texts and ESP. In S. Holden (Ed.), *English for specific purposes* (pp. 13–17). London: Modern English Publications & Macmillan.

Mudraya, O. (2006). Engineering English: A lexical frequency instructional model. *English for Specific Purposes*, 25, 235–256.

Musgrave, J., & Parkinson, J. (2014). Getting to grips with noun groups. *ELT Journal*, 68, 145–154.

Narjaikaew, P., Emarat, N., & Cowie, B. (2009). The effect of guided note taking during lectures on Thai university students' understanding of electromagnetism. *Research in Science and Technological Education*, *27*, 75–94.

Nation, P. (2010). *Language curriculum design*. London: Routledge.

Nesi, H. (2005). A corpus-based analysis of academic lectures across disciplines. In A. Ife & J. Cotterill (Eds.), *Language across boundaries* (pp. 201–218). London: Continuum.

Nesi, H., & Gardner, S. (2012). *Genres across the disciplines: Student writing in higher education*. Cambridge: Cambridge University Press.

OECD [Organisation for Economic Co-operation and Development]. (2014). *Education at a glance 2014: OECD Indicators*. Paris: OECD.

Oxford advanced learner's dictionary. (2015). Retrieved from http://www.oxford learnersdictionaries.com/

Oxford learner's dictionary of academic English. (2014). Oxford: Oxford University Press.

Paquot, M. (2010). *Academic vocabulary in learner writing*. London: Continuum.

Park, J. S.-Y., & Wee, L. (2009). The three circles redux: A market-theoretic perspective on world Englishes. *Applied Linguistics*, *30*, 389–406.

Pearson Education. (2012). *PTE academic score guide*. Retrieved from http://pear sonpte.com/wp-content/uploads/2014/07/PTEA_Score_Guide.pdf

Pecorari, D. (2008). *Academic writing and plagiarism: A linguistic analysis*. London: Continuum.

Pecorari, D. (2013). *Teaching to avoid plagiarism: How to promote good source use*. Maidenhead, UK: Open University Press.

Pecorari, D. (forthcoming). ESL vs. EFL writing: Blurred boundaries. In J. I. Liontas (Ed.), *The TESOL encyclopedia of English language teaching*. Hoboken, NJ: Wiley.

Pecorari, D., Shaw, P., Irvine, A., & Malmström, H. (2011). English for academic purposes at Swedish universities: Teachers' objectives and practices. *Iberica, 22*, 55–78.

Pecorari, D., Shaw, P., & Malmström, H. (in preparation). Testing the academic vocabulary list.

Pecorari, D., Shaw, P., Malmström, H., & Irvine, A. (2011). English textbooks in parallel-language tertiary education. *TESOL Quarterly*, *45*, 313–333.

Pennington, M. C., & Hoekje, B. J. (2010). *Leading language programs in a changing world: An ecological approach*. Bingley, UK: Emerald.

Petrić, B. (2007). Rhetorical functions of citations in high- and low-rated MA theses. *Journal of English for Academic Purposes*, *6*, 238–253.

Phillipson, R. (2008). Lingua franca or lingua frankensteinia? English in European integration and globalisation. *World Englishes*, *27*, 250–267.

Räisänen, C. (2002). The conference forum: A system of interrelated genres and discursive practices. In E. Ventola, C. Shalom & S. Thompson (Eds.), *The language of conferencing* (pp. 69–93). Frankfurt: Peter Lang.

Read, J. (2015). *Assessing English proficiency for university study*. Basingstoke, UK: Palgrave Macmillan.

Reinders, H., & White, C. (2010). The theory and practice of technology in materials development and task design. In N. Harwood (Ed.), *English language teaching materials: Theory and practice* (pp. 58–80). Cambridge: Cambridge University Press.

Rowley-Jolivet, E. (2004). Different visions, different visuals: A social semiotic analysis of field-specific visual composition in scientific conference presentations. *Visual Communication, 3,* 145–175.

Rowley-Jolivet, E., & Carter-Thomas, S. (2005). The rhetoric of conference presentation introductions: Context, argument and interaction. *International Journal of Applied Linguistics, 15,* 45–70.

Samraj, B. (2016). Research articles. In K. Hyland & P. Shaw (Eds.), *The Routledge handbook of English for academic purposes.* London: Routledge.

Schmidt, R. W. (1990). The role of consciousness in second language learning. *Applied Linguistics, 11,* 129–158.

Schmitt, D., & Schmitt, N. (2005). *Focus on vocabulary: Mastering the Academic Word List.* New York: Longman.

Schmitt, N., Schmitt, D., & Clapham, C. (2001). Developing and exploring the behaviour of two new versions of the Vocabulary Levels Test. *Language Testing 18,* 55–88.

Shaw, P., & McMillion, A. (2008). Proficiency effects and compensation in advanced second-language reading. *Nordic Journal of English Studies, 7,* 123–143.

Shawer, S. F. (2010). Classroom-level curriculum development: EFL teachers as curriculum-developers, curriculum-makers and curriculum-transmitters. *Teaching and Teacher Education, 26,* 173–184.

Silva, T. (2013). Second language writing: Talking points. *Journal of Second Language Writing, 22,* 432–434.

Simpson-Vlach, R., & Ellis, N. (2010). An academic formulas list: New methods in phraseology research. *Applied Linguistics, 31,* 487–512.

Sinclair, J. M. (1991). *Corpus, concordance, collocation.* Oxford: Oxford University Press.

Spaulding, S., Mauch, J., & Lin, L. (2001). The internationalization of higher education: Policy and program issues. In P. O'Meara, H. D. Mehlinger & R. M. Newman (Eds.), *Changing perspectives on international education* (pp. 190–211). Bloomington: Indiana University Press.

Stapleton, P., & Helms-Park, R. (2006). Evaluating Web sources in an EAP course: Introducing a multi-trait instrument for feedback and assessment. *English for Specific Purposes, 25,* 438–455.

Stoller, F., & Robinson, M. (2014). An interdisciplinary textbook project. In N. Harwood (Ed.), *English language teaching textbooks: Content, consumption, production* (pp. 262–298). Basingstoke, UK: Palgrave Macmillan.

Sutton, A., & Taylor, D. (2011). Confusion about collusion: Working together and academic integrity. *Assessment & Evaluation in Higher Education, 36,* 831–841.

Swales, J. M. (1981). *Aspects of article introductions.* Birmingham: Language Studies Unit, Aston University.

Swales, J. M. (1990). *Genre analysis: English in academic and research settings.* Cambridge: Cambridge University Press.

Swales, J. M. (1996). Occluded genres in the academy: The case of the submission letter. In E. Ventola & A. Mauranen (Eds.), *Academic writing: Intercultural and textual issues* (pp. 45–58). Amsterdam: Benjamins.

Swales, J. M. (1997). English as *Tyrannosaurus rex*. *World Englishes, 16*, 373–382.

Swales, J. M. (1998). *Other floors, other voices: A textography of a small university building*. Mahwah, NJ: Erlbaum.

Swales, J. M. (2002). Integrated and fragmented worlds: EAP materials and corpus linguistics. In J. Flowerdew (Ed.), *Academic Discourse* (pp. 150–164). London: Longman.

Swales, J. M. (2004). *Research genres: Explorations and applications*. Cambridge: Cambridge University Press.

Swales, J. M. (2009a). *Incidents in an educational life: A memoir (of sorts)*. Ann Arbor: University of Michigan Press.

Swales, J. M. (2009b). When there is no perfect text: Approaches to the EAP practitioner's dilemma. *Journal of English for Academic Purposes, 8*, 5–13.

Swales, J. M., & Feak, C. B. (1994). *Academic writing for graduate students*. Ann Arbor: University of Michigan Press.

Swales, J. M., & Feak, C. B. (2009). *Abstracts and the writing of abstracts*. Ann Arbor: University of Michigan Press.

Swales, J. M., & Feak, C. B. (2012). *Academic writing for graduate students: Essential tasks and skills* (3rd ed.). Ann Arbor: University of Michigan Press.

Tajino, A., James, R., & Kijima, K. (2005). Beyond needs analysis: Soft systems methodology for meaningful collaboration in EAP course design. *Journal of English for Academic Purposes, 4*, 27–42.

Thompson, P., & Tribble, C. (2001). Looking at citations: Using corpora in English for academic purposes. *Language Learning and Technology, 5*, 91–105.

Thompson, S. (1994). Frameworks and contexts: A genre-based approach to analysing lecture introductions. *English for Specific Purposes, 13*, 171–184.

Thompson, S. (2003). Text-structuring metadiscourse, intonation and the signalling of organisation in academic lectures. *Journal of English for Academic Purposes, 2*, 5–20.

Thurstun, J., & Candlin, C. (1997). *Exploring academic English: A workbook for student essay writing*. Sydney: NCELTR.

TOEFL (n.d.). Understanding your TOEFL iBT test scores. http://www.ets.org/toefl/ibt/scores/understand/

Tribble, C. (2009). Writing academic English: A survey review of current published resources. *ELT Journal, 63*, 400–417.

Truscott, J. (1996). The case against grammar correction in L2 writing classes. *Language Learning, 46*, 327–369.

Tuksinvarajarn, A., & Watson Todd, R. (2009). The e-pet: Enhancing motivation in e-portfolios. *English Teaching Forum, 47*, 22–31.

Wang, J., Liang, S.-L., & Ge, G.-C. (2008). Establishment of a medical academic word list. *English for Specific Purposes, 27*, 442–458.

Ward, J. (2001). EST: Evading scientific text. *English for Specific Purposes, 20*, 141–152.

Ward, J. (2009). A basic engineering English word list for less proficient foundation engineering undergraduates. *English for Specific Purposes, 28*, 170–182.

Wesche, M., & Paribakht, T. (1996). Assessing second language vocabulary knowledge: Depth versus breadth. *Canadian Modern Language Review, 53*, 13–40.

West, M. (1953). *A general service list of English words*. London: Longman, Green & Co.

Whitelock, D., Twiner, A., Richardson, J.T.E., Field, D., & Pulman, S. (2015). OpenEssayist: A supply and demand learning analytics tool for drafting academic essays. In J. Baron, G. Lynch, & N. Maziarz (Eds.), *LAK15: Proceedings of the fifth international conference on Learning Analytics and Knowledge* (pp. 208–212). New York: ACM Press.

Widdowson, H. G. (1978). *Teaching language as communication*. Oxford: Oxford University Press.

Wingate, U. (2015). *Academic literacy and student diversity: The case for inclusive practice*. Bristol, UK: Multilingual Matters.

Yakhontova, T. (2001). Textbooks, contexts, and learners. *English for Specific Purposes, 20*, 397–415.

Yeo, S. (2007). First-year university science and engineering students' understanding of plagiarism. *Higher Education Research & Development, 26*, 199–216.

Index